DOING BUSINESS IN
ROMANIA

CBI
*Initiative
Eastern Europe*

DOING BUSINESS IN ROMANIA

**TOUCHE ROSS
SINCLAIR ROCHE & TEMPERLEY**

KOGAN PAGE

Note: This book has been written on the basis of information and law current as at March 1992.

First published in 1992

Apart from any fair dealing for the purposes of research or private study, or criticism or review, as permitted under the Copyright, Designs and Patents Act, 1988, this publication may only be reproduced, stored or transmitted, in any form or by any means, with the prior permission in writing of the publishers, or in the case of reprographic reproduction in accordance with the terms of licences issued by the Copyright Licensing Agency. Enquiries concerning reproduction outside those terms should be sent to the publishers at the undermentioned address:

Kogan Page Limited
120 Pentonville Road
London N1 9JN

© Confederation of British Industry, 1992

British Library Cataloguing in Publication Data

A CIP record for this book is available from the British Library.

ISBN 0 7494 0690 9

Typeset by DP Photosetting, Aylesbury, Bucks
Printed and bound in Great Britain by Clays Ltd, St Ives plc

Contents

The Contributors 8

Foreword 11
Theodor Stolojan, Prime Minister of Romania

Preface 13
Alan J Lewis, CBE, Chairman, CBI Initiative Eastern Europe

PART I: A BUSINESS REVOLUTION? 15

1. The Country and its Potential 17
   Brittain Engineering Ltd

2. Economic Transformation 36
   Touche Ross

3. A New Legal Framework 42
   Sinclair Roche & Temperley

4. Business Culture 50
   Touche Ross

5. Market Intelligence 57
   Touche Ross

6. Trading Partners 61
   Sinclair Roche & Temperley

7. Foreign Investment 68
   Sinclair Roche & Temperley

PART II: THE BUSINESS INFRASTRUCTURE 75

8. Commercial Law 77
   Sinclair Roche & Temperley

9. The Convertibility of the Leu   82
   Charterhouse

10. Prices, Rents and Wages   88
    Charterhouse

11. Banking and Financial Services   93
    Charterhouse

12. Accounting Standards   99
    Touche Ross

13. The Privatisation Process   103
    Sinclair Roche & Temperley

14. Privatisation in Practice   108
    Touche Ross

15. Property   113
    Sinclair Roche & Temperley

16. The Fiscal Framework   118
    Touche Ross

17. Technology and Communications   128
    Touche Ross and the Romanian Development Agency

18. The Environment   134
    Sinclair Roche & Temperley

19. The Labour Market   139
    The Romanian Development Agency

PART III: THE OPTIONS FOR BRITISH BUSINESS   147

20. Planning   149
    Touche Ross

21. Marketing   157
    Brittain Engineering Ltd

22. Agencies and Distributorships   163
    Sinclair Roche & Temperley

23. Export and Import   167
    Touche Ross and the Romanian Development Agency

24. Trade Finance   172
    Commodities International

25. Licensing and Franchises   176
    Sinclair Roche & Temperley

26. Forming a Company   180
    Sinclair Roche & Temperley

27. Financing a Company   188
    Charterhouse

PART IV: CASE STUDIES   195

1. Romanian Manufacturers SA   197
2. Shell Romania   204
3. The Wadkin Group   209
4. Glaxo   214

APPENDICES   219

1. Opportunities by Sector   221
   Brittain Engineering Ltd
2. Sources of Grants and Aid   232
3. Bibliography and Sources of Further Information   240

Index   251

The Contributors

Sinclair Roche & Temperley is a leading international commercial law firm based in London, with offices in Hong Kong and Singapore. In 1992 the firm established a representative office in Bucharest to service its Romanian and international clients. Sinclair Roche & Temperley has an established network of legal correspondents and contacts with government and commercial organisations throughout Central and Eastern Europe. Partners have been involved in a substantial number of joint ventures and other projects involving foreign investment in Romania and other Central and Eastern European countries. The firm is acting as advisor to the Romanian National Agency for Privatisation on privatisations of a number of enterprises as part of the Romanian pilot privatisation scheme.

Touche Ross & Co and the ***Deloitte & Touche*** practice in Romania are part of Deloitte Touche Tohmatsu International, one of the world's largest accounting, auditing, tax and management consulting firms. The firm has taken the leading role in setting up Romania's Early Privatisation Programme and has extensive experience of assisting Western clients entering the Romanian market by providing advice on many areas including joint ventures, valuations, personnel, government relations, environmental factors, IT and customs software applications. Deloitte Touche Tohmatsu International has offices in all the major Central and Eastern European capitals, including Bucharest, staffed by both Western and national professionals.

Charterhouse is a leading international merchant and investment banking group with significant corporate finance, development capital, risk management and stockbroking activities. Soon after the

December 1989 revolution, Charterhouse recognised the need to offer its expertise to Western companies interested in opportunities in Romania. In conjunction with four other leading European financial institutions, it founded Industrial Finance Reconstruction Corporation (IFRC), a financial services and consultancy company with offices in Bucharest. IFRC has already advised a number of major western corporations on approaching the Romanian market, appraising business opportunities, financing business with Romania and structuring joint ventures and other transactions with Romanian companies.

Brittain Engineering Ltd is an export company specialising in business with Central and Eastern Europe and acts as agents and distributors for a selected number of manufacturers. The company has a long history of trade in Romania and is a qualified supplier to the Romanian aircraft and nuclear engineering industries. It is currently setting up a subsidiary in Bucharest.

Foreword

This book provides British readers with a considerable amount of relevant information on the reality of Romania today, a country where a series of far-reaching changes have occurred in rapid succession.

The Romanian Government has been constantly aware that consolidating the mechanisms of the market and stimulating economic activity are major prerequisites for stability and progress, and for Romania to gain her natural status as a free country in a democratic world. The top priority of our economic programme has been to create an adequate environment for promoting trade and international cooperation and for attracting foreign investment.

Following the Romanian Revolution of December 1989, the people of Romania decided that democracy, respect for private property and the rule of law were to be the future of their country. Only two years ago the notion of democracy was an empty slogan in Romania, and the distortions caused by a centralised economic system had plunged the country into a severe crisis.

In a remarkably short period of time, important progress has been made towards creating the appropriate legislative and institutional framework for transition to a market economy. The Romanian Parliament adopted the fundamental law of the country – the Constitution. In line with the economic reform targets state-owned, centrally controlled enterprises were transformed by law into commercial companies and autonomous state-owned companies; private enterprise was allowed and encouraged; the privatisation of commercial companies and the agrarian reform were launched; the Foreign Investment Law was passed and enacted; foreign trade was liberalised; the internal convertibility of the national currency for current account transactions was introduced; and the banking system was re-organised on market-oriented principles.

All this is proof of my country's determination to change its economic mechanism. Following the enactment of the Privatisation Law and the Foreign Investment Law, Romania has opened up to mutually beneficial international cooperation. The effort to build a proper legal framework is being carried forward by the preparation of the Bankruptcy Law, the Anti-Trust Law and a comprehensive assistance programme for private enterprise.

The time has come to make full use of the existing opportunities, to work together efficiently and profitably.

I regard the CBI Initiative Eastern Europe as a positive response by the British business community to the economic policy of the Romanian Government. Our clear aim is to identify the incentives for enhancing those private initiatives that are capable of setting in motion individuals and the nation as a whole towards a prosperous society.

The links between the United Kingdom and Romania have a long and fruitful tradition. My message to the readers of this book is to rest assured that the British way of doing business has a good name in Romania; the British are widely regarded in my country as reliable and trustworthy partners. Now, more than ever before, business people have many promising opportunities to consider.

This book provides a perceptive account of the reforms under way in Romania, breaking new ground for a better understanding of the present-day reality of my country. Romania's opening to the outside world favours a further strengthening of economic ties with the UK as an increasingly important and active business partner.

Theodor Stolojan
Prime Minister of Romania
May 1992

Preface

Romania has emerged as a democratic country with an accepted legal and constitutional framework within which to live and do business. To an outsider, politics in Romania may seem extreme but the freedom of expression is an established constitutional right. The post-Ceauşescu era has brought many positive fundamental changes to Romanian civil and economic life.

The priority has been to introduce, through a massive programme of legislation, a sound legal and fiscal system, before switching to a market economy. In many respects, Romania's legal framework is better developed than some of the higher profile Central European countries. Some vestiges of the state planning system still remain but market forces predominate.

Romania has the lowest per capita debt of any country in Eastern Europe. Its population is over twice the size of Belgium and the country is 70 per cent self-sufficient in energy. Parts of the economy are growing quite healthily particularly in light industry and agriculture, which are key sectors for Romania's economic development.

Very few price controls remain and all newly created private firms and firms with foreign capital are exempt from price controls. A liberal trade regime has also been introduced, in which tariffs are virtually the only tool of intervention.

Large sums of money are beginning to flow into Romania, which reflect external confidence in the underlying strength of the economy and in the government's commitment and ability to transform the economy successfully. International aid and loan agencies are providing support to upgrade major parts of the economy. This should speed up the process of privatisation and the transformation of the country's structure.

This book is designed as a source of pragmatic business advice, drawing on the expertise of Touche Ross, Sinclair Roche and Temperley, the Romanian Development Agency, Charterhouse Bank and Brittain Engineering. The CBI thanks them for the very substantial efforts they have made. In addition, Commodities International has given us the benefit of its knowledge of trade finance in Romania and David Potter wrote the appendix on grants and aid.

Relatively few Western companies have realised the growth potential of the Romanian market. There are notable exceptions and some of these are featured as case studies in this book. The CBI thanks Romanian Manufacturers, Shell, the Wadkin Group and Glaxo for their contributions.

Romania's topography and wealth of natural resources, coupled with a skilled and relatively cheap labour force, will undoubtedly prove attractive to foreign investors. Although there can be no guaranteed returns on any investments, there are many business opportunities. Unless British business establishes its presence now and takes a long-term view, the rewards will inevitably go to our more daring trading rivals. It is our hope that this book will give British companies a competitive advantage when exploring and developing business in this new and exciting market.

Alan J Lewis, CBE
Chairman, CBI Initiative Eastern Europe
April 1992

Part I

A Business Revolution?

1

The Country and its Potential
Brittain Engineering Ltd

Romania came back to the attention of public opinion when, in December 1989, its people shed their blood to shake off 43 years of communist oppression. The country is slowly but certainly working its way to a multi-party democracy, based on a market economy, which should eventually guarantee that the long nightmare is over and people are again free, in every sense of the word.

A report from the members of a British mission in 1991 came to the conclusion that 'with well directed support initially, Romania has the features which should enable it to aspire to equality with most of the countries in Western Europe'. The report listed among the main reasons for reaching this conclusion the fact that 'there is a pool of well educated, intelligent young people, adaptable, eager and quick to learn'. This may indeed be the most important asset the country has.

After some initial hesitation, the Petre Roman government and its successor, the Theodor Stolojan administration have embarked on wide-ranging reforms including price liberalisation, liberalisation of foreign trade, privatisation, encouragement of foreign ownership and investment in the economy, banking reform and, maybe most important of all, unification of exchange rates, internal convertibility and a controlled floating of the national currency, the leu.

These reforms have been carried out in the context of several economic difficulties. The latest forecast is that gross national product will drop by 6.6 per cent in 1991, followed by further drops in 1992 (5.1 per cent) and 1993 (3.9 per cent), with growth resuming only in 1994 (+2.6 per cent). A major problem is the relative lack of foreign credits and aid.

Romania has, nevertheless, a few major advantages over some of the other emerging democracies:

- A capacity, given the right policies in agriculture, to feed its own people and create substantial surpluses for export. In this they are matched only by the Ukraine, Hungary and Serbia.

- Relatively less reliance in the past on the Soviet and other East European markets and, in particular, on supplies of raw materials from the Soviet Union. Even though some industrial mammoths were not based on local mineral or raw material supplies, a large number of them were not specifically designed for USSR sources, and the Romanians have some experience, given the money, of sourcing these from Third World or even developed countries. Conversely, relatively fewer products are designed specifically for the East European markets.

- A better knowledge of and exposure to Western specifications and quality assurance systems, particularly in engineering (aircraft, nuclear engineering, oil and petrochemical plant manufacture and shipbuilding) industries. In this they are exceeded only by the Yugoslavs, although some of their neighbours are likely to catch up with them before too long. However, the trained people are there: in many factories the systems are in place and – once they are freed from political and bureaucratic interference and sort out their material supplies – can change the results quite dramatically. Since April–May 1990, the new State Committee for Standards and Quality has been campaigning to introduce throughout industry quality assurance systems to ISO 9000 series (BS5750) which should be in place for the single market at the end of 1992.

GEOGRAPHY

Romania covers an area of approximately 237,500 square kilometres, bounded to the north and north-east by the Ukraine and the Republic of Moldova, to the east by the Black Sea, to the south by Bulgaria, to the south-west by Yugoslavia and to the west by Hungary.

The country's relief reminds one of a fortress: a plateau (Transylvania) in the centre, surrounded by mountains – the Carpathian

The Country and its Potential   19

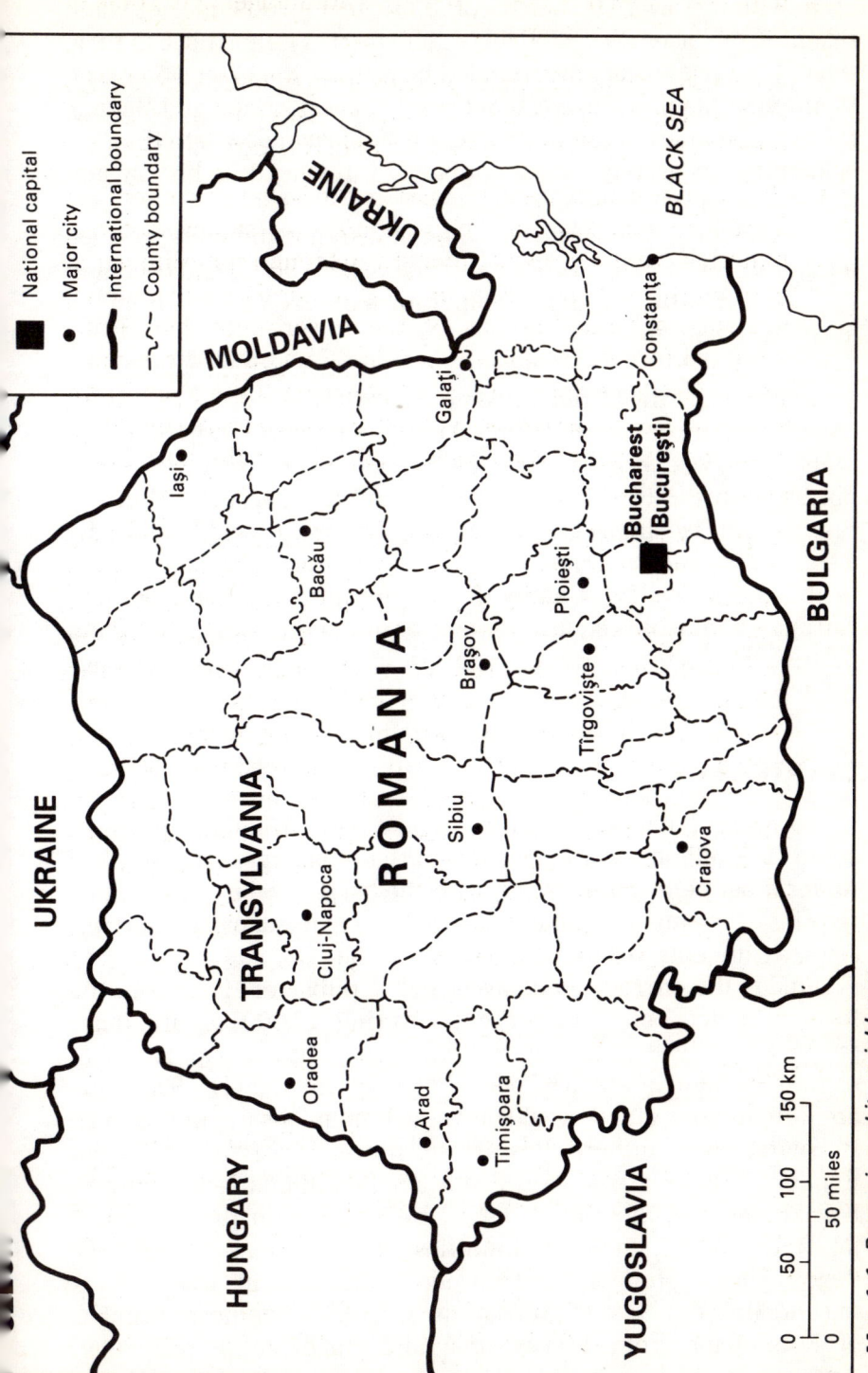

Map 1.1 *Romania and its neighbours*

arch with an average height of 3300 feet (1006 metres) and reaching in places over 8300 feet (2530 metres) - and hills. In turn, the upland regions are surrounded by plains - the extension of the Pannonian plain in the west and south-west (Crişana and Banat), the Danube valley in the south and the Moldavian downs in the east. Romania's geography has undoubtedly influenced its history and the character of its peoples.

The climate is temperate continental with hot summers, average temperatures of 21°C (70°F) but rising to 32° (90°F) and over, and cold winters with an average temperature of −2°C (28°F), dropping at times to −20° to −35°C.

Virtually all Romania's land surface is drained to the Danube. The lower course of the Danube river, from the Cazane defile to Silistra, constitutes the border with Yugoslavia and Bulgaria and, from Reni to the Black Sea, with the Ukraine. The main rivers are the Prut (the border with the Republic of Moldova and the Ukraine), Moldova, Bistriţa and Siret in the east, the Mureş, Criş, Someş and Timiş in the west, and the Jiu, Olt, Dâmboviţa, Ialomiţa in the south. At its mouth to the Black Sea, the Danube forms the most extensive delta in Europe - about 2600 square kilometres of lagoon, swamp and damp pasture, home to numerous rare species of birds, fish and other wildlife.

DEMOGRAPHY

Romania's population is estimated at just under 23 million of which some 19.9 million (over 86 per cent) are Romanians, 2 million (just under 9 per cent) Hungarians, with the balance being made up by Gypsies, Germans, Ukrainians, Serbs, Croats, Russians, Bulgarians, Jews, Armenians, Greeks and others.

Outside the current boundaries, the Republic of Moldova in the former Soviet Union, at present covering 13,000 square miles (approximately 34,000 square kilometres), has a population of some 4.3 million of which 67 per cent (or approximately 2.9 million) are Romanians. A further 460,000 plus Romanians live in northern Bucovina and southern Bessarabia, now part of the Ukrainian Republic. There are an estimated 250,000 Romanians living in Kazakhstan and Siberia (deported by Stalin from the territories taken in 1940), small communities of Romanians in Bulgaria, Yugoslavia and Hungary, and Macedo-Romanians in Greece, Albania and Macedonia. At the turn of the century a significant number of Romanians from Transylvania and Bucovina in particular, emigrated, mainly to the USA and Canada, and Israel has a large community originating from Romania.

In 1990, 10.8 million people were in employment: 28 per cent in agriculture, 37 per cent in industry, 6 per cent in construction, with the balance being involved in education, health, administration, transport, commerce and other occupations. Since then a considerable number of people over 55 have taken early retirement, and unemployment, in September 1991 standing at 238,000, is likely to increase substantially in the immediate future.

Over 60 per cent of the population now live in towns. The capital, Bucharest, has some 2 million inhabitants, and 15 towns each have over 150,000 inhabitants. In order of size these are: Brașov, Constanța, Iași, Timișoara, Cluj-Napoca, Galați, Craiova, Ploiești, Brăila, Oradea, Arad, Sibiu, Bacău, Târgu Mureș, Pitești.

Most Romanians are nominally Eastern Orthodox, with some 1.5 million Uniate (Eastern Catholics). There are sizeable Roman Catholic and Protestant communities, especially among the Hungarian and German minorities, with various Protestant sects, Jewish and Muslim communities making up the balance. Education is compulsory up to the age of 16 and a large proportion of the student population goes on to higher education at universities, technical universities and academies, both state funded and, since 1990, private establishments. The first foreign language is English, followed by German, French, Russian (compulsory for many years) and Italian.

BRIEF HISTORY

Before the Revolution

The Romanians trace their ancestry back to Dacian (Thracian) tribes who inhabited the territory in prehistoric Roman times, and to Roman settlers in the 2nd century AD, to which were added elements of later invaders – Slavs, Magyars, Celts, Goths, Tatars and Turks.

The modern Romanian state was born of the union of the two Romanian principalities, Wallachia and Moldavia in 1859, when the two *ad hoc* assemblies elected Alexandru Ion Cuza to the throne of both. In 1866 the throne was offered to Prince Charles of Hohenzollern-Sigmaringen, a relative of the Prussian kaiser. In 1877-78 the united principalities joined the Russo-Turkish war (fought in Bulgaria) and thus secured full independence from the

Ottoman Empire. Formally recognised by the European powers under the Treaty of Berlin in July 1878, the country also incorporated the Danube delta, Snake Island in the Black Sea and Dobrudja.

Romania fought in the Balkan Wars of 1912 and 1913 and during World War I (after two years of armed neutrality) joined the Entente in 1916, thus ending on the winning side.

The collapse of the Austro-Hungarian and Russian Empires brought about the integration of the provinces of Transylvania, Bucovina and Bessarabia into a 'Greater Romania', changes which were enshrined in the treaties of Saint Germain, Trianon and Neuilly.

Romania had been a constitutional monarchy since 1866, and the 1923 Constitution enshrined all subsequent amendments, including universal male suffrage irrespective of nationality and religion (women were enfranchised in 1937).

In 1938 Romania became a corporatist state under King Carol II's direct control (the 'Royal Dictatorship'). In April 1939 in the aftermath of Munich, the Romanian government, under pressure from the Axis to take sides, in vain asked Britain and France to guarantee the nation's integrity. Romania's defence strategy – based on the alliance with Czechoslovakia, Yugoslavia, Poland, France and Britain, but to an even greater extent on the antagonism between Germany and the USSR – was thrown into disarray by the Molotov-Ribbentropp Pact in August 1939. Although Romania did not declare war in September 1939, the government decreed general mobilisation and armed neutrality, allowing the Polish government and large sections of the army to withdraw via Romania to the Middle East.

In June 1940 the USSR, in accordance with the Molotov-Ribbentropp Pact, occupied Bessarabia and northern Bucovina. In July a German 'military mission' arrived in the country, in August the Vienna Diktat handed Northern Transylvania to Hungary and, in September, the King handed power over to General Ion Antonescu, abdicated in favour of his 19-year-old son, Michael I, and left the country.

After appalling excesses, including pogroms in Iași and Bucharest and a spate of political assassinations by the Iron Guard, a fascist movement allied to and supported by Germany, General Antonescu introduced a military dictatorship and expelled, imprisoned or killed all the leaders of his erstwhile allies, despite German protests.

The Soviet-German pact did not last and, in June 1941, Germany attacked the Soviet Union. In order to recover the territories lost in

1940 Romania joined the war against the USSR and achieved that goal in less than a month. The war with the USSR was very popular until the army crossed the Dniestr river and went on to Stalingrad.

In 1943 secret negotiations started between representatives of the traditional parties, the King and the Allies. In August 1944 the Palace Guard arrested Marshal Antonescu and Romania declared war on Germany and the Axis powers. Yalta, and subsequently Potsdam, however, settled the fate of Romania: it was to become part of the Soviet 'sphere of influence'.

In November 1946 in the first post-war election the nation voted overwhelmingly for the National Peasant Party (PNT) and the National Liberal Party (PNL) but, 'miraculously', they lost to the communist dominated 'Block of Democratic Parties'. There followed the outlawing of the PNT and of the other traditional parties. A peace treaty in 1947 restored northern Transylvania to Romania (from Hungary) but left Bessarabia and northern Bucovina to the Soviet Union and southern Dobrudja to Bulgaria. At the end of 1947 King Michael was forced to abdicate. Thus ended Romania's short-lived attempt to restore democracy. In March 1948, new elections held under the regime of terror produced the prescribed result. The country became the Romanian Peoples' Republic with a new Constitution drafted in April 1948. (Later, it was renamed the Socialist Republic of Romania.)

In February 1948 Romania signed a treaty of friendship and mutual assistance with the Soviet Union, in January 1949 it joined the Council for Mutual Economic Assistance (Comecon) and in 1955 the Warsaw Pact. The period 1948–55 saw the expropriation of virtually all property and the suppression of any dissent: large numbers of people were sent to internal exile and political prisoners ran into hundreds of thousands, either languishing in prisons or forced to work in slave labour camps. The death toll from all this has not yet been computed, but the most conservative estimates put it at well over 100,000.

After Stalin's death in 1953, the 'national' faction in the Party started asserting itself, timidly at first, then more and more boldly, with the removal from power of the Comintern contingent. The Party refused to tow the line in relation to China, or to commit Romania to the integrationist plans of Comecon. In 1966, Ceauşescu, the General Secretary of the Party, stated that the Romanian Communist Party was continuing the struggle for complete independence. In 1967 he refused to break diplomatic relations with Israel and established diplomatic relations with the

Federal Republic of Germany. In 1968 he opposed the intervention of Warsaw Pact forces in Czechoslovakia and restored ties with Yugoslavia. He also refused to allow the presence of Soviet or any other Warsaw Pact troops on Romania's soil, even for short periods for exercises.

A relatively liberal emigration policy towards Jews, Germans and other minorities and even some 'less politically desirable' ethnic Romanians, the introduction in 1968 of joint venture legislation long before the other East European countries, membership of GATT, the IMF, the World Bank and other bodies, all combined to ensure that Romania received preferential economic treatment. This took the form of favourable commercial links with the EEC, Most Favoured Nation Status with the USA (eventually lost in the late-1980s) and ample government-to-government and commercial bank credits which, unfortunately, were misallocated as in other East European countries.

However, from 1971 onwards the regime showed its true colours and turned into the most repressive in Eastern Europe. In the circumstances, it is less surprising that it all ended in bloodshed than that this happened as late as December 1989. Leaving aside the influence of events everywhere else in Central and Eastern Europe, there were solid internal reasons for the 1989 Revolution. There had always been some form of resistance to the communist regime, although the main form of protest was sullen submission and virtual sabotage, plus, whenever the opportunity arose, leaving the country altogether.

Serious unrest occurred in 1977 in the Jiu Valley, a mining district. The revolt was put down, miners' leaders imprisoned and Securitate officers sent into mines as foremen and technicians to keep an eye on the ordinary workers. On 15 November 1987, workers at both the truck and tractor works in Brașov went on strike, descended on the town centre and sacked the county Party headquarters and the County Hall. The uprising was put down by force, leaders were imprisoned or sent to psychiatric hospitals and, again, the factories were flooded with Securitate officers and informers.

On 16 December 1989, the people of Timișoara – Romanians, Hungarians, Germans, Serbs and others alike – decided to oppose the removal of Pastor Tökes László from his parish church and his deportation. This rapidly degenerated into a shooting incident and the entire town was on the streets the following day. Many people, mainly young were killed, Timișoara was cut off from the rest of the country and for a while it seemed that it was all over. Ceaușescu carried on with a planned visit to Iran, leaving everything in the capable hands of his wife, who anyway was reputed to be the power behind the throne. Once back in the country, the second mistake was that Ceaușescu called a mass meeting in Bucharest on 21 December to talk to the crowds. Instead, the rally turned into an anti-communist uprising and by 22 December, the army joined the people and power was in the hands of a 'National Salvation Front'. The fighting subsided only a few days later when Nicolae and Elena Ceaușescu were summarily judged by a military tribunal and executed on Christmas Day 1989.

After the Revolution?

The debate goes on as to whether December 1989 was a Revolution, a *coup-d'état*, or both. What can be said is that it was the dramatic phase of a process which, with ups and downs, has continued since then.

With the demise of the Ceaușescu dictatorship the potential power vacuum was filled by the National Salvation Front, followed later by the Council for National Union, which, under the interim presidency of Ion Iliescu and a provisional government led by Petre Roman, governed the country up to the May 1990 elections. January–May 1990 saw the revival of old parties, banned under communism, the creation of new parties and formations, the rebirth of a free press, the transformation of the National Salvation Front from an interim body into a political party and, on the negative side confrontations, including physical violence, against the leaders and activists of the opposition, as well as a raid by miners in Bucharest.

The apparent volatility of Romanian politics should be set in the context of the country's emergence from a brutal and corrupt regime. There was limited scope for an opposition movement to develop: under Ceaușescu, for instance, no one outside the immediate family circle could be trusted. In such circumstances, it should not be surprising that politics has a much higher emotional content than is normal to Western eyes.

Unlike some other countries, the Communist Party in Romania had no real indigenous roots and relatively few intellectuals before 1945 embraced 'the cause'. The Party was brought to power by the Red Army. The repression against all potential alternative leaders was therefore more thorough than elsewhere, emasculating the old political class, all independent communist thinkers and any other non-conformists. The repression of the late-1940s and 1950s was matched by that in the 1980s. Consequently, no alternative structure could evolve in the Party and certainly not outside it. Dissent there certainly was, and many prominent Party members were plotting the downfall of Ceaușescu, but there was relatively little preparation for the aftermath.

Add the lack of a large emigration, with no mass exodus such as after the 1956 Hungarian Revolution or the Prague Spring of 1968, and one can see that little support could come from Romanians outside the country. Some other countries benefited from support from the Catholic Church. Romania is largely Eastern Orthodox and their brethren in faith are in a worse state than themselves.

The regression from the liberalisation of the 1960s and the reintroduction of severe Stalinism in the 1980s left the country ill-prepared for the shock of dismantling the command economy, with no private enterprise whatsoever prior to 1989 to take some of the strain.

Finally, unlike anywhere else, the Communist Party, after the demise of its central leadership, simply 'disappeared' and never tried to reform itself. A large number of the membership were only nominal communists so their change of heart comes as no surprise, but the activists and middle leadership stayed in place by virtue of their jobs in administration and are active in politics. Quite a few have just retired and some are now entrepreneurs in the thousands of private companies that have been sent up since 1990.

The May 1990 elections were fought by an ill-prepared opposition, which had only started organising just over four months earlier, and an amorphous National Salvation Front which had not yet defined its philosophy and its place in the political spectrum. The incumbents therefore had an in-built advantage which resulted in a landslide, both in the presidential and (bicameral) parliamentary elections. The only other party to come out with a reasonable performance was the UDMR, the Hungarian minority's party, but, based on an ethnic vote, the latter has probably peaked and so, unless they can in future attract the votes of other groups, are unlikely to improve significantly on these results. The traditional parties, National Liberal and National Peasant-christian democratic trailed far behind. The life of the parliament was limited to two years in which time it was to act as a constituent assembly and tackle the most urgent reforms in the economy and in social life.

The electoral campaign was a lively affair, but, lacking a true identity and drawing on the less savoury traditions of politicking, the ruling party in particular made promises which could not be kept and which came back to haunt them later. Thus there was talk of a middle way, neither communist nor capitalist, vaguely referred to as the 'Swedish Model', involving a painless transition to a market economy, all contradicted subsequently by the practical steps that were required and taken.

The ruling party's overwhelming majority in parliament also enabled it to push through legislation, with some severe side-effects. On the one hand, the lack of an effective opposition meant that not all legislation was properly debated and some parts of it proved subsequently inadequate. The choice of the agenda was made to suit the executive rather than anything else. On the other hand, the blame for all the difficulties and lack of progress could only be laid at the door of the governing party – none of it could be apportioned to the opposition, not even on the grounds of obstruction.

In the two-year life of this parliament, major items of legislation were passed, principally the new Constitution promulgated in December 1991, a Law on Agrarian Reform, a Company Law, laws on privatisation and on foreign investment, social legislation, a first step in setting up a coherent system of taxation, and a reform of the banking system. The new parliament, which will be elected in July 1992, will undoubtedly introduce a Commercial Code, which has unfortunately been left to one side, with some potentially serious consequences for practical relationships between partners inside and outside the country.

Another consequence of the early elections in 1990 and the ruling party's virtual monopoly on power – in parliament, central and local administration and, to all intents and purposes, in the economy – is the prominence that street politics played. Periodic demonstrations by dissatisfied workers, strikers, monarchists, students and others demonstrated the growing unpopularity of the administration. The occupation by students and others of University Square in Bucharest was broken up in June 1990 by miners brought from the Jiu Valley and President Iliescu at the time thanked the latter for their 'contribution' to the restoration of public order. The draft was cashed in September 1991, when the same miners came back to Bucharest in a Mark II performance and brought about the resignation of the Roman government.

The Stolojan Administration, which succeeded Petre Roman's in October 1991, comprised three members of the National Liberal Party, and one each from the Democratic Agrarians and the

Ecologists, which made it a less one-sided government. The Prime Minister (a banker) declared that he will not seek election to parliament and will leave politics altogether when his mandate runs out. Refreshingly, he started telling the unvarnished truth about the state of the economy. The price liberalisation process was finalised and internal convertibility was introduced with a partially controlled float of the leu, the national currency. With properly thought-out macroeconomic measures and control of the money supply, the way should be open for the start of the climb out of trouble. So far, Romania has adhered reasonably well to policies and targets agreed with the IMF, so more help from international bodies, including (crucially) a currency stabilisation fund, should be forthcoming. The World Bank has forecast that the economy could start growing again by mid-1993.

There is little doubt that Romania is heading in the general direction being followed by all Central and Eastern European countries. The main questions are: how, at what price, are there any major obstacles on the way and, crucially, is there a danger of backtracking?

The local elections in February 1992 saw a swing from the National Salvation Front to the main opposition, united as the Democratic Convention, particularly in the main cities, such as Bucharest, Timişoara, Ploieşti, Constanţa, Braşov, Sibiu and others.

Since then, a realignment in Romanian politics has been under way. The National Salvation Front has split, with the majority backing the new statutes and policies proposed by the radical faction led by Petre Roman and a significant minority, with left wing tendencies, forming a new 'FDSN-Democratic National Salvation Front' grouping.

The leadership of the National Liberal Party have decided to leave the Democratic Convention which now groups together the National Peasant-christian democratic, the Civic Alliance and the Social Democrat Parties, the Democratic Union of Hungarians in Romania and some eight other smaller parties and associations.

The performance of the Romanian National Unity Party (the main Romanian nationalist party) and the Socialist Labour Party and their allies (the avowed successors to the Romanian Communist Party) in the forthcoming elections will be important pointers to future developments in Romania's political life.

At the time of writing, it is difficult to predict the outcome of the elections to both the lower house, the Parliament, and the upper house, the Senate. It is however certain that the balance of power will be altered; that the main protagonists will be the mainstream National Salvation Front and the Democratic Convention; that the next government will be a coalition; and that reform will continue, albeit with some changes in emphasis and personalities involved.

In the political sphere there are still outstanding problems to be solved. The separation of powers in the state, the trial of communism and increasing the powers of the legislative versus those of the executive are only the most glaring examples. The tendency to centralise everything in the capital would certainly have to be abandoned and regional centres allowed to develop with minimum interference. Reform has to be tempered by care for the social consequences. The Romanian people, however, have demonstrated that they can stoically tolerate a high degree of pain if they are told the plain truth.

Sooner rather than later, extreme left and right wing parties, of whatever hue, their propaganda and any vestiges of racism and xenophobia will have to be outlawed, and human and minority rights entrenched in the Constitution or not, strictly enforced. Romania is a signatory to the European Declaration on Human Rights so it is a matter of practical steps, including where necessary legislation, rather than first principles.

The potential territorial dispute with the now independent Ukraine over northern Bucovina and southern Bessarabia and the re-unification or otherwise with the Republic of Moldova will require statesmanship by all the parties concerned so that negotiated solutions can be reached.

There seems to be no danger of backtracking – the programmes of the major political parties all point the same way – but, again, implementation and consistency are the main ingredients and only time will tell.

THE ECONOMY

Before World War II, Romania was the only country in Eastern Europe in which Britain and British business had a sizeable interest and foothold, based largely on the dynastic link and oil. Indeed, Britain has always enjoyed a certain aura in the country and British business can therefore draw on a large pool of goodwill.

Natural resources

Romania's main wealth has always been based on agriculture and animal husbandry: 60 per cent of its territory is agricultural, over 25 per cent is covered by forests and the balance is mainly permanent pasture.

Oil has been a very important resource, with the first well sunk in 1848 and commercial production starting in 1854. Since then, extraction has steadily increased reaching 8.7 million tonnes per annum in 1936 (3.5 per cent of world production), 11-13 million tonnes in the late-1960s and early-1970s, but dropping back to no more than 7-7.5 million tonnes in 1991 (compared with internal requirements of some 16 million tonnes per annum). Estimated proven recoverable reserves are 175 million tonnes.

Natural gas, at 25 billion cubic metres per annum in 1991 (28.3 in 1990), also no longer covers internal requirements (30 billion cubic metres per annum), and the only practical outside source of gas is the pipeline from the former Soviet Union. Using current technologies, natural gas production will fall by some 1-1.5 billion cubic metres per annum (estimated reserves are 235 billion cubic metres), so if there is no contraction in the chemical industry and improvements in energy efficiency, imports will have to grow considerably in the foreseeable future.

Large deposits of bauxite (now heading for depletion) form the basis of the aluminium industry. Sizeable deposits of uranium ore, virtually alongside, were seized upon by the Romanian administration in the 1970s to justify the choice of Western (Canadian) technology in nuclear power generation rather than the Soviet option favoured by all Romania's neighbours.

Other minerals, the extraction of which goes back for over 2000 years, are coal (38 million tonnes in 1990, with estimated reserves of 2870 million tonnes of hard coal and 1100 million tonnes of lignite), iron ore (practically depleted), lead (24,700 tonnes per annum), zinc (35,500 tonnes per annum), copper (31,700 tonnes per annum), gold, silver, chalk, quartz, bentonites, clay, kaolin, calcite and, in particular, salt (reserves for 500 years).

Agriculture

In the past, Romania was (together with the Ukraine) the breadbasket of Europe. The forced collectivisation of agriculture under the communist regime destroyed the peasant farmer class and transformed them into agricultural proletarians, with most youngsters drifting away to towns to increase the urban proletariat.

Although some 40 per cent of the population still lives in villages, most are part-time farmers, supplementing their income with work on building sites, state farms, local industries, the railways, etc. The end result is that the country can no longer feed itself, despite the fact that by all standards it could sustain 2-3 times its population and create sizeable surpluses for export. A step in the right direction has been made with the land reform in 1991, as yet incomplete. This will in due course lead to an improvement, but its success will depend to a large extent on the new banks, agricultural machinery manufacturers, fertiliser producers, and so on, which will have to gear their products to the requirements of smallholders. Agriculture and food processing represent one of the most promising areas for official help and foreign investment.

The main crops are corn, wheat, barley, oats, sunflower, rape, fruit and vegetables, tobacco, cotton and hemp. Although the area devoted to vineyards is the ninth largest in the world, Romanian wines are virtually unknown in the West. People say that they are too good for foreigners and are best drunk by themselves. The country is ideal for raising cattle, sheep, pigs and poultry, but again much will have to be done to improve the breeds, ensure fodder for the long winters, improve distribution, processing and retailing and not least improve prices to farmers.

Fish farming is underdeveloped, with the main source of freshwater fish in the Danube delta. Carp, pike, trout and, of course, sturgeon and caviar, are the most popular along with the famous Danube mackerel.

Forestry

With more than a quarter of the country covered by forests, timber, pulp, paper and woodworking industries have a strong basis. In the last years of the communist regime, reforestation was all but abandoned and, in the immediate future, this is the most urgent task to ensure renewable resources and prevent soil erosion.

Mining

As in so many of Romania's industries, the policy of autarchy in the production of oil extraction and mining equipment has isolated the country from the latest developments in technology and hardware. The new government is taking some steps to grant concessions for exploration and extraction, both for oil and the other mineral resources. It appears that in the oil industry some 15 fields, both offshore and on land are being offered in the first instance, with bids

32   *Romania: A Business Revolution?*

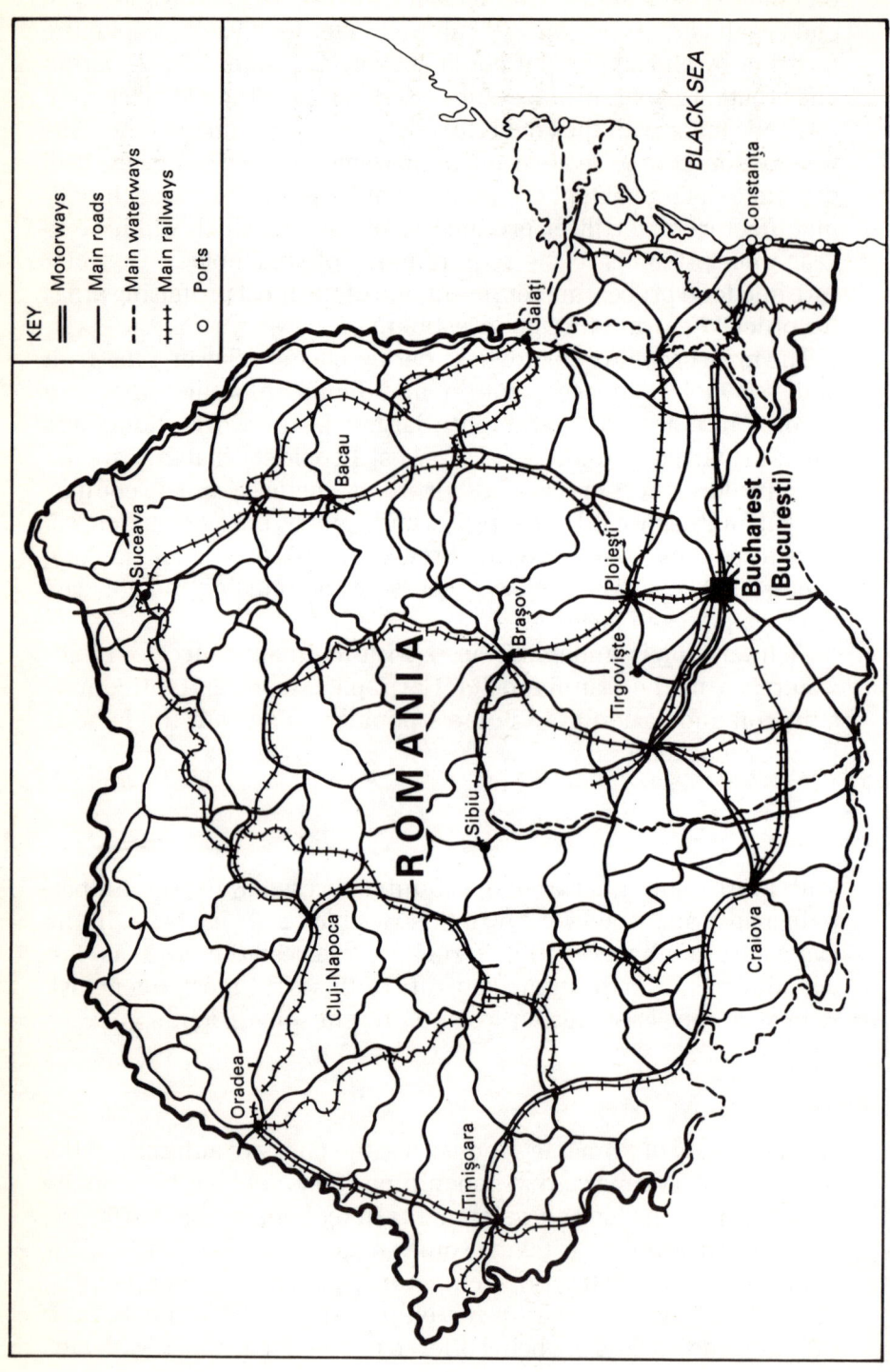

coming mainly from the UK, USA, Mexico, The Netherlands and France.

Feasibility studies are being prepared for coal and other extractive industries and the next few months should see developments in that area.

Power

Power stations generated some 64,100 million kilowatt-hours in 1990, 15 per cent less than in 1989, and further reductions were recorded in 1991. This should have been sufficient for an economy the size of Romania's but for the extremely low energy efficiency of its industry. In the circumstances, a substantial (over 20 per cent) part of the country's requirements have to be imported, primarily from the former USSR and Yugoslavia, but also from further afield.

Most of the electricity is generated by coal (23 per cent), oil (27 per cent) and gas (40 per cent) fired power stations, supplemented from hydroelectric stations on the Danube and the other main rivers. Construction of a heavy water type nuclear power station, with five 685 megawatt Candu reactors, was started in 1979 but completion has been delayed for a variety of reasons, mainly lack of money. When completed, this should cover some 30 per cent of Romania's requirements and recently Canada has approved a loan to enable work to go ahead, with more money promised when progress is recorded.

Industry

The inter-war years saw a rapid industrialisation of Romania, apart from a break during the 1929–32 depression.

After the communist takeover, the Stalinist pattern of industrialisation was adopted, as in all the other countries which fell into the Soviet sphere of influence in the late-1940s, with little or no regard for mineral or energy resources, tradition, availability or otherwise of adequate labour, together with exaggerated emphasis on heavy industry, petrochemicals, bulk chemicals, and so on.

The 1960s and early-1970s saw rapid growth in industrial production, based in the latter period on heavy borrowing which led eventually to a payment crisis and the decision by the Ceauşescu regime to repay all debt in the 1980s. The lack of spares, adequate raw materials and further investment in upgrading technologies, and the failure to replace obsolete equipment and modernise products reduced industry to a sorry state, with industrial output falling by some 20 per cent for two successive years.

Foreign trade

Romania's foreign trade has suffered from: (a) a deliberate decision since 1990 to ban exports of products in short supply in the country

Table 1.1 *Industrial production*

Product	Unit	1990 (approx)	1990 as % of 1989
Raw steel	thousand tonnes	9,686	67.7
Aluminium and aluminium alloys	thousand tonnes	178	63.4
Lead	thousand tonnes	20	49.6
Zinc	thousand tonnes	11	38.4
Petrol	thousand tonnes	4,667	76.8
Chemical fertilisers	thousand tonnes	1,742	62.2
Cement	thousand tonnes	10,383	78.3
Pesticides	thousand tonnes	11	64.4
Synthetic rubber	thousand tonnes	102	68.4
Bearings	thousand pieces	100,654	70.5
Tractors	pieces	25,556	104.5
Motor cars	pieces	62,490	70.3
Buses	pieces	1,186	84.5
Furniture	million lei	15,587	88.6
Paper	thousand tonnes	432	77.9
Refrigerators	thousand pieces	363	85.9
Radio sets	thousand pieces	478	74.2
Television sets	thousand pieces	401	78.5
Medicines	million lei	4,157	85.1
Fabrics	million square metres	882	75.9
Knitwear	million square metres	184	77.1
Apparel	million lei	22,167	84.5
Footwear	thousand pairs	74,279	76.5
Soap	thousand tonnes	33	113.9
Detergenets	thousand tonnes	86	78.9

and to increase imports of food and consumer goods; (b) the impact of the dismantling of the command economy; (c) the recession in the West; and (d) troubles experienced by some of its traditional customers (eg, Iraq, the ex-USSR and others).

Total imports increased in 1990 versus 1989 by 55 per cent, while exports fell by 19.5 per cent. With former Comecon countries, imports increased by 19 per cent and exports fell by 17.15 per cent but with developed countries, imports grew by a staggering 151.6 per cent while exports fell by 16.6 per cent. The trend seems to be confirmed in 1991, which explains the growth in external debt and the desperate need for more assistance and short-, medium- and long-term loans. As it is, medium- and long-term debt stood, at the end of the first six months of 1991, at US$70 million with IMF credits at $812 million.

Patterns of UK/Romanian trade

Despite all the difficulties experienced in the last two years, Romania has risen since 1990 from seventh place to sixth in the league table of the UK's Central and Eastern European export markets.

The UK ranks about sixth in Romania's trade with the West, a bare 5.5 per cent of Romania's total trade with developed countries. Although the UK's exports to Romania trebled in 1990 compared to 1989, the UK's ranking did not change – trade with other countries increased by the same ratio.

In the first six months of 1991 UK exports to Romania slipped from 6 per cent of the total imports from the West in 1990 to 4.9 per cent. One cause could be the lack of any credit lines throughout the year, while the UK's competitors have taken full advantage of theirs. There is ample room for improvements in bilateral trade, with little or no overall increase – just by tipping the balance to the UK's favour at the expense of its competitors.

In 1990, UK exports stood at £86 million and imports at £61 million. Exports comprised chemicals (14.4 per cent of the total), transport equipment and vehicles (10.3 per cent), power generating equipment (10 per cent), textile yarns and fabrics (8.5 per cent) and non-ferrous metals (7.3 per cent). Imports comprised clothing (26 per cent), furniture (16 per cent), electrical machinery (6 per cent) and ferrous metals (5.9 per cent).

2

Economic Transformation

Touche Ross

UNDER CEAUŞESCU

For 40 years the Romanian economy was run according to the Soviet system of central planning. Resources were allocated centrally, not by the market. All large enterprises were nationalised. Small business was restricted and huge monopolies dominated the economy. Managers were selected on grounds of political reliability, not commercial ability. Distribution was a matter of bulk breaking and consumer markets were characterised by shortages of poor quality goods.

In the 1980s economic policy continued to be dominated by forced industrialisation and 'systematisation' – the ordering of people's daily lives to fit their ruler's preconceived notions. Ceauşescu created huge new industrial complexes with no regard for economic logic, and laid waste to villages in a collectivisation programme on a scale not seen outside Stalinist Russia.

When industrial enterprises are established and developed for reasons of government prestige and vanity rather than the utility of their output, they are liable to become 'value-subtractors'. That is, the economic value of their output is less than the sum of the inputs employed. In Romania this was true on a grand scale. For instance, in the 1930s Romania had the biggest oil industry in Europe, but declining reserves and lack of investment deprived it of this pre-eminence. Ceauşescu decided to restore the industry, and based on nothing more than a hunch he invested huge sums in oil exploration in the Black Sea. No new oil was found and the money was wasted.

His drive to build a heavy industrial sector which would make Romania an economic power left no resources for the producers of consumer items to buy raw materials or invest in new technologies. Ceaușescu's visions created even more havoc in the countryside. In the drive to systematisation, a thousand villages were destroyed and millions of lives disrupted as part of a plan to create a series of 'agro-industrial towns'.

In common with the other Eastern European countries, the failure of Romania's economic system was becoming increasingly evident at the end of the 1970s. Unlike its neighbours, however, Romania made virtually no progress in the 1980s towards reforming its system. A New Economic and Financial Mechanism (NEFM) was introduced in 1979, but it was limited in scope, and even more limited in implementation. As a result, the plans and projections of the State Planning Committee (SPC) became ever more unrealistic, and misreporting of production became endemic at all levels. One of the tasks of the new regime has been to prepare more accurate statistics about the Romanian economy during the 1980s, and this work is only now bearing fruit. Meanwhile, Romania entered the 1990s with an economy in crisis, and a state apparatus which responded by exerting ever-tighter control over the daily lives of its citizens.

The two bright spots in this bleak picture were energy and debt. As mentioned before, Romania had Europe's largest oil industry in the 1930s, and with Western technology and expertise the industry can perhaps be put back on its feet. Romania's gas reserves are also the largest in Eastern Europe, and account for half of its domestically produced energy. Romania's energy production has long been outpaced by its energy consumption, however, and this was the cause of a rift with Comecon in the 1960s. Comecon demanded a slowdown in Romania's drive to build a heavy industrial infrastructure, and when Romania refused it was excluded from 'soft currency' (ie lower than world price) Soviet energy supplies.

This led directly to a rapid accumulation of debt to Western suppliers. A forced rescheduling in 1982 determined Ceaușescu to end Romania's vulnerability to foreign financiers by eliminating its external debt. This was achieved by the end of the decade, to the extent that Romania held foreign currency reserves of $2 billion. The debt was eliminated by halting imports and boosting exports, which in practice meant sacrificing the availability of consumer goods and investment inputs for industry, and exporting items which were greatly needed at home.

Thus Romanian living standards declined throughout the 1980s. Food was rationed while production surpluses were exported.

Average calorie intake fell from 3260 in 1980 to 3070 in 1990. Male life expectancy declined, as did access to medical help. Energy consumption was rationed, with only a few hours of electricity supply each day, even in winter. Consumer goods were scarce, with only 13 telephones per 100 people, for instance, and 35 cars per 1000. Living standards were lower than anywhere in Europe except Albania, and lower than many Third World countries.

THE PILLARS OF REFORM

Throughout Eastern Europe, reforming governments have had to tackle five key issues: commercial regulations, prices, trade, privatisation and the financial system. The roles of these issues can be summarised thus:

- Commercial regulations are needed (among other things) to enforce contracts, reduce fraud, and produce tax systems based on fair and rational principles.

- Free prices give signals to economic agents about where to invest their time and money most effectively.

- Free trade and currency reform ensures that price signals are in line with world prices, and expose enterprises to the stimulus of international competition. They also improve the economic position of both trading partners through the effects of comparative advantage.

- Privatisation ensures that managers act in the interests of the owners of their enterprises (and not just the interests of their managers and workers) in a way that governments never manage to. It also allows complacent and inefficient monopolies to be broken up.

- Financial reform curbs government spending (particularly on subsidising enterprises) and monetary growth in order to contain inflation.

In the early days, Romania did not seek Western advice in drafting is reform programme. In early-1990 the new government freed prices and allowed the import of consumer goods. As Western economists had predicted, these steps unleashed inflation and ran down the country's hard currency surplus. The policy was reversed later in the year. But with hindsight, such a breathing space may have been essential to prepare the hard-pressed Romanians for the slow and painful adjustment of their economy to market principles.

Romania wanted to establish an effective commercial framework of legislation and regulation before unleashing the forces of the market. In April 1991 a new foreign trade law was passed, and Romania's tax and property laws are considered relatively liberal. But in some other ways, the country is only just starting out on the road to reform.

The government was forced to free prices faster than it would have liked because it could no longer afford the subsidies required to hold them down. Prices more than doubled in November 1990, and again in April 1991. A third stage of price reform was introduced in July 1991, by which time the prices of all but 14 basic products and services were liberalised.

As regards currency reform, in socialist economies hard currency tends to be extremely valuable. Governments monopolise its supply by setting unrealistic rates to citizens who want to buy it. Easing this restricted access to foreign currency is essential to trade, but carries inflationary dangers. The leu was devalued to Lei35 to $1 in November 1990, and to Lei60 in April 1991, but the black market rate was around Lei250. In November 1991 the leu was made internally convertible. It immediately lost two-thirds of its value and was trading at around Lei200 against the US dollar.

In January 1990 Foreign Trade Organisations (FTOs) lost their monopoly on foreign trade. However, they are likely to continue to dominate this trade for some time by virtue of their contacts and expertise. By the end of 1991, export controls had been lifted from all but a handful of essential items. All quantitative restrictions on imports had been abolished, and the tariffs protecting domestic industries were relatively low.

Turning to privatisation, a land law passed in 1990 allowed citizens to reclaim agricultural land confiscated by the communists. The government aimed to have 80 per cent of farmland in private hands by the end of 1991 in order to make the country self-sufficient in basic foods in 1992.

Small firms can pass directly into private hands by means of leasing arrangements. Of the country's 24,000 commercial units, 12,193 had been transferred in this way by the end of June 1991. Leases expire after two years, when the new owners acquire control. Many more commercial enterprises have been started from scratch: by April 1991 there were 134,143 authorised private entities.

Romania's first privatisation law covering large firms was passed in July 1990, and established the National Privatisation Agency. Many inadequacies were apparent in the law, however, and with the assistance of Western firms a new law was drafted, and was passed by parliament in July 1991. The new law established two types of fund which would acquire the assets of around 6000 enterprises comprising 53 per cent of Romania's industrial equity. These firms would start to be transferred to the funds in summer 1992.

Romania's banking system was fundamentally reformed between October 1990 and April 1991. The National Bank of Romania was stripped of commercial activities, and made independent of the government with regard to its responsibilities for the conduct of monetary policy, including setting interest rates and regulating the financial system. Measures were also taken to introduce competition into commercial banking.

FOREIGN ASSISTANCE AND INVESTMENT

The IMF agreed in April 1991 to provide a one-year standby credit of $545 million. By early-1992 Romania had drawn down $456 million of this facility, and had also received $355 million in balance of payments support. In November 1991 the IMF published a report on Romania's progress over the previous year which praised the significant achievements made in very difficult conditions.

The Export-Import Bank of Japan is extending a $100 million credit to Romania as part of a World Bank-led loan. But in November the World Bank announced the postponement of a $300 million loan because of Romania's political crisis. The loan was to be used for energy imports.

Starting in April 1991, the G-24 was to grant Romania $1 billion to invest in priority areas, including coal and oil production. Half of this was to come from the EC (in two $250 million tranches), and the rest from EFTA countries, Japan and Canada. The EC disbursed its first tranche in November 1991, but was prevented from releasing the second tranche for technical reasons when the other parties failed to provide their shares. The EC Commission obtained special dispensation in December 1991 to release its second tranche, and urged its G-24 partners to speed up their contributions.

In May 1991 Romania became the sixth country eligible for support from the UK's Know-How Fund.

In 1991 foreigners invested $267 million in 7787 Romanian companies. Only 38 of those companies received more than $1 million. Germany led the way in numbers, investing in 1136 firms, with Italy investing in 821, Turkey in 745, the US in 450 and France in 348. But in money terms France led the way, investing $93 million (35 per cent of the total), compared with Germany's $80 million (30 per cent). Traditional Franco-Romanian links were emphasised during a visit to Bucharest by French President Mitterand. Pullman Hotel, Colgate Palmolive, Coca-Cola, Siemens, Alcatel, Tatay, Trionics and Tangarut are among those companies undertaking new projects.

ECONOMIC PERFORMANCE

GNP in 1990 was 15 per cent down on 1989, at $89.8 billion. The decline continued in 1991, with output down a further 5 per cent at $85.3 billion. Industrial output fell 35 per cent in 1991, although in some sectors production has climbed back to 1989 levels.

Inflation has been brought down after the initial take-off in 1990, but for 1991 as a whole the rate was 217 per cent. Reducing the government budget deficit is an essential element of tackling inflation. The deficit in 1991 was Lei65 billion, nearly double the Lei37 billion endorsed by parliament.

Approximately 266,000 people were unemployed at the end of 1991 (2.7 per cent of the work-force). The figure could well reach 1 million by the end of 1992.

Although Romania is facing significant difficulties in moving towards a market economy, a start has been made towards revitalising the Romanian economy. Many prices have been liberalised and subsidies removed, import and export barriers are fairly low, privatisation measures are in hand, and foreign investors are being courted.

3
A New Legal Framework
Sinclair Roche & Temperley

In common with many other European countries, Romanian law is based on a civil law system and is substantially codified. The adoption of a new Constitution in November 1991 has served to supplement and update the historical codified legal framework as contained in the Civil Code (first adopted in December 1865) and the Commercial Code (September 1887).

In addition to the modification of the two codes by the Constitution, the move from a command to a free market economy since the Revolution of December 1989 has required the government to introduce a vast range and quantity of legislation aimed at creating and regulating a new legal framework within which developing business may flourish.

For the foreign investor, the interaction of and relationship between, newly adopted laws and the codified framework can often appear unclear and uncertain. However, to some extent, such uncertainty merely serves to highlight the speed at which the government is seeking to introduce a market-driven economy and it is fully expected that the 'gaps' in the newly adopted legislation will be supplemented by more complete reforms as the Romanian economy and legislative process continue to develop.

This chapter seeks to clarify the current uncertainties and to provide a brief outline of the developing legal framework, particularly as it affects foreign businessmen seeking to invest in Romania.

THE LEGISLATIVE FRAMEWORK

The Constitution

Romania's new Constitution, adopted on 21 November 1991, has attempted to address many of the issues encountered in a country where the economy is moving rapidly towards a system driven by the forces of private enterprise. Rights of private individuals to freedom of speech, the right to vote and the right to work are among the fundamental issues addressed. Plurality in politics is also recognised and fully endorsed.

Of importance to foreign investors, the Constitution clearly states (in a number of places) that in the event of incompatibility of the Constitution with internationally recognised legal principles, the internationally recognised principle is to prevail. With the government having already stated its intention to seek admission to the European Community in due course, the Constitution has already gone some way towards addressing the question of potential conflicts between EC and domestic legislation.

The Civil Code

Based on the Napoleonic Civil Code and adopted in December 1865, the Civil Code essentially concerns the rights, capacity and status of individuals in Romania.

Although never fully repealed, the Code has been fundamentally modified over time to reflect the requirements of a socialist society. Because of the rapid social and economic changes since 1989, the Civil Code is now largely outdated and is currently being redrafted under direction from the Justice Ministry. However, with so much legislation being drafted in order to implement the process of change to a market economy, the Civil Code has not merited a high priority in the reform process and, at present, no date can be estimated for the adoption of a new Code.

The Commercial Code

Adopted on 1 September 1887, the Romanian Commercial Code was, for many years, the principal legislation governing commercial activity in the country.

The original Code has been modified on several occasions (particularly in the period between the two World Wars) and in 1938 was almost entirely replaced by a new version. However, the

Code of 1938 was never widely accepted within Romania and the original Code, never having been formally repealed, continued to be followed. Throughout the period of socialist government until 1989, the terms of the Commercial Code were largely ignored, business being conducted through state organisations in accordance with government policy.

Since January 1990 the terms of the Commercial Code have once again come to the forefront in regulating business in Romania. With the adoption of a new Company Law, Foreign Investment Law, Land Law and Privatisation Law (to name only a few), the Commercial Code has, obviously, now been largely altered. However, it continues to provide the basic framework for the creation of contracts, security and the regulation of commercial transactions.

Transformation Law

Passed in August 1990, the Law on State Owned Enterprises Restructuring (the 'Transformation Law') represents one of the major steps in the transformation of the Romanian economy towards private ownership.

The Transformation Law marked the initial step of 'transforming' the state-controlled command economy into a free market economy by creating new state-owned companies through which business should be undertaken – unlike the former situation where business was undertaken directly through state-operated monopolies. The Law vested the assets of all companies formed under it in the companies themselves rather than in the state and, in effect, marked the first step towards privatisation under the Privatisation Law of 1991.

Although the share capital of the companies set up under the Transformation Law continues to be owned by the state, the Law is unambiguous in stating that the property of a company belongs to that company and that it is at the absolute discretion of the management of the company as to how a company uses such property. Unfortunately, in practice, the management of many of the companies set up under the Law has been unable to reconcile the concept of a company (having its share capital owned by the state), owning its assets and being able to deal with them in its own right, with the former concept of state ownership of assets (where, of course, there was no separate company structure – only a state-controlled monopoly with no ownership rights in the assets used). This can cause problems for many potential investors in their discussions and negotiations with Romanian managers.

While the government is continuing to seek to remove any misunderstanding on the part of management, potential investors should be aware that ministerial consent is no longer normally required when making an investment – only board and, in some circumstances, shareholder approval.

In addition, the Transformation Law established the National Privatisation Agency in preparation for privatisation of state-owned commercial companies established under the Law. By way of partially effecting small privatisations, the Transformation Law also provides a framework within which privately owned trading companies can take business concessions from the state and state-owned enterprises. However, the Law does not allow for such privately owned companies to purchase assets for the purposes of carrying on their own businesses; such acquisition being regulated by the Privatisation Law.

Foreign investment

As will be discussed in Chapter 7, the Foreign Investment Law (passed in its current form in April 1991) regulates all foreign investment in Romania – with the exception of investment by virtue of participation in the privatisation process. Accordingly, the law is of fundamental importance to all potential foreign investors.

Clearly defining business interests within which a foreign investor may participate, the Law establishes the regulatory framework for making investments under the control of the Romanian Development Agency. The provisions extend to tax incentives and concessions on importation of equipment and on profits. While not without weaknesses, the Law is generally recognised as providing a clear framework within which foreign investors must operate.

Trading companies

For a foreign investor wishing to set up a business within Romania – other than by way of a representative office only – the Law Concerning Trading Companies (the 'Company Law') is of fundamental importance in regulating the structure of the local business vehicle.

Although most foreign investment is, in fact, conducted through limited liability companies, the Company Law provides for five different types of corporate structure:

- General partnerships, through which the partners assume joint and several unlimited liability.

- Limited partnerships, by which the active partners have joint and several unlimited liability and any sleeping partner has a liability up to the limit of the value of his stock only.
- Sleeping partnerships, similar to the limited partnership.
- Joint stock companies, similar to a UK public limited company, in which the members' liability is limited to the value of their stock holdings.
- Limited liability companies, in which a member's liability is limited to the amount of his shareholding, as with the joint stock company.

From the foreign investor's point of view, the legal framework is not yet in place to support a partnership structure and, with unlimited liability for an active partner, the attraction of investing through means of a partnership is minimal.

The limitation of liability by investing through a joint stock or limited liability company is an obvious incentive to an investor. However, the additional attraction of the limited liability company over a joint stock company is that the minimum share capital requirement is substantially less than for the joint stock company (Lei100,000 as compared to Lei1 million). Additionally, the regulations affecting limited liability companies are less onerous than for joint stock companies.

Privatisation

Following the creation of state-owned trading companies under the Transformation Law, the Privatisation Law – passed in August 1991 – sets out the framework within which it is intended that the transfer of state-owned trading companies to private ownership will be effected.

The National Privatisation Agency (set up under the Transformation Law) is responsible for the implementation of the privatisation process – which presents significant opportunity for foreign business investment through acquisition of strategic shareholdings and/or absolute control of existing businesses – initially through a pilot scheme and latterly through State and Private Ownership Funds.

Intellectual property

Having adopted domestic legislation affecting patents (1974), trademarks (1967) and copyright (1956), the Romanian government has now adopted a new Patents Act which takes effect from 21 January 1992.

The new Act repeals the previous Patents Act of 1974 and is aimed at redressing the inconsistencies of the previous legislation regulating patents within the framework of a communist society. The new legislation recognises that the exclusive right to use an invention may be protected in Romania by a patent granted by the State Office for Inventions and Marks – a specialised government agency with exclusive powers regulating the protection of industrial property in Romania.

The length of patent protection depends on the nature of the invention, but may be for a period of up to 20 years in the case of a new invention. If the invention is a complimentary invention – that is, an invention which cannot be used except in conjunction with a pre-existing invention – the term is limited to the term of protection in respect of the invention which is improved (although protection may not be for less than ten years).

From a foreign investor's point of view, the new Patents Act protects foreign investors through the application of the Conventions to which Romania is a party. These include, in particular, the Paris Convention of 1883 (to which Romania acceded in 1920). The protection of a patent held by a foreign investor from a Convention country has priority from the date of the first deposit overseas if, within 12 months of the date of deposit, the inventor also applies for a patent of the same invention within Romania.

Employment regulation

The Romanian Constitution sets out the basic principles of employment which, in effect, are (a) a right to employment for every person and (b) certain minimum protections by law.

Legislation extends to provisions covering employment standards, collective bargaining, human rights, health and safety at work, remuneration and financial recompense for unemployment through the Social Security Fund.

While a foreign investor may employ a Romanian citizen without any authorisation, employment of foreign nationals is restricted to management or specially skilled employment (under the Foreign Investment Law).

As regards regulation of employment terms, an employee must agree a contract of employment, which may be either collective or individual. In either event, the contract must contain certain specific minimum details being, essentially:

- the minimum legal age for employment;
- the minimum wage;
- provisions relating to holiday entitlement, bonuses, sickness benefits and special working conditions; and
- details of scope of employment activity and the minimum required levels of skill.

The right to participate in a trade union and the right to strike are also recognised and regulated under existing Romanian employment legislation.

Banking

Law No 33 of 1991 – the Banking Law – creates a two tier banking structure in Romania. The National Bank of Romania has been assigned the role of central bank with authority for issuing regulations under monetary, credit, foreign exchange and payment policies. All other banking activities are undertaken by commercial banks under the supervision of the National Bank.

A limited amount of foreign investment in the banking sector has already been effected, with a number of private banks having been established with some level of foreign participation.

Property law and land ownership

Of fundamental importance to many foreign investors, the lack of a fully effective property law remains an unsatisfactory aspect of the developing legislative process. Although the Constitution guarantees rights of private property against the state, there are still restrictions on ownership of land by foreign citizens. Further consideration is given to the rights of property ownership in Chapter 15.

Environmental legislation

At the time of writing, a new Environmental Law is under consideration by the Romanian government. The principal objectives of the draft legislation (which will be of interest to many foreign investors, particularly in connection with heavy industries and the petrochemical industry) are:

- preventing and reducing environmental pollution;
- maintaining and improving the environment; and
- redeveloping property previously damaged by environmental causes.

The Ministry of the Environment will be the central body responsible for establishing and structuring rules and regulations for the implementation of the legislation, and for imposing penalties for any breach of the environmental regulations. The Ministry will also be responsible for establishing a compulsory registration and authorisation system where businesses which are intending to participate in any activities that may adversely affect the environment must seek registration and approval before proceeding with the implementation of any proposal.

OTHER LEGISLATION AND OUTLOOK

In addition to the outline of legislation already given, Romania has already adopted laws affecting (among other matters) competition (initial competition legislation was introduced in the Transformation Law), accounting, social security and convertibility of currency.

Stated objectives of the government include an acceleration of the land restitution process and it is in this area that the most radical developments are to be expected.

To date the government has attempted to introduce wide-ranging legislation for the stimulation of a free market economy and for encouraging foreign investment. However, it is realised that without effective legislation regulating land ownership, it will be difficult to achieve a continued growth of the market economy.

4

Business Culture
Touche Ross

Romanian enterprises suffered under probably the most rigid postwar planning system of any of the Eastern European countries and, moreover, saw this become more stifling as time went on. From the mid-1970s onwards Romania experienced a kind of second Stalinist period in which imports and contact with foreign organisations were restricted while the regime demanded exports; in which higher productivity was expected as useful investment was curtailed in favour of Ceauşescu's grotesque vanity projects; in which greater organisational efficiency was desired even as the system merged plants into larger and larger structures where local initiative was discouraged; in which workers were supposed to be increasingly involved in developing the economy by motivated effort while the reality was that the work-force was often forced to work at the weekend without payment to ensure the fulfilment of plan targets.

The legacy of the last 15 years of communist rule is factories often with badly run down capital stock, managements used to improvising to hold things together rather than planning for the future, alienated workers with great skill at getting the most out of antiquated equipment, bad working conditions for both blue and while collar staff and an acquaintance with technical, but often not managerial, solutions to problems.

The dismantling of the planning structure, the liberalisation of trade and the breaking up of many of the larger monoliths into smaller organisations has started to expose managers across Romania to the necessity for lower level decision making so that the situation now is more complex than just after the Revolution. There are wide variations in managerial and organisational competence between regions (with the area around Timoşoara generally regarded as the best) and industries (with light industry being the most dynamic) as well as trade orientation (export factories usually having better workers, managers and quality control) and between different managerial styles. In consequence, foreign companies interested in a sector of Romanian industry should not give up hope having visited one unpromising plant.

STRUCTURES – THE PRACTICAL CONSEQUENCES
State enterprises

There are two basic types of state enterprise – *regia autonoma* and *societate comerciale*.

Regia autonoma can be translated roughly as 'state corporation'. These 600 or so organisations include public utilities, defence producers and other strategic industries supplying raw materials and intermediate goods. They represent the heaviest and most capital intensive parts of industry and have less freedom of action from the state than the *societate comerciale*. They cannot be privatised under present laws, and joint ventures involving them are more likely to be scrutinised by the Ministry of Industry or other interested bodies.

There are over 6000 *societate comerciale* or 'commercial companies'. They have shares (albeit currently held by the state) and are intended for ultimate privatisation. Almost all consumer goods are produced by these companies as well as a large proportion of industrial goods. The size of the enterprises is generally smaller, often because large entities have been broken up after the Revolution. Examples of such break-ups are to be found in textiles where the largest clothes producing organisation in Europe was broken into seven entities, and in car production where the largest car company, Dacia, was split up into the core business of producing cars and peripheral businesses such as engine production, distribution and services.

Many commercial companies have broken their links with the old specialist Foreign Trade Organisations (FTOs) and now conduct trade either on their own behalf or through new private intermediaries. Differences between factories can be great. Probably the best shoe factory in Bucharest admits to discarding up to 10 times as much of its production intended for export due to quality problems as a similar factory in the west of the country. This despite the fact that the Bucharest factory has a good management team, exemplary worker discipline and has developed an in-house tannery using imported equipment to make sure that quality problems due to leather are reduced.

Managers are often aware of the theoretical solutions to many of their basic problems in quality and organisation and are keen to improve their knowledge but are unable to put what they know into practice for lack of resources. In addition, management time is often swallowed up in managing the severe problems of the debt queue that has built up, finding raw materials of all types, as well as trying to comply with new laws and decrees.

It needs to be noted that many of the more dynamic managers from state enterprise have left, however, to start up their own firms or work for foreign companies. Others were removed after 1989, having climbed their way to the top more through contacts in the Communist Party than through competence, and are being replaced either through election by the workers or through an open competition process involving a selection board. These various processes, together with the provision of training and experience abroad through international agencies, is leading to changes in the people in charge of state companies with younger people coming to the fore.

Co-operatives

There are around 2300 co-operatives in Romania, usually involved in the processing of agricultural products and the manufacture of craft goods such as carpets, certain types of clothes and ceramics. Traditionally the co-operatives exported through their own FTOs and this continues to a greater extent than with industrial organisations due to the relatively small size of most co-operatives and their isolation from direct contact with foreigners.

Private companies

The change in the system for registering private entrepreneurs makes it difficult to define exactly the private sector. There are some 60,000 private companies of all types registered under the new system, of which about three-quarters are operational. To these must be added another 50,000 registered under the old system either as family businesses or small businesses, and more than 100,000 people who are classified as self-employed.

The sector is now growing fast, particularly in trade, distribution and services, which around 65 per cent of the firms claim as their activity. Less than one-fifth are currently involved in manufacturing although that statistic must be seen in the perspective of the low levels of capital available until now for private entrepreneurs. As privatisation of companies and assets gets underway from 1992, the private sector's weight in the economy will grow and its focus will shift more towards production. Already private companies deal with about a quarter of retail turnover and a fifth of foreign trade. Many firms have grown explosively – one company founded with less than Lei100,000 was recently reported to have had an annual turnover in 1991 of around Lei10 billion.

Joint ventures

The passing of perhaps the most liberal foreign investment legislation in Eastern Europe in 1990 has led to the establishment of a large number of joint ventures in Romania.

In 1990 around 1500 were formed, with an initial capital of $129 million; in 1991 around 6500 were formed with capital of $150 million. There was a daily increase of around 20-25 at the end of the year. Even when the miners came on their second trip to Bucharest in September 1991, the level of registrations slowed only for a few days. Most of the joint ventures are relatively small (90 per cent have less than $50,000 initial foreign capital), although some of these originally small firms are now growing, large concerns – something the official figures do not record.

Since the middle of 1991 another trend has become apparent – the arrival of large multinational corporations setting up multi-million dollar ventures – so that there are now more than 40 with more than $1 million initial foreign capital. They represent a second wave of investment concentrated more in infrastructure and production including firms like Coca-Cola, ABB, Alcatel, Siemens, Colgate-Palmolive, Shell, Goldstar and Bouygues. Alongside these investments are numerous representative offices of large firms. This has led to estimates of foreign investment over the next 5 years of around $500-$700 million a year.

MENTALITIES

Too much is often made of the supposedly ingrained characteristics of managers and workers in Romania, usually by those who have had a couple of bad experiences in trying to transact business in the country. Romania has its fair share of stupid, difficult and lazy people, of course, but they can be avoided by careful screening of partners, as in any country. Given the right incentives and conditions, Romanians display all the motivation and creativity one would hope for. Problems of bureaucracy are more likely to stem from badly designed management structures, built to implement a plan rather than respond to a changing world, and from a lack of clarity on both sides about exactly what is required when.

There are some differences of approach, however, that do need to be borne in mind when dealing with Romanian organisations.

Prices and values

The lack of contact with international prices and costs, the very low salaries and the minimal purchasing power of the leu against other currencies can make Western prices seem exorbitant to many Romanians. A manager may be horrified, for example, when a consultant expects hundreds of pounds a day, plus expenses, for advice when the manager's own salary is much less than a hundred pounds a month. At the same time, because of the different approaches to valuing assets – Romanian enterprises generally value themselves on the cost of their assets – a foreign company may find itself very unpopular or disbelieved when it suggests that the value of an enterprise is very low or non-existent due to a lack of real profitability. Romanian managers are aware of their own inexperience in pricing and valuation and worry, therefore, at the prospect of foreigners taking advantage of them. Some foreigners have done so, which means that an emphasised display of integrity during business dealings, together with the provision of evidence for costs and prices in the West are recommended when discussing these issues.

The largest part of the Romanian university-trained managers will have taken their degrees in technical subjects like mechanics, hydrology and architecture rather than economics or management. It is not surprising to find, therefore, that most business people, particularly in state companies, find the technical aspects of deals the most interesting. Financial aspects can tend to be relegated to the bottom of agendas. First, an organisation will want to be satisfied that a product or deal makes technical sense to them, and only then will other details come into focus. This implies that either technical people get sent before or with deal makers, or that sales people are well briefed on product, specification and parameters.

The severity of the implementation of communist laws and the dearth of case law referring to the new regulations means that

Romanians often deal with questions very literally and are not comfortable interpreting the spirit of provisions – or may simply assume that the least favourable option is the most likely. Some organisations and employees of joint ventures will want detailed clarifications from a ministry or other authority concerning a law before they move ahead with a deal for fear of liability in the event of a mistake. This is often identified as 'bureaucratic ways' or stubbornness but in the reform period, as the legal structure and system develop, it is not surprising that Romanians have some anxiety about breaking laws with which few people are fully familiar, and which change frequently. A good lawyer or accountant is recommended to minimise the effects of this.

COMMUNICATIONS

Perhaps the single biggest frustration of doing business in Romania can be getting and keeping in contact with partners and one's own staff. Along with other countries in the region, the communications infrastructure is in bad condition and limited in extent, even if attempts are being made now to upgrade the various channels. It is important, therefore, to give some thought to how to ensure that information can flow both to and from Romania.

Taking into consideration the two-hour time difference, some companies arrange for the UK side to call to Romania at a fixed time each day or week to exchange news and faxes. Alternatively, direct dial telephone lines can sometimes be obtained by the Romanian partner by application to a telephone company, Rom Telecom. If not, the Western partner may agree to pay for vital documents to be sent out of the country by one of the several international courier companies now working in Romania, like DHL, TNT or UPS. It may also be appropriate to assist in the supply of useful materials like fax paper, stationery or printer ribbons to ensure that problems of availability do not hold back deals.

With regard to foreign languages, French and English are the most commonly spoken, with English increasingly having the edge. Most enterprises should have no difficulty providing someone to translate or interpret. However, when it comes to negotiations, it is advisable to have your own person to be able to pick up nuances of what is being said and to catch behind-the-hand comments, both of which give feedback on the progress of the discussion. Make use of time-outs to hear what your translator has picked up.

Expect meetings to last rather longer than in the West, due to the need for translation and also as both sides will need to understand what the other side means by certain expressions or words. In addition, use examples of the operation of the deal you are discussing to make sure that both sides have the same ideas about what will happen, and have not made different basic assumptions about the way such deals normally work. A 'normal' deal for a Romanian company may be different from what you regard as such.

5
Market Intelligence
Touche Ross

In order to run the most authoritarian regime of Eastern Europe, the Romanian Communist Party took great pains to obstruct the free flow of information of all types, both within the country and to the outside world. For example, typewriters were registered to suppress the samizdat that plagued other regimes. Information on large parts of manufacturing industry was declared a state secret. That, added to the particularity of the information required by the plan (generally relatively basic production data), led Romania to become an information desert which is still a problem today, even if the restrictions on most types of information have been abolished.

Such information which does exist is often out of date, not comparable to Western data or not comparable to figures produced before the Revolution when statistics were an offshoot of propaganda as much as of elucidation. While that has started to be redressed by the initiation of various local and foreign projects to provide business information, it still has to be said that more work needs to be done by potential investors and traders in Romania than in the other countries of Eastern Europe.

OBTAINING INFORMATION

As very few sources of information can be relied on too heavily to provide all the perspectives on the Romanian market that a foreign company requires to make an informed judgement, it is a good idea to take information from as many sources as are available in order to be able to cross check trends that emerge in one source, using both qualitative and quantitative data. Since many sources of information do not attempt to publish or sell the information they collect or provide, it can be advisable to have someone to do the leg work, making contact with all possible holders of information on the problem in question to see whether they can contribute to clarifying the situation.

Most Romanian organisations are helpful to those trying to track down information and would usually refer you to someone else if they cannot help themselves. The people to talk to in ministries and companies are either the international division or the protocol department. Creativity can reap rewards. One oil company which found the official geological data on a certain area it had bought of little use, then paid the students and teachers at the geology faculty at Bucharest University to do more general geological research on the same area to clarify the situation - with great effect. Given the low cost of labour, it may be appropriate to pay for a market study using questionnaires, interviews or polling.

SOURCES

External

Before going to Romania it is worth visiting the Eastern European Trade Council to look through the large amounts of information of all types they have available on all the countries of Eastern Europe. This extends from trade directories and reference books, through copies of Romanian legislation and business magazines, to summaries of BBC reports on the economy and the various newsletters on Eastern Europe. As a point of information, and a free one at that, there is nowhere better to start. In addition, it is worth getting a copy of the DTI's country profile, hints for exporters and the various other sheets of information that they have (for example on English companies already represented in Bucharest). The DTI's export intelligence service might also be useful on an on-going basis for early notification of trade opportunities. The Romanian Embassy in London is worth calling to see what materials they have available at any particular time. A talk with the commercial attaché may throw up a few decent contacts not available on paper. Local chambers of commerce, particularly the LCCI may have many interesting documents, especially on trade, and may well have organised a trade mission to Romania, in which case a report may exist of useful contacts in Romania and members of the mission could be consulted for suggestions.

As the European Community PHARE programme is now spending a lot of money in Romania on consulting and procurement of certain products, it is worth keeping in contact with sources that cover forthcoming tenders.

As legal and accounting firms are increasingly involved in Romania, some of them now provide free documentation on doing business in the country which often has useful data, particularly on the legal situation.

The first Western newsletter specifically devoted to Romania is now being published in America and is called *Romanian Economic Newsletter*. As the name suggests, it is primarily oriented towards economic developments. There is now quite a large choice of newsletters and magazines dealing with Eastern Europe in general, the best known of which are published by PlanEcon, Business International and the *Financial Times*. Business International also provide a research service.

Internal

On arriving in Romania there are a number of places to start the information search. The Romanian Development Agency (RDA), which has the responsibility for promoting foreign investment and trade, can supply for free some information on laws, the general business environment and advice on some specific matters which concern foreign companies. Industry specialists are available to keep up with identifying potential partners and even with opening discussions. Where information is not held by the agency, the staff will usually either obtain it from elsewhere, or refer an inquirer to the relevant source.

The British Embassy is another good starting point to find out about the local market conditions. They have probably already had some experience with most kinds of problems put before them by British companies and so can provide relevant information rather than speculation. The Embassy also produces its own small newsletter. For those who also speak French, it is worth getting a copy of the French Embassy's newsletter *Le Fils*. The French Ministry for Foreign Trade also sell a good *Dossier d'Information* on Romania for Ffr500 which has some sectoral studies as well as information on laws, etc.

The Romanian Chamber of Commerce has some publications including a kind of trade directory, in English, which can be obtained on payment.

The National Commission for Statistics produces a year-book of several hundred pages in Romanian and a summary in English, with data on all manner of social and economic trends. In addition, it produces a monthly economic bulletin in Romanian and English, an industrial survey, a price survey and some sectoral studies. All of these are available at low prices.

The Ministry of Industry, and its component branch ministries organised by sector, hold large amounts of information that might be of use. It is worth contacting the protocol department where there are English-speaking staff and discussing your information needs. Given time, data can include details on interesting companies falling under the responsibility of the Ministry and concerning the sector as a whole.

Other ministries may, or may not, be able to supply information easily on their area of competence. For example, the Ministry of Trade and Tourism produce the book containing the tariff levels for all goods imported into Romania, and this can be bought from them.

One method of getting in touch with foreign companies much preferred in Romania is through trade fairs. The two biggest are TIB, which deals with all types of goods and takes place each October, and TIBCO, which deals with consumer goods only. There are also several fairs dealing, for example, with medical goods.

There are a large number of research institutes that are organised largely along industrial sector lines. These are best contacted through the RDA or the Ministry of Industry.

Rompres produces a daily newsletter called *Economic Highlights* with exerpts from the press. This can be obtained on subscription from them.

The Romanian company WEBO produces a magazine called *Western Perspective* which offers useful reference information for visitors to Bucharest.

There is a four-page English language newspaper produced daily called *9 O'clock News* which has a business and economic page with some interesting articles. This can be obtained by subscription, although in Bucharest there are usually free copies in major hotels.

In the Romanian language there are a number of specialist newspapers dealing with economic and business questions. They can be a bit theoretical but sometimes have useful bits. The main ones are *Tribuna Economica* and *Economistul*, and there are also advertising-driven news sheets with names like *Fast Business* and *Partenerul*. All the serious dailies have economic and business articles of varying interest. They include: *Libertatea, Romania Libera, Adevarul, Azi* and *Cotidianul*.

6

Trading Partners
Sinclair Roche & Temperley

This chapter describes the development of Romania's external trade with its main trading partners in the former Comecon countries of Central and Eastern Europe on the one hand, and the United States, Western Europe and the Middle East on the other.

FOREIGN TRADE AND INVESTMENT 1850 TO 1947

Before World War II, Romania was a predominantly agricultural country. Despite a wealth of raw materials, industry was slow to develop.

The petroleum industry began in the 1850s and the first refinery was established at Ploesti in 1858. Production increased steadily to a total of almost 2 million metric tonnes in 1913, by which time 57 per cent of Romania's oil yield was exported. By 1914, the main components of industrial production were food products (49 per cent), oil and petroleum products (29 per cent), forestry products and construction materials (14 per cent) and metal and energy production (8 per cent).

At this stage, Germany had overtaken Austria-Hungary as Romania's largest trading partner. Grain exports made up 68.6 per cent of total exports followed by petroleum and forestry products. The development of Romanian industry was hampered by poor transport and credit systems as well as the free trade policies of successive Romanian governments. Industrialisation depended largely on foreign capital which dominated particularly the oil, metal and forestry industries.

After World War I an active protection policy was introduced and foreign capital lost considerable ground. Between 1920 and 1940 Romania was the world's fifth largest agricultural producer and, by 1937, agriculture still accounted for 55 per cent of the net national product, a large proportion of agricultural produce being exported. Industry made significant progress in the inter-war period. By 1938 only 21 per cent of capital invested in Romanian industry was foreign, Britain being the biggest foreign investor followed by France, the United States, Italy and Germany. As regards external commerce, Germany again established itself during this period as Romania's principal foreign trade partner, importing raw materials and grain in return for industrial goods and arms.

ROMANIA, COMECON AND THE WEST

The communist government which took power in 1947 immediately began to remodel the Romanian economy and to trade on Stalinist lines. Romania was brought within the Soviet trading bloc by an economic collaboration treaty in 1945 and became a founder member of Comecon in 1949. The objectives of Comecon were to 'assist in the economic development of its members' and to further 'deepen and perfect the co-operation and development of socialist economic integration'.

In 1958, the withdrawal of Soviet troops from Romania coincided with the beginnings of an increasingly independent Romanian economic and foreign policy. In the late-1950s and early-1960s foreign trade was re-orientated towards the West with some Western firms showing a willingness to grant credit to Romania. The total value of imports from the West grew from 21.5 per cent in 1958 to 40 per cent in 1965 and exports to Western countries increased from 24 per cent to 33 per cent during this period, while both imports from and exports to the Soviet Union fell significantly.

In the early-1960s Romania withstood pressure from other members of Comecon for greater integration of the economies of the member countries and, at the same time, Romanian leaders emphasised the country's diplomatic independence and established closer relations with China and Western countries in defiance of the Soviet Union. Diplomatic tension with the Soviet Union, however, did not reflect any move away from Stalinist economic policies by the Romanian leadership, its hallmarks being continuing concentration on investment in heavy industry, neglect of agriculture and the absence of any concessions to consumer demand. Successive five-year plans throughout the 1960s and 1970s set increasingly ambitious industrial targets and rates of growth, without much regard to availability of raw materials or quality of products, although increasing independence from the Soviet Union brought new commercial ties with the West. Romania joined the World Bank and IMF in 1972 and reached agreement with the European Community on preferential treatment in trade in 1973. In 1971 Romania was the first Comecon country to permit joint ventures with foreign partners. Western credit flowed freely at this time and, by 1982, Romania's foreign debts stood at approximately US$13 billion. Trade with the Soviet Union and other Comecon countries declined yet further with a corresponding rise in trade with the West, the Middle East and the Third World.

By the mid-1970s food shortages had set in as a result of the chronic neglect of agriculture in favour of heavy industry, and industry itself stagnated under tight central control so that, in the 1980s, Romania found it necessary again to re-orientate its foreign trade towards Comecon and the Third World. Over the period 1982 to 1986 Romania's trade with the Soviet Union increased from 17 per cent to 34 per cent of the total, with exports including steel, industrial machinery, rolling stock, consumer goods, oil equipment and weapons in return for imports of electricity and raw materials often on barter terms. Romania continued to maintain its neo-Stalinist economic policies, even as the rest of Eastern Europe embraced *Perestroika* and *Glasnost*.

FOREIGN TRADE IN THE 1990s

Table 6.1 shows the changing pattern of Romania's foreign trade over 1989, 1990 and the first nine months of 1991.

Table 6.1 *The balance of trade, 1989–91*

	1989	1990	To end-Sep. 1991
Exports			
Roubles (million)	4545	2474	753
US dollars (million)	5949	3600	2355
Imports			
Roubles (million)	5096	4194	515
US dollars (million)	3465	5436	3534
Balance			
Roubles (million)	–551	–1720	+288
US dollars (million)	+2484	–1836	–1179

It is apparent from the table that Romania's rouble-dominated trade with other Comecon members, particularly the former Soviet Union, has declined dramatically since the fall of the Ceaușescu regime. This is consistent with the pattern throughout Central and Eastern Europe although it should be borne in mind that the reduction in rouble-denominated transactions is attributable not only to the quantitative reduction in trade between former Comecon members but also to the fact that Romanian trade between these countries is now largely carried out in hard currency.

While Romania ran a hard currency trade surplus in 1989, the position has now been reversed and it seems likely that Romania will have a net deficiency in its foreign currency account during at least the early stages of its transition to a market economy. While the volume of both exports and imports denominated in hard currency has declined over the period shown in the table, exports of most products have declined more than imports, the resulting deficit putting serious pressure on Romania's very limited foreign currency reserves.

Romania's main foreign currency exports are fuel, mineral raw materials and metals, accounting for almost 50 per cent of total hard

Table 6.2 *Principal trading partners, 1990*

Exports
Former Soviet Union	25.2%
Germany	11.0%
Italy	8.8%
USA	5.8%
France	3.4%
Czechoslovakia	3.2%
Turkey	2.8%
The Netherlands	2.7%
Hungary	2.6%
China (PR)	2.6%
Yugoslavia	2.3%

Imports
Former Soviet Union	23.6%
Germany	11.4%
Saudi Arabia	8.3%
Iran	5.9%
USA	4.6%
Poland	4.3%
Egypt	3.6%
Czechoslovakia	3.1%
Yugoslavia	2.3%
Bulgaria	2.3%

Table 6.3 *Trade with the UK (£ million), 1985–90*

	1985	1986	1987	1988	1989	1990
UK exports	78.5	82.0	55.7	50.1	38.9	85.7
UK imports	102.9	86.7	92.5	100.9	117.7	56.1

currency exports in 1990; these are followed by consumer industrial goods representing approximately 20 per cent of the 1990 total. Well over half the 1990 exports denominated in roubles were comprised of machinery and equipment. Romania's main hard currency imports in 1990 were also in the category of fuel, mineral raw materials and metals and, on its rouble account, machinery and equipment followed by fuel and mineral raw materials. Romania's main trading partners in 1990 are shown in Table 6.2.

In July 1991 the United States extended its trade agreement with Romania for a further ten years, although Romania now no longer enjoys Most Favoured Nation status with the USA.

Table 6.3 shows the development of the UK's trade with Romania. Thus in 1990, the UK achieved a trade surplus with Romania for the first time in almost a decade due to the fall in Romanian production and increased reliance on imports. The UK's main exports to Romania in 1990 were chemicals, transport and transport equipment, power generating machinery and non-ferrous metals. Imports from Romania were mainly textiles and furniture.

ROMANIA'S TRADE WITH THE EUROPEAN COMMUNITY

Trade with the EC currently represents 45 per cent of Romania's foreign trade.

Romania officially recognised the EC in 1990 when it also established diplomatic relations by setting up a permanent mission in Brussels. Shortly afterwards an Agreement on Trade and Commercial and Economic Co-operation was signed. Negotiations are under way for the eventual association of Romania with the Community by which Romania hopes to secure treatment as favourable as that accorded to Czechoslovakia, Hungary and Poland. In particular, Romania is seeking elimination of the quantitative restrictions on imports of textiles and other individual products by the Community and reductions in EC tariffs.

The Romanian government has established an interdepartmental committee to assist in further negotiations with the EC which will comprise representatives of the Ministries of Foreign Affairs, Trade and Tourism, Economy and Finance, Industry, Agriculture, Transport, Environment, Justice and Culture, the Romanian Development Agency and the National Privatisation Agency. This committee, chaired by the Minister for Trade and Tourism, will co-ordinate all negotiations with the EC designed to secure associate status for Romania.

FOREIGN INVESTMENT

Romania passed a new Foreign Investment Law on 1 March 1991. The detailed terms of the Law are examined in Chapter 7. The Romanian Development Agency has reported that in January 1992 over 8000 joint ventures had been established with a registered capital of US$289 million. Of the joint venture companies registered, 39 have a registered capital of over US$1 million. According to 1991 statistics the main foreign investors were: France $34.7 million; the USA $32.0 million; Germany $29.0 million; the UK $23.6 million; and The Netherlands $17.0 million.

While the violent demonstrations by miners in Bucharest in late-1991 and the consequent replacement of the Roman government had a serious negative impact on the confidence of foreign investors, foreign investment now appears again to be on an upward trend and investor confidence will no doubt be further boosted by the results of the local elections of February 1992.

CONCLUSION AND PROSPECTS

The post-1990 changes required to establish a market economy in Romania and upheavals elsewhere in Central and Eastern Europe have resulted in serious dislocation of the patterns of Romanian foreign trade established between 1947 and 1989. Romania has been obliged to find new markets for many of its products in place of its former Comecon partners. Proportionately, however, Romania has been less heavily dependent in the past on intra-Comecon trade than most other Central and Eastern European countries and may find the transition to new markets less traumatic than some of its neighbours.

Romania's foreign debt is also low in comparison with that of other former Comecon countries so that Western export credit institutions may in future be more ready to extend cover and Western banks more ready to lend to Romania than to other countries in the region. The future long-term health of Romania's foreign trade and balance of payments will, however, depend on the country finding suitable export products to make up for dwindling oil reserves and limiting its dependence on imported food, raw materials and consumer goods.

7

Foreign Investment

Sinclair Roche & Temperley

Fundamental to the transformation of Romania's former command economy to a free market economy is the promotion of foreign investment into the country. Such investment will provide a much-needed source of hard currency for financing the economy and will bring with it, in many cases, industrial development, exposure to foreign markets and exposure to Western management and training techniques.

This chapter is intended to outline the framework within which foreign investment in Romania may be effected and to provide a working guide for businessmen intending to invest in Romanian business.

HISTORICAL PERSPECTIVE

In the early-1970s Romania was the initiator among Eastern European countries in formulating a joint venture law aimed at attracting foreign capital to Romania. A number of agreements were signed, including the continuing joint venture with British Aerospace for the production, under licence, of BAC 1-11 jets. However, not all investors viewed the regime benevolently and foreign investment under the old legislation (Decree-Law No 424) was effectively reduced to a mere trickle due to the isolationist policies pursued by the government under the presidency of Nicolae Ceauşescu.

One of the first measures implemented by the new regime following the December 1989 disturbances was the enactment of Decree-Law No 96 of 1990. This provided a basic framework for foreign investment, reinforcing some of the provisions of the earlier joint venture law. In particular, 100 per cent foreign ownership of companies was allowed, as was remittance of hard currency profits.

However, in spite of some joint ventures being established within the framework, the foreign investment regime as set out in the 1990 law did not cover all aspects of foreign investment and joint ventures and, consequently, the law was superseded by Decree-Law No 35 of April 1991 – the Foreign Investment Law (which became effective on 3 April 1991).

FOREIGN INVESTMENT LAW

Areas of participation

The Foreign Investment Law – also known as the Joint Venture Law, although it does not relate specifically to joint ventures – allows a foreign investor to:

- establish a new company, subsidiary or branch, either wholly owned or with Romanian participation, in accordance with Romanian Company Law No 31 of 1990;
- participate in the share capital of an existing company;
- participate in a concession, lease or administration of an 'Autonomous State Enterprise';
- acquire proprietary rights over moveable and immovable property (but excluding land ownership rights);
- acquire industrial and intellectual property rights;
- purchase production facilities and other buildings (but excluding residential buildings not related to the investment); and
- participate in agreements for the exploration and production of natural resources.

Investment may be made in cash; by the provision of machinery and equipment or services; by the payment of profits from other business activities carried out within Romania; or by any combination of the foregoing.

Restrictions on investment

The only restrictions placed on the scope of the foreign investment activity are that the activities must not:

- infringe environmental protection regulations;
- affect national security and defence interests; or
- harm 'public order, health and good morals'.

As regards participation in Romanian businesses, the participation of foreign investors may consist of:

- investment in freely convertible currency, without limitation;
- contribution of plant, machinery and equipment (up to a maximum value of 60 per cent of the issued share capital of the joint venture company – the value of contributions in non-cash form must be evidenced by a valuer's report or receipts);
- services, management training and expertise or industrial and intellectual property rights; and
- profits obtained in freely convertible currencies or in lei from business activities carried out in Romania.

The law includes a specific expropriation guarantee aimed at giving comfort to foreign investors. The guarantee takes the form of an undertaking from the government not to nationalise or expropriate investments other than in instances where such expropriation or nationalisation is in the public interest (and then only subject to payment of compensation equivalent to the affected investment). However, it is important to note that the expropriation guarantee does not extend to protection of investors against restitution claims from third parties (a matter which is likely to receive further consideration by the government in future months).

Incentives

By way of providing further incentives to the foreign investor, the Law also provides for certain specified tax holidays and import duty concessions. The tax holidays range from two years (for investments in trade, tourism, banking and insurance) to five years (for investments in industry, agriculture and construction). There may also be further tax concessions following the initial tax holiday, depending on the activity of the enterprise.

Although the Law appears attractive in this respect, the tax concessions have, in fact, been widely criticised by investors as being insufficient in scope and ineffective in actually giving any tax savings. Prospective investors are of the opinion that the tax holiday period should be extended and that, in any event, the tax holiday should only become operative once profits are generated by the business. At present, the tax-free holiday takes effect from the date that the project commences operation. The Romanian authorities may find the level of foreign investment rising if further consideration is given to promoting more favourable tax holidays for investors.

Similarly, tax incentives are given for importation of raw materials, exportation of finished goods, research and development expenditure and reinvestment of profits.

Rights of investors

As regards the rights of a foreign investor under the legislation, a foreign investor may participate in the management of the investment although the business may not employ foreign nationals other than in a management or specialised technical role. There are no restrictions on an investor as regards his rights to employ and dismiss employees although the employment of a local work-force (and in particular the rationalisation of the work-force in the event of acquiring an interest in the capital of an existing company) is, of course, something which is likely to be addressed in negotiations with a Romanian partner.

An investor is entitled to transfer abroad any freely convertible currency profits. Of annual profits in lei due to a foreign investor, 8 to 15 per cent (depending on the investment's field of activity) of the investor's capital investment can be transferred abroad in convertible currency – through currency exchanges conducted by the Romanian Bank for Foreign Trade and other authorised banks.

Previously at odds with one another, the official and unofficial rates of exchange were unified by the government in November 1991. However, while introducing what was widely regarded as a necessary and progressive step, the government further decreed that, having unified the rates, all hard currency held in Romania (with the exception of share capital) must be converted into lei at the official rate of exchange. The National Bank of Romania has subsequently announced that hard currency accounts of foreign investors, opened before 8 November 1991, may remain open but that no further sums may be credited to such accounts.

As regards share capital, a foreign investor's contribution may be credited to a hard currency account opened specifically for receipt of sums paid in respect of share capital. No hard currency profits may be credited to the account, although, if the business has sufficient profits available, an investor may pay dividends from the account.

The overall effect for investors of the government's decree and the National Bank's decision is that only limited profits may be converted from lei and repatriated in hard currency. There is no opportunity to retain hard currency profits within Romania.

It is also essential to note that, subject to any double taxation agreements, a withholding tax of 10 per cent is levied on all profits repatriated to a foreign investor. Profits retained within Romania are taxable only under the recent Tax on Profits Law (which is, in any event, applicable whether or not it is intended to retain or remit profits). Dividends are also taxed at 10 per cent, whether remitted out of Romania or not. Interestingly, however, loan capital may be contributed by an investor to the Romanian business venture and, in such circumstances, interest payments made by the borrower may be made without deduction of any withholding tax in Romania.

Registration and the role of the Romanian Development Agency

In addition to regulating the type and scope of investment, the Foreign Investment Law also contains a number of operational provisions relating to the registration requirements for foreign investment.

The basic requirement of the Law is that the Romanian Development Agency (the 'RDA') must approve and regulate all foreign investments. In effect, the approval procedure requires the RDA (which is a public institution directly subordinate to the government and charged with 'implementing the government programme for reform and economic development by inducing and harnessing foreign capital resources') to respond to an application within a specified period of its submission by the investor, the application providing information on the investor and a draft of the investment proposal.

Prior to proceeding with any investment in Romania, a foreign investor must lodge an application with the RDA seeking approval of the investment. The application must indicate the field and form of the proposed investment and must state the amount of capital to be invested. The application must be supported by certain evidence concerning the investor including:

- Confirmation from the investor's local chamber of commerce (or other similar competent office) of the investor's existence as a legal entity, its objects and share capital.
- Evidence of the investor's solvency (provided by the bank at which the investor has its principal account).
- A copy of the balance sheet of the investor in respect of the immediately preceding financial year.
- A copy of the memorandum and articles of association of the investor.
- A certified power of attorney empowering a specific individual to act on behalf of the investor and to produce all documents in its name.

The RDA will co-ordinate the application process through any relevant ministries – it is not necessary for the investor to make any direct application to any relevant ministry at this stage.

Within a period of 30 days from the date of the application, the RDA must respond to the investor or, if no response is forthcoming, the investor may proceed with the investment – which will be based upon the terms of either the RDA's response or the application if no response has been received.

Following the initial application procedure an investor is then free to proceed with the investment within the scope of the Law. If the investment involves the establishment of a local company, the investor must comply with Court and Commercial Registry procedures (see Chapter 26) before the investment vehicle will acquire legal status in Romania.

Finally, on completion of the investment, the investor is entitled to apply to the RDA for an 'Investor's Certificate' issued under the Foreign Investment Law. This Certificate constitutes evidence of the investor's status as a 'foreign investor' and confirms the various tax and other incentives available to the business.

Part II
The Business Infrastructure

8

Commercial Law

Sinclair Roche & Temperley

Romania has had a Commercial Code regulating commercial activity within the country since September 1887 and a Civil Code since 1865. Although largely altered by recent legislation affecting, for instance, company law, privatisation and foreign investment, the two Codes remain as the basic sources of legislation regulating two aspects of law which are of particular importance to foreign investors – contract and security.

The purpose of this chapter is to focus on the law of contract and the creation of security interests in relation to investments made by a foreign investor. It also considers how competition laws may affect a foreign investment.

CONTRACT

The Commercial Code is divided into four separate sections comprising, in total, 34 titles. Section One contains the relevant articles relating to the law of contract.

The Code makes clear that parties have absolute freedom of contract – that is, there can be no restriction on the content of a contract which parties may wish to enter into.

In common with English law parties must, of course, have the capacity to enter into a contract (insofar as they must have legal persona) and they must have power to effect a contract. For instance, where a Romanian company is entering into a joint venture with a foreign investor, the Romanian company will not have the capacity to contract if it has not previously obtained the consent of its shareholder representative body to the transaction (in this instance, it will be normal for the Romanian Development Agency ('RDA') to ensure that such approval has been obtained before consent to any investment will be given).

Creation of a contract

Presuming that the parties have both the legal persona and the power to enter into a contractual relationship, how is a contract effectively constituted under Romanian law? There are two basic criteria for the formation of a contract: (1) the contract must be in writing; and (2) there must be consideration.

The fact that a contract must be in writing is self-explanatory. However, what is not so clear is the concept of 'consideration', which does not equate to the English concept but, rather, to the French concept of consideration.

Whereas the English concept means that a party must receive a benefit for entering into a contract, the Romanian concept is essentially that there must be a proper cause for entering into the contractual relationship. As such, it is not essential that a party should receive a benefit for entering into an agreement but only that there should be a real reason for entering into that relationship in the first place. In practice, the 'reason' for entering into a contract will be that a benefit accrues, but it is important that potential investors should be aware of the fact that a legally binding situation may arise without any 'consideration' (in the English sense) being given or received.

As regards the creation of a contract through written offer and acceptance, investors should be aware that a contract is constituted only when notification of acceptance is received by the offering party and not when it is made by the accepting party.

Liability and damages

Although it is normal for a company's statutes to exclude liability for a failure to perform due to circumstances of *force majeure*, it is normal for a contracting party to be required to perform its obligations under a contract within a reasonable period of time. A failure to so perform entitles the other contracting party to withdraw from the contract (having first given the defaulting party notice of intention to withdraw and a reasonable period to remedy the default).

Where the right to withdraw is properly exercised, the defaulting party will be liable in damages for any loss suffered by the other party.

SECURITY

The creation of a security interest by any party under Romanian law is of essential importance to all prospective investors. For instance, security may be required by a third party financier supporting an investor, or by an investor from a joint venture partner in support of that party's obligations under a joint venture contract.

Security over immovable property

The Romanian Civil Code allows a company to create a mortgage over immovable property, including rights to land and buildings. The creation of a mortgage must be:

- by agreement;
- in writing; and
- before a notary.

The security created must relate to specific and clearly identifiable immovable property and must be for the purposes of securing a specific debt – that is, a debt which is specific in amount and not only specific in identifying the transaction to which the debt relates.

After creation, the mortgage must be registered with the notary and must also be registered against the specific immovable property over which the security interest has been created. Registration against property is effected by registering the mortgage with the relevant notary in the district in which the property is situated.

A security interest may be validly created for a period of 15 years, although this period may be extended by agreement of the parties at the expiry of its term.

In common with UK legislation, a mortgage may be set aside on the basis of it having created an unfair preference over the interests of other creditors – ie it may be unenforceable if it creates a more favourable position for one creditor as against others.

Retention of title

Where a foreign party is supplying goods to a Romanian business under the terms of a contract governed by Romanian law, it is also important to note that a security interest may be created under the terms of the supply contract: such security interest constitutes, in effect, a retention of title in favour of the supplier. This may also be of relevance when an investor is selling goods manufactured by a joint venture operation in Romania.

Security over movable property

As regards security over movable property, security may be created: by giving up possession of the movable property; or by retaining possession, with the security interest being created by a written, but not a notarised, contract.

Where security is created by contract, it is normal (but not essential) for one copy of the contract to be left with the state notary. Failure to submit a copy to the notary will not affect the validity of the security interest. However, the deposit of the contract does give a priority right to the security holder against third parties.

Security in respect of debts due

Finally, as regards security, it is also possible to create a security interest over debts due to a borrower by third parties. In order to create effective security by this means, the security interest must be notified to the third party debtor, failing which the security interest created will not be effective.

COMPETITION

In common with many other former communist countries, the activities of many Romanian businesses have, until now, amounted in effect to monopolies dominating particular industrial sectors within Romania. Consequently, in investing in such a country, a foreign investor will be concerned to know of competition laws which may adversely affect that investment.

In Romania, the first attempt at creating an effective competition law came with the passing of the Transformation Law in 1990. One of the principal provisions of this Law was to ensure that existing large monopolies were broken up and that competing businesses were created within separate sectors of industry. However, with the exception of the breakdown of monopolies under the Transformation Law, Romanian law has not yet addressed the question of competition in the manner which would normally be understood by British businesses - ie by the creation of an equivalent body to the Monopolies and Mergers Commission. Rather, Romanian competition law has attempted to seek to address the question of unfair practices between businesses rather than regulate and avoid the creation of dominant interests.

However, with Romania likely to seek associate status within the European Community as soon as possible, it would seem that it is only a matter of time before Romania will adopt competition legislation regarding control of monopolies and mergers in accordance with current EC practices.

As regards the treatment of unfair practices, the Law on Unfair Competition (Law No 11 of 1991, in effect since 30 January 1991) sets out a regulatory framework affecting unfair competition in Romania. Article 4 of the Law defines the following unfair practices:

1. employing an employee of a competitor where such an employee was previously employed by a competitor on an exclusive basis;

2. the obtaining of secret or confidential information from an employee of a competitor;

3. entering into contracts on advantageous or discounted terms with the intention that such a contract should adversely affect competition;

4. passing off - ie seeking to sell a product by attempting to confuse such a product with the product or products of a competitor.

Complaints in respect of unfair practices may be raised by any person or company that has suffered loss or damage in consequence of the practice concerned. As regards timing, a complaint must be made within one year of the 'injured' party becoming aware of the unfair practice and, in any event, must be made within three years of the date on which the unfair practice occurred.

Enforcement of the legislation is effected by local Chambers of Commerce, each of which has powers to levy fines (of up to Lei100,000), impose prison sentences (of up to two years) and order payment of damages (to be paid, if required, from the sale proceeds arising from the sale of any goods manufactured by the competitor).

9
The Convertibility of the Leu
Charterhouse

THE LACK OF HARD CURRENCY

Like other Eastern Europe currencies, the Romanian leu is not freely convertible. The present Romanian government's reform strategy aims to make it so within the next two years in order to facilitate trade and investment, and to bring the Romanian economy in line with Western economies. However, foreign exchange policy has oscillated considerably since the revolution of December 1989, as the Romanian government has been unable to build up the hard currency reserves it considers necessary to achieve free convertibility.

When the National Salvation Front government came to power at the end of 1989, Romania had the advantage of being a net creditor in hard currency. This was the result of President Ceauşescu's policy during the 1980s of repaying all of Romania's foreign debt in order to prevent any interference in Romanian affairs by Romania's creditors. In doing so, Ceauşescu starved the Romanian economy of badly needed imports of both consumer and capital goods and pursued a policy of forced exports, leading to trade surpluses of over $2.7 billion in 1988 and 1989.

When the Ceauşescu regime fell, the relatively advantageous position which the new government enjoyed *vis-à-vis* other Eastern European countries – no external debts and a favourable balance of payments with the West – was soon lost and Romania now faces persistent problems of lack of hard currency hindering plans to introduce free convertibility of the leu. The reasons for this are the following:

1. The government that replaced Ceaușescu's regime came under increasing pressure to use its hard currency reserves to import badly needed consumer goods - primarily fuel, foods and pharmaceuticals.
2. The productivity of Romanian industry fell by 57 per cent in 1990, leading to a significant fall in hard currency exports to the West.
3. Higher hard currency payments for energy imports, particularly from the Soviet Union.
4. The Gulf crisis, which severely affected Romania because of its large credits to Iraq, most of which were to be paid back in crude oil supplies.
5. The National Salvation government that came to power in December 1989 embarked on a policy of reform and liberalisation hoping to obtain the support of the multilateral credit agencies. Although in March and April of 1991, the IMF pledged over $1.2 billion in funds for Romania, primarily to purchase strategic imports and to stabilise the Romanian economy during the conversion to market forces, and the European Community committed ECU80-110 million under the PHARE (Poland--Hungary Assistance Restructuring Economy) programme to finance imports and technical assistance, to date, only a fraction of that support has arrived, primarily because of the continual doubts expressed by the United States about the Romanian government's commitment to market reform.

Consequently, the Romanian government has been unable to move quickly towards its objective of free convertibility of the leu, and any efforts made in that direction have been hindered by the persistent lack of hard currency reserves.

MOVES TOWARDS CONVERTIBILITY

Prior to the Revolution of 1989, all transactions involving foreign currencies in Romania were undertaken by the Romanian Bank for Foreign Trade and by the powerful state-controlled Foreign Trade Organisations (FTOs), which in practice retained complete control on all hard currency revenues generated by Romanian enterprises. In general, Romanian companies were not allowed to retain any of the hard currency they generated through exports (although some were officially allowed to retain a small percentage), and foreign exchange transactions were effected at different exchange rates for different industrial sectors, centrally established by the Romanian Bank for Foreign Trade.

The reforming government that came to power at the end of 1989 created two official foreign exchange rates – one governing commercial transactions, the other for small transactions in cash at *bureau de change* offices, primarily for tourists. Both exchange rates were broadly similar, with the tourist rate being approximately Lei5 higher per dollar than the official commercial rate.

The commercial exchange rate was set at Lei21 per US dollar for the first months of 1990 and then was allowed to fall to Lei35 in November of that year. In 1991, the rate was again allowed to fall to Lei60. All these exchange rates massively overvalued the leu, discouraged enterprises from exporting, and generated significant competition among Romanian enterprises for imports, for which the allocation of hard currency was still centrally determined. Consequently, the Romanian government only permitted and allocated the necessary hard currency for imports if they were considered to be national priorities. In that respect, the continuation of a policy of centrally determined exchange rates ensured the survival of a system of central allocation of hard currency reserves.

In February 1991, the government allowed a third exchange rate in addition to the commercial and tourist rates. This new rate was known as the inter-bank or auction rate, and closely resembled a free market rate, fluctuating between Lei250 and Lei300 to the US dollar, depending on the supply and demand for hard currency at daily hard currency auctions held between Romanian enterprises at certain Romanian commercial banks. The inter-bank rate, however, was not allowed to govern official transactions – it was permitted for enterprises that wished to buy hard currency to finance imports or to sell their hard currency surpluses.

In the autumn of 1991, the government fundamentally changed its foreign exchange policy, establishing internal convertibility of the leu. The dual system of commercial and inter-bank rates was abolished, and a new single official exchange rate was introduced, initially established at Lei180 per US dollar. Simultaneously, all the hard currency held by companies in Romania was forcibly purchased by the National Bank of Romania at the new official rate, and the inter-bank auctions ended. Finally, all sales in hard currency in Romania were banned. The reasons for the change of policy were the following:

1. the government's inability to encourage firms to export under the previous system;
2. its inability to build up sufficient hard currency reserves under the previous system;
3. worries at the increasing 'dollarisation' of the economy which was a result of the artificially high official exchange rate established by the government.

With the new rules governing the supply of foreign exchange, companies that require hard currency have to make an application to the National Bank of Romania and to deposit with the Bank the corresponding amount in lei. For amounts up to US$10,000, the hard currency is immediately made available. For larger amounts, an approval from the National Bank is necessary. Although the Bank has 20 days to grant an approval, it can establish priorities in approving requested sums, energy imports being its first priority.

Western businessmen in Romania have been critical of the government's reforms of autumn 1991. The conversion of all hard currency accounts held in Romania into lei at the new exchange rate is seen as an infringement on the economic freedom of enterprises operating in Romania and perceived as a sign that Romania may still revert to its illiberal past. In addition, joint ventures in Romania can no longer sell products and services for hard currency, increasing the risk for foreign investors of currency devaluation and limiting the possibility for companies to repatriate profits made in Romania. On the other hand, the principal merit of the reform lies in the more realistic level at which the government has fixed the new unified conversion rate of the leu.

Under the present system, the National Bank establishes daily amounts of hard currency for sale to the commercial banks and Romanian enterprises, based on an estimate of the demand for hard currency for imports. For a period of time, companies managed to obtain the amount of hard currency they had requested. Now, for certain types of imports, the hard currency is already difficult to obtain. In addition, although the daily official rate was Lei193 per US dollar by early-1992 and has now fallen to just under Lei200, the rate for private persons at the *bureaux de change* has already fallen to over Lei350. Companies often resort to changing money with the *bureaux de change*, which, although illegal, assures them access to hard currency. Finally, the black market is again active with transactions taking place at well over Lei350 per dollar.

The real success of the currency reform will be evident if and when the Romanian National Bank manages to build up sufficient hard currency reserves to make the currency freely convertible. Although officials claim that since the reforms were implemented the National Bank's hard currency reserves have been steadily, if gradually, increasing, no official figures are available to show the up-to-date position.

RETENTION OF PROFITS

Whereas during the Ceauşescu regime, Romanian companies were in practice not allowed to retain any of the hard currency they generated through exports, the two governments that succeeded Ceauşescu's inititally adopted a more liberal approach. After the Revolution of December 1989, Romanian companies were allowed to retain up to 50 per cent of hard currency earnings in hard currency interest bearing accounts, either with Romanian banks or with foreign banks operating in Romania. It was the existence of these hard currency accounts that enabled companies to create a market in hard currency at the inter-bank auctions.

Joint ventures with foreign investors were initially exempt from any retention quotas, and are normally obliged to open both hard currency and leu accounts with a Romanian bank. Transfers between the two accounts must take place at the bank's official exchange rate.

Because of the relative freedom granted to foreign investors operating in Romania by the Foreign Investment Law, there was considerable outrage when, in the autumn of 1991, the government's foreign exchange reform involved the forcible conversion of all hard currency assets held in Romania, including those held by joint ventures, at the new official conversion rate.

Whereas under this reform all Romanian state-owned enterprises had no choice but to convert hard currency deposits, both joint ventures and private Romanian companies were allowed three months to dispose of their hard currency held in Romania. Those enterprises that wish to retain a capital base in convertible currency in Romania are allowed to keep the hard currency portion of their share capital in frozen hard currency accounts, although they are no longer allowed to use that currency for current account transactions in Romania.

REPATRIATION OF PROFITS

The Romanian Foreign Investment Law allows joint ventures to repatriate all hard currency revenues generated, and between 8 and 15 per cent of the foreign party's initial cash investment in a joint venture per annum in lei, converted at the official exchange rate. The percentage depends on the sector of the joint venture:

- 15 per cent for investments considered to be of 'special importance', as defined by the Romanian government;
- 12 per cent for joint ventures in extraction, agriculture, construction, communications and transport industries;
- 10 per cent for investments in the banking and financial sector;
- 8 per cent for all other sectors.

These regulations are still in place, providing joint ventures comply with the November 1991 currency regulations.

Although the Romanian repatriation laws initially generated considerable interest among foreign investors, the new currency regulations introduced in November 1991, which ban sales in hard currency, severely limit the ability for joint venture companies to repatriate profits made in Romania.

In addition, the present enforced leu denomination of all transactions within Romania has greatly increased the devaluation risk faced by foreign investors, and the exposure to devaluation of the leu remains a prime concern for them.

10

Prices, Rents and Wages
Charterhouse

STANDARDS OF LIVING

Most Westerners travelling in Romania are shocked by the general lack of consumer goods, the obsolete infrastructure and general backwardness of services. Under the Ceauşescu regime, standards of living in Romania were considered to be the worst in Eastern Europe, with the possible exception of Albania, and even now they have not improved significantly.

Throughout the 1980s, standards of living declined considerably in Romania. The regime pursued a policy of forced exports to repay and prepay foreign debt, restricting imports of most consumer goods. Food was rationed, while Romania's pork and other surpluses were forcibly exported for hard currency. The authorities imposed particularly severe restrictions on the household consumption of energy and, in most parts of the country, only a few hours per day of electricity and heating oil were allowed, even during winter, while inefficient state industries consumed the bulk of energy imports. At the same time, the life expectancy for men, and the the access to medical treatment, all declined substantially during the last decade of the Ceauşescu regime. The average calorie intake in Romania declined from 3259 to 3067 between 1980 and 1990.

The provisional government which came to power at the end of 1989 realised that both its own popularity and the prospect of a successful reform programme depended on its ability to satisfy the population's pent-up demand for consumer goods and to reverse the dramatic decline in living standards experienced in the 1980s. Consequently, Romania's hard currency reserves were immediately used to import basic consumer goods, especially food, heating oil and electricity, while exports of certain consumer goods were prohibited. Items such as bread, milk, eggs, fresh vegetables and meat became generally available in the early months of 1990, although certain subsidised products remained scarce. As food production and prices were gradually liberalised, more food articles became available, although at more expensive prices.

The initial aim of the provisional government was to improve living standards for the active population during the reform period, and to protect certain disadvantaged groups, such as orphans or mothers of many children. The working week was reduced from six days to five days, and other measures included additional holidays, subsidies for young couples, and improved social insurance for the population. Real incomes were boosted considerably by the government, although the output of Romanian industry collapsed.

By the summer of 1990, the Romanian government realised that a general objective to improve living standards was incompatible with the macroeconomic objectives of its reform programme. It therefore changed its strategy by identifying specific segments of the population that most needed a safety net, and containing the general desire for an improvement in living standards.

A moratorium on basic wage increases throughout the economy was introduced to reduce inflationary pressures. This, coupled with successive price liberalisations, caused a general decline in living standards after the breathing space of early-1990. The government's 1991 Budget included a social safety net which only covered those specific segments of the population most vulnerable to the effect of the price liberalisation, and the government acknowledged that even for these groups, adjustment had to have its costs.

With an annual inflation rate of approximately 180 per cent in 1990, the standard of living of most Romanian citizens declined substantially. The transition to a market economy is still having its effect on living standards and Romanians will probably have to wait a number of years before achieving living standards in line with Western Europe or even other Eastern European countries. Meanwhile, certain groups of the population are already benefiting more than others from the move to a market economy. Expensive luxuries such as whisky, hi-fi systems and Western cars are already to be seen in the shops and streets of Bucharest.

Romanians still suffer from a vastly inadequate health-care system, despite efforts by the international community to increase the supply of all sorts of vital medical equipment. Patients often share beds and other medical facilities in hospitals, and the supply of basic materials such as syringes are still not sufficient to meet the medical needs of the population.

Although statistics on the ownership of durable consumer goods since the 1989 Revolution are not available, a fall in the production of goods such as washing machines, television sets and refrigerators over the last two years indicates that these goods have become less easily available. In 1990, Romania had approximately 13 telephones per 100 people, which puts it well behind other Eastern European countries such as Hungary and Bulgaria. The Romanian government is putting considerable effort into modernising its telephone system and has recently entered into agreements with Siemens and Alenia for the provision of new telephone exchanges and international satellite facilities.

RECENT EVOLUTION OF PRICES, RENTS AND WAGES

Before the Revolution of December 1989, prices in Romania were centrally controlled and did not play an allocative role in the economy. Prices were kept fairly stable over the years by a system of government subsidies, which shielded Romanian citizens and uncompetitive state industries from increases in world prices. Shortages were common, resulting in long queues for consumer goods, large pent-up demand, and a monetary overhang among the population.

In early-1990, the provisional government took some initial measures to liberalise certain prices. The prices of agricultural products sold directly to peasant markets, which previously had been subject to a number of restrictions, were freed, and newly created private firms, including joint ventures, were allowed to price their products and services freely. This was followed by a more thorough price liberalisation in November 1990, accompanied by a devaluation of the currency from Lei20 to Lei35 per US dollar. Prices of all goods and services produced by three or more producers were freed, with the exception of:

1. A group of 77 raw materials and intermediate goods, the prices of which were increased to reflect world prices at the new exchange rate that followed the devaluation of the leu.

2. Prices for 40 essential consumer goods and services, which were maintained at then current levels, such as heating energy and electricity, rents and basic foods.

In addition, it was decided that the prices of goods produced by only one or two producers would be negotiated between the producers and the Ministry of Finance.

Overall, the November 1990 price liberalisation freed approximately 50 per cent of prices, although, if measured by the volume of transactions, far fewer than 50 per cent took place at market prices. In addition, the government introduced a system of partial compensation for wage-earners and pensioners which further reduced the impact of price liberalisation.

In April 1991, a more complete price liberalisation was allowed to take place, in conjunction with a further devaluation of the currency to Lei60 per US dollar. The prices of raw materials and intermediate goods were increased again to reflect world prices at the new official exchange rate. The prices of household energy products were increased although they were still controlled. The prices of all food products were freed, with the exception of only 12 essential products (including milk, bread and eggs) for which price ceilings were maintained. However, these price ceilings were set at levels prevailing in the free peasant markets, and therefore already represented increases of up to 150 per cent on the former prices. In addition, controls on the prices of goods produced by less than three producers were gradually abandoned. In total, the April 1991 price liberalisation freed the prices of approximately 80 per cent of goods in Romania.

In July 1991, a further price liberalisation was introduced: all prices were freed except those of 14 basic consumer goods – 5 basic food items and 9 other items, including heating oil and rents.

Rents of state-owned houses and apartments continue to be fixed by the government, although a limited private real estate market is in existence, primarily because the government has allowed some tenants to purchase their living accommodations. Rents in the private market are uncontrolled both for commercial and residential users.

During the Ceaușescu years, wages in Romania were dependent on enterprises meeting plan targets and were set at unrealistically high levels. Consequently, workers often received incomplete or late payments. The National Salvation Front government abolished this system. Wage increases during the early months of 1990, combined with higher benefit payments, contributed to an increase of approximately three per cent in the average real wage in the economy in 1990. This, together with a dramatic decline in industrial output and an expansionary monetary policy, added to the monetary overhang and fuelled inflation. Consequently, in July 1990 the government and trade unions agreed a moratorium on wages, in an effort to control inflationary forces.

Wage rates in Romania are still low compared to other East European countries, and the average wage in manufacturing in the state sector is just over Lei10,000 per month. Wages in the private sector, however, are free and are often over 50 per cent higher than in the state sector.

DIFFERENCES ACROSS THE COUNTRY

Driving out of Bucharest towards the southern border with Bulgaria, one is struck by a clear contrast between the living conditions of those areas of the countryside which Ceauşescu did not take an interest in, and the large towns and cities. Water supply facilities in the countryside are often far from adequate, due to a lack of investment in purifying and distribution installations. Countryside roads tend to be narrow and difficult, and often consist of simple dirt tracks.

Country people tend to suffer even more from erratic electricity and other energy supplies than town dwellers. Living conditions in many rural parts of Romania seem not to have changed over the centuries, and horse-driven carts are still a common means of transportation as are wells a common source of water supply.

However, in some respects country life in Romania is more tolerable than in the urban areas. Peasant markets were the first to be liberalised in 1990, and country dwellers have benefited considerably from this. Price rises have been less severe in private peasant markets than in the cities, where an efficient private food distribution system is still not operational. The variety of products for sale on the peasant markets has also increased considerably since the 1989 Revolution. In addition, the partial land privatisation introduced in 1990, giving former landowners a right to limited acreage, has benefited both countryside and cities, by encouraging greater production of foods for sale both at peasant markets and in the cities.

There are large regional differences across Romania. For example, the old German towns of Transylvania, and the Banat, enjoy considerably higher standards of living than most towns in Wallachia. Living conditions are, however, most squalid in the highrises built to accommodate the growing populations of industrial towns such as Ploiesti and Rimnicu Vilcea.

11

Banking and Financial Services

Charterhouse

NEW BANKING STRUCTURE

The Romanian banking system was reformed fundamentally in October 1990 and April 1991 when the framework of a commercial banking sector was established. Prior to that, the banking sector was made up of the National Bank of Romania and four specialised banks - the Romanian Bank for Foreign Trade, the Investment Bank, the Bank for Agriculture and Food Industries and the Savings and Loans Bank.

The National Bank of Romania was a conventional central bank, with responsibility for issuing currency and administration of the state budget accounts, but it also performed certain commercial banking operations, such as taking deposits from state corporations and making loans to enterprises. The other banks had a monopoly in their areas of activity, such as foreign trade, the provision of finance to industry, the provision of credits to the agricultural and agrobusiness sectors, and the taking of personal savings.

The reform of April 1991, which in theory established a two-tiered banking system, stripped the National Bank of Romania of all its commercial banking activities, and transferred its commercial banking portfolio to a newly created Romanian Commercial Bank. In addition, the National Bank was made independent in the performance of its duties, with the Governor and the Board of Directors appointed for renewable eight-year terms by Parliament on the recommendation of the Prime Minister.

The National Bank of Romania is now only responsible for the conduct of monetary policy, including the setting of interest rates for regulating the financial system, and for exchange rate policy, including the issuance and implementation of foreign exchange regulations. In addition the National Bank manages the state's foreign exchange reserves and acts as banker to the government. The monopoly on foreign exchange and gold transactions previously held by the Romanian Bank for Foreign Trade has now been abolished.

The main goal of the government's reforms has been to move towards a more liberal banking system, and to end the rigid system of central credit allocation which had governed the Romanian banking system since 1948. Another objective of the reform has been to end the sectoral specialisation of the state banks. However, although the banks are no longer effectively forced to remit profits to the state budget, the scope of the banking reforms has been limited by a traditional lack of competition between banks and a habit of monopolistic banking in certain sectors. For example, the *de facto* monopoly of the Savings and the Loans Bank in drawing retail deposits has not been broken by the other banks. Finally, although the National Bank has officially lost its commercial banking operations, it is still a major provider of credits to state enterprises because loss-making enterprises continue to be supported by the Ministry of Finance.

The Romanian banking sector has undergone these crucial market reforms at a time when the financial system has been affected severely by an extremely high level (approximately Lei70 billion) of non-performing loans between companies. In order to solve this, a 'General Compensation Scheme' has been devised, under which the commercial banks are responsible for determining the net debt position between enterprises. Once this is established, net debtors will have their debts refinanced by the banks, with government guarantees for up to six months, after which they will be treated as normal commercial debts.

LOCAL BANKS

In spite of the general reform of the banking system over the last two years, the sector is still dominated by the former state banks which remain all-powerful in their respective specialisations.

The Romanian Bank for Foreign Trade ('RBFT')

Prior to the reforms of 1990-91, this bank performed all foreign currency transactions, was the banker to the state Foreign Trade Organisations and managed the country's foreign exchange assets. Although the monopoly on foreign exchange transactions has now ended, the RBFT is still the all-powerful trade bank. This is primarily because other Romanian banks have been unable to establish a network of foreign correspondent banks, representatives and agents, and because they lack the know-how to do so. In addition, export credit agencies and foreign commercial banks often insist on a confirmed letter of credit from the RBFT in trade transactions with Romania. The only banks to compete with the RBFT in this sphere are the foreign banks operating in Romania.

The RBFT is now a commercial bank, with 30 per cent of its shares to be held by a Private Ownership Fund, and will be privatised in due course. In addition, because of its know-how and foreign contacts, the RBFT hopes to offer a wider range of services than it has done in the past, including privatisation and financial advisory services.

The Investment Bank

This bank has been the traditional provider of finance to all state enterprises, with the exception of those involved in agriculture and food processing.

The Bank for Agriculture and Food Industries

This bank had a monopoly on the provision of credits to agricultural and food-related businesses, and is still the most active bank in its sphere of operations in spite of increasing competition from private and co-operative banks.

The Savings and Loan Bank

This bank takes deposits from the public and offers a limited amount of credits to finance the purchase of houses. It previously had a monopoly in this sector, supported by a large network of local branches.

The Romanian Commercial Bank

This bank began operating in 1991, having inherited the

commercial operations of the National Bank, although its specific role within the Romanian banking sector is not clear.

The Investment Bank and the Bank for Agriculture and Food Industries are the two banks the monopolistic role of which is being eroded the most quickly, primarily because of the wide scope of their operations. These banks are facing the increasing competition from the emerging private commercial banking sector.

The formation of three private banks since the 1989 Revolution, under Law 54 regarding private initiative which allows private enterprises to establish banks, represents a new direction for the Romanian banking sector. These banks are Bankcoop SA, Mindbank SA, and Tiriac Bank SA, the latter being headed by Ion Tiriac, the former Romanian tennis star. Ion Tiriac raised Lei3 billion in equity for the bank through an offer of shares in both dollars and lei to the Romanian public in November 1990. The offer was greatly oversubscribed with 9000 applicants for shares, suggesting that the financial sector in Romania could regain the vibrancy of pre-World War II years, when there were over 100 banks operating in Romania.

Bankcoop and Mindbank are both co-operative banks. Bankcoop was founded by Romania's consumer co-operative union – the country's largest private organisation active in services and light industry – and by the co-operatives which provide credits to Romania's farmers. Mindbank is the Bank for Small Industry and Private Enterprise. It was founded by the Central Economic Union of Trade Co-operatives and by Centracoop, a central co-operative organisation. It aims to provide financing to small enterprises in the private sector and to co-operatives.

FOREIGN BANKS

Two foreign banks in Romania have carried out hard currency transactions for a number of years, primarily relating to trade finance (letters of credit) and the arranging of credits for the Romanian government.

The first foreign bank to establish a branch in Romania was Manufacturers Hanover Trust (1974). It has experience of the Romanian market and trade-related activities. Société Générale followed with a Bucharest branch in 1980 and offers a similar range of services.

The scope of the operations of the foreign banks is limited by the fact that the banking system reforms of the last two years have not extended to permitting foreign banks to take lei-denominated deposits and performing other functions in the local currency. On the other hand, the Romanian Foreign Trade Bank and other Romanian banks have started to provide services in hard currency and to hold foreign currency accounts.

In addition to the two banks mentioned above, the Romanian Bank for Foreign Trade has established offshore joint venture banks with foreign partners to act as its representatives in the West. The Anglo-Romanian Bank Ltd is based in London and is a joint venture with Barclays Bank International and Manufacturers Hanover Trust. The Banque Franco-Roumaine SA is a joint venture with eight French banks headed by Crédit Lyonnais, and Banca Italo-Romena was founded with Banco di Sicilia and Instituto San Paolo di Torino. Finally, the Misr Romanian Bank SAE is a 50/50 joint venture with Bank Misr in Cairo. In addition, Frankfurt-Bucharest Bank – a German-Romanian joint venture – operates in Frankfurt and provides a wide range of banking services in hard currency.

INTEREST RATES

Before 1989, interest rates were kept very low and their structure was complicated. The Savings and Loan Bank paid approximately 2.5 per cent per annum for household deposits in 1989 and it in turn received 3.0 per cent from the National Bank. Other banks obtained credits from the National Bank at 1.5 to 1.8 per cent per annum and paid the same rates on enterprise deposits.

In 1990, interest rates were marginally increased and simplified, in an attempt by the government to reduce the monetary overhang and other inflationary forces. This was clearly insufficient and in early-1991 the government decided to liberalise interest rates further, in a policy designed to complement the liberalisation of exchange rate policy. The National Bank allowed interest rates to be freely determined between banks and their customers.

However, the National Bank continues to monitor margins between lending and deposit rates in an attempt to prevent spreads from becoming too wide, and has reserved for itself the right to intervene if it believes spreads are not reasonable.

The Savings and Loan Bank now offers its customers interest rates of 18 per cent on lei-denominated sight deposits, and of 25 per cent on term deposits for a year. No further interest rates are quoted on deposits for over a year, although the bank is planning to introduce gradualised interest rates for term deposits of less than a year.

New commercial loans in Romania are made at interest rates of between 35 and 40 per cent. Because of the high inflation rate in Romania – approximately 180 per cent in 1990 – and the consequent negative real interest rates, it is difficult to obtain credits with Romanian banks, although officials claim that Romanian banks are anxious to support well structured projects.

Interest rates on hard currency accounts in Romania are in line with international rates.

12
Accounting Standards
Touche Ross

BACKGROUND

Under the former totalitarian regime, state companies utilised the traditional state plan accounting which involved a strict cash basis of accounting with no recognition of accruals or provisions. The concept of profit or loss was irrelevant to state companies, the main concern of which was the level of production. This practice continues to a great extent and, accordingly, there is a need for Romanian accountants to be trained in Western accounting ideas. It is also imperative that the accounting profession be given formal recognition as soon as possible so that properly qualified accountants will be available to both prepare and audit the financial statements of enterprises operating within Romania. In the meantime, it will remain necessary for foreign investors to employ foreign accountants to ensure that financial statements prepared by joint ventures or Romanian subsidiaries comply with international standards and will be acceptable, for example, as a basis for raising finance.

Despite these problems, it should be noted that the first legislative steps have been taken with the passing in late-December 1991 of the new Accounting Law. The implications and limitations of the new law are discussed in this chapter.

THE ACCOUNTING LAW

Romanian accounting law and practice is at a very preliminary stage. Although the first legislation on the subject, the Accounting

Law, came into force on 1 January 1992, this law provides nothing more than a broad framework for the Romanian accounting system, since its provisions are limited generally to setting out what accounting documentation should be prepared and by whom, and setting deadlines by which financial statements should be lodged with the public authorities each year.

The Accounting Law anticipates that there will be a formalised accounting profession made up of expert accountants, and requires that further draft legislation in this context be issued within the first few months of 1992. The Ministry of Finance has been given until June 1992 to issue regulations setting out relevant accounting standards and bookkeeping methods. Until such time as these regulations are promulgated, there must be some uncertainty as to the proper accounting methods to be adopted by Romanian companies, joint ventures and branches of foreign companies. It is likely, however, that basic accounting records familiar in the West will prove acceptable and that a standard accounts code similar to the French *'Plan Comptable General'* will be introduced.

Concerning financial statements, trading companies set up under the Company Law (other than limited liability companies with no more than 15 shareholders) are required under that Law to be audited, and the Accounting Law confirms this requirement. The Accounting Law, however, does not contain any detailed provisions regarding auditing standards and again investors must await regulations issued by the Ministry of Finance.

General provisions

The Accounting Law applies to all forms of enterprise including public institutions, trading companies and individuals carrying on business. It also applies to Romanian branches of foreign companies and foreign branches of Romanian companies. Accounts are to be prepared for the benefit of the enterprise itself as well as for its shareholders, creditors, the tax authorities and the public. Accounting information provided each year to the public authorities is also to be used in preparing the national budget and in order to assess the Romanian economy as a whole.

The Accounting Law is to be generally administered by the Ministry of Finance which, as mentioned earlier, is required to issue bookkeeping and accounting standards in the near future. Accounting standards for banks are to be prepared by the National Bank of Romania and approved by the Ministry of Finance.

Accounting requirements

Accounts must be kept in the Romanian language and currency, except that foreign currency operations must be accounted for in both lei and the foreign currency.

Most companies are obliged to carry out double-entry bookkeeping. Members of a company's accounting department who undertake bookkeeping duties must be university graduates in economics, although accounts may be kept and prepared by qualified accountants.

A profit and loss account and tax computation must be drawn up monthly and submitted to the General District Department of the Public Finances and to the Municipal Department of Bucharest. This requirement, which seems to be somewhat onerous, corresponds with the requirement under the present Profits Tax Law. The books of account and source documentation must be kept by each company for 10 years following the end of the relevant accounting period for which they were prepared, although payroll records must be kept for 50 years. Accounts may be kept on computer provided the relevant bookkeeping regulations are observed.

Audited financial statements – a balance sheet, profit and loss account and management report – must be prepared for each accounting period (which must correspond with the calendar year) and these must be filed by 15 April in the following year with the same authorities as those to which the monthly profit and loss accounts have to be submitted. The audited financial statements must be retained for 50 years. If a company ceases its activities its accounting documents must be handed over to the state archives.

It is not yet clear whether the format of financial statements is to follow, as widely predicted, the French *'Plan Comptable General'*, which differs in detail from accounts familiar to UK users. However, the financial statements must provide a true, clear and complete image of the company's financial position. This requirement seems in principle to be compatible with international accounting standards.

Valuation methods

The Accounting Law deals very briefly with the valuation of assets and liabilities for accounting purposes. Again this topic will be covered by Ministry of Finance regulations to be issued in the first half of 1992.

The Law states that real and personal assets are to be valued in the accounts at cost (either the cost of purchase or of production) or market value, but does not require that the lower of these values should be used.

Loans and other financial obligations are to be recorded in the balance sheet at their 'nominal value'.

Penalties for non-compliance

Penalties are prescribed for contraventions of the Accounting Law, including failure to record assets or transactions in the books of account, and non-observance of regulations issued by the Ministry of Finance. The latter regulations will cover the maintenance of books of accounts; the requirement to retain accounting records and to replace lost or stolen records; and the making of an annual inventory and the preparation of the annual audited financial statements.

13
The Privatisation Process
Sinclair Roche & Temperley

Romania's objective of creating a free market economy took a further step towards being realised with the approval of the country's Privatisation Law on 14 August 1991 (Law No 58 of 1991).

Often considered by potential investors to be a less attractive and more slowly developing investment opportunity than other Central and Eastern European countries (for example, Czechoslovakia and Hungary), the Romanian government has attempted to redress the situation by seeking to implement an ambitious Privatisation Law and programme, looking to the examples (and lessons learned) of more advanced privatisation programmes throughout Central Europe.

The purpose of this chapter is to outline the framework of the Law, emphasising the role of the National Privatisation Agency, and the way in which the Law may affect foreign investors.

OUTLINE OF THE LAW

In its finally adopted form, the Privatisation Law does not attempt to set out any specific privatisation timetable but rather 'provides the legal framework through which to effect the transfer of ownership from the state to the private sector' (Article 1). To this end, the Law has four principal objectives:

1. to set out the procedure for distribution of certificates of ownership to Romanian citizens;

2. to set out the methods for privatisation of commercial companies;

3. to set out the methods for undertaking an asset sale or sale of shares in companies to employees; and

4. most importantly for foreign investors, to provide a mechanism by which investors may acquire an interest in companies through the purchase of shares or assets.

Private Ownership Funds

In the first place, the Law provides for the setting up of five Private Ownership Funds, to be established as joint stock companies within the framework of the Company Law (Law No 31 of 1990). The five Funds will initially own, in aggregate, 30 per cent of the share capital of each commercial company affected by the legislation, and certificates of ownership in the Funds will be issued to all Romanian citizens resident in Romania and aged 18 or over on 31 December 1990. Initially, Romanian citizens will not own shares in Romanian companies directly (although the Law does provide for a sale of shares in companies being privatised by way of public offering which must, consequently, require direct ownership in due course).

Although the Law includes detailed provisions relating to administration of the Funds, the basic aim of the Private Ownership Funds is to administer the 30 per cent shareholding on behalf of the public. To achieve this aim, the Funds are entitled (and expected) to provide a management input to each company in which they own shares. At the time of writing, the government has already appointed advisers to consider who should be responsible for running the Funds.

State Ownership Fund

In addition to the five Private Ownership Funds, the Law details provisions for the formation of a State Ownership Fund as a public 'establishment'. The role of the State Ownership Fund will be to own and administer the balance (70 per cent) of the share capital not owned by the five Private Ownership Funds. The State Fund will be under an obligation to implement a continuing process of privatisation of the 70 per cent shareholding retained by it initially, and this includes an obligation to privatise at least 10 per cent of its remaining interest in each company in each year, either by transfer (through sales) to investors or to the Private Ownership Funds. The role of the State Ownership Fund will continue only for as long as that Fund retains an interest in the share capital of commercial companies.

Implementation of the privatisation programme

As regards private investment (whether from foreign or domestic investors) in Romanian commercial companies, the Romanian government has realised that the process of setting up the Funds and transferring ownership to the public will be a lengthy one, even with the best intentions of achieving early privatisation. Accordingly, specific provision is made in Article 42 of the Law to authorise the National Privatisation Agency (the 'NPA') - the government agency established for the preparation and implementation of the Privatisation Law - to implement, prior to the organisation of the Funds, an early scheme of privatisation of not more than 30 of the total number of commercial companies to be privatised under the Law (the total number being approximately 6000 companies).

This provides an early opportunity for foreign investors to become involved in the Romanian privatisation process. Sales of shares by the NPA may be effected either through a public offering, an open auction or auction to pre-selected bidders, a sale through direct negotiation with an investor (including trade investors or management and employees) or any combination of such processes. In any event, the NPA will be responsible for depositing the consideration received on an interest-bearing account, to be held on trust until such time as the Funds are set up.

As regards the companies to be sold through the early privatisation scheme, the NPA has (as of January 1992) already undertaken an initial assessment of companies and pilot privatisation schemes have been initiated with funding from the EC PHARE programme and the UK Know-How fund.

In addition to the privatisation process in respect of share sales of commercial companies as set out above, the NPA has been given the task of effecting sales of assets of commercial companies by means of auction (to Romanian or foreign parties), and the Agency is preparing a list of assets to be so sold.

Employee participation

In considering any investment, a potential investor should always consider the motivation and efficacy of the work-force of the 'target' of the investment proposal.

A fundamental aspect of the Privatisation Law is the emphasis given to employee participation in the privatisation process (particularly in Articles 47, 48 and 49). Employees are given a preferential right to purchase (at a discount) up to 10 per cent of the shares offered for sale on credit and deferred payment terms. Of the companies involved in the pilot privatisation programme, virtually all employees and managers have expressed strong interest in being involved in share ownership and it is essential that, in targeting any company for investment through the privatisation process, any investor should consider the intentions of the workforce and possible share incentives.

Similar rights are available to employees in connection with the sale of assets.

FOREIGN OPPORTUNITIES

In due course, significant investment opportunities will arise for foreign investors, as the Funds acquire control of companies under the legislation. The Private Ownership Funds holding shares in a particular commercial company are authorised, under Article 51, to negotiate share sales on behalf of the State Ownership Fund and such a situation obviously affords an opportunity for a foreign investor to invest in 100 per cent of the share capital of a commercial company (subject to employee pre-emption rights).

Participation in the privatisation process (whether by way of share or asset acquisition) is open to non-Romanian parties without restriction and potential investors need not undergo the preliminary registration process with the Romanian Development Agency (which is, under the Foreign Investment Law, obliged to issue an Investor's Certificate – although upon completion of, rather than prior to, the investment).

CONSTITUTION AND ROLE OF THE NPA

Constituted by the 'Transformation' Law (Law No 15 of 1990) prior to the passing of the Privatisation Law, the NPA is a governmental agency, charged with regulating the transfer of ownership of shares and assets from state to private ownership.

The role of the NPA is to:

1. set up and structure each Private Ownership Fund;
2. devise and implement a method for distribution of certificates of ownership;

3. compile a list of Romanian citizens eligible to participate in the privatisation process;

4. guide, manage and control the early privatisation programme; and

5. provide advisory assistance to companies being privatised, including support for the formulation of privatisation plans for companies and conducting negotiation of sales with interested parties, particularly during the initial programme.

Under Article 23 of the Transformation Law, any negotiation for sale and transfer of share capital of a commercial company set up under that law must be exclusively through the NPA. If completed without registration, a transaction will be null and void. Consequently, it is essential that, in making any proposal for acquisition through privatisation, an investor must conduct negotiations through the NPA and keep the Agency advised of its interest in any target company. Particularly, the NPA should be approached with any proposal regarding a company which is not being privatised within the scope of any early privatisation programme but which is targeted by an outside party for privatisation directly (for instance, in consequence of a long-term trading association).

14

Privatisation in Practice

Touche Ross

The legal framework for privatisation is positioning Romania with some of the conditions for successful investment. However, any investor will also wish to know the practical approach which the authorities and enterprise management are adopting to the implementation of the Privatisation Law. This chapter reviews this broader picture for foreign investors. It also looks forward to future operating conditions which foreign companies and investors can expect to find.

The privatisation programme Romania is pursuing, in common with other Eastern European countries, has both top-down and bottom-up aspects. The key purpose of the combined approach is to reduce the size of the state sector in national production.

The top-down approach involves the sale of state-owned companies to foreign or domestic private buyers, through trade sales, public flotation, public auction or management/employee buy-outs. In Romania the law allows all these approaches, or a combination, to be pursued. The bottom-up approach encourages a new class of small entrepreneurs through a variety of incentives. Often, the traditional top-down approach has attracted much of the international attention while the efforts being made to restore vitality to the small business sector have played second fiddle. Arguably, the opposite emphasis should be placed since the establishment of a new and pervasive entrepreneurial class is essential for economic success. Romania is making particular efforts to stimulate the growth of this group.

BOTTOM-UP PRIVATISATION

To lay the conditions for small business development, the Romanians have established an extensive programme of inducements through the Company Law, incentives for investment and profit retention and repatriation, permissive tax regimes and a host of training initiatives. In addition, in a determined effort to ensure entrepreneurs have both the physical and business assets to develop their businesses, the Romanian government is actively proposing to release assets from the state sector into the private sector.

Already, more than 4000 assets – typically small businesses or business units such as shops, hotels, small factories and warehouses – have been identified for disposal by auction within 6 months. They are available to Romanians and foreigners alike. Subject only to the provision of certain opportunities for employees to make a bid, the auction programme for the disposal of such assets will allow the highest priced bidder to acquire the asset through a transparent and accessible process. The Romanian government is keen to make this programme work quickly.

TOP-DOWN PRIVATISATION

In the top-down programme a two-phase approach has been adopted. The main phase, due to be launched in the summer of 1992, will involve privatisation of 99.5 per cent of Romania's commercial companies. This will be done through a system of institutions similar to unit trusts but with the capability to discipline managements. This capability will complement the transfer of ownership which will already have begun through the issue of 30 per cent of the nominal equity in these businesses to Romanian citizens. The Funds will have to manage the programming of companies or whole industrial sectors for privatisation. This should allow them, under the overall responsibility of the National Privatisation Agency, to set commercial priorities into the programme and to undertake the restructuring and company support which may be necessary before privatisation.

As a precursor to this, however, an early privatisation programme for about 30 companies is already in progress. This is intended to set the tone for the whole programme both by selecting companies which are likely to survive in the private sector and by exploring alternative methods to privatisation. About 20 companies are already in the programme and advisers are currently working on the privatisation of at least 10 of these. At this stage, the method of privatisation cannot be anticipated but trade buyers are likely to be a preferred method, not least because of the access they offer to investment funds and to management skills, particularly in marketing.

A feature of the top-down element of the Romanian privatisation programme is the initial focus on small and medium-sized enterprises. Privatisation in other parts of Eastern Europe has often been bogged down by focusing on the apparent jewels of the state sector, only to find that the shimmer is lost in detailed review. As a result the process can become discredited. In Romania rigorous criteria have been employed in selecting companies for the early privatisation programme in an attempt to provide attractive commercial propositions for new owners. This has led to the selection for early privatisation of, for example, companies in the consumer industries sector with relatively stable markets. Where companies in heavier industries have been selected, the criteria (which have included financial performance, the lack of exposure to former Comecon markets, a promising market share and long-term sector prospects) were designed to improve the chances for a successful transition to the private sector.

The consumer industries represented in the early privatisation programme are in strong sectors. They include:

- tourism (Litoral, Ont Carpati, CTT);
- brewing and spirits (Ursus, Valco); and
- textiles, footwear and porcelain products (Simat, Pantera, Famos, Apullum).

Among the heavier industries (typically larger companies), sectors such as vehicle parts manufacturers (Apsa SA) and suppliers to the public utilities (Electromontaj) are represented.

In all of the companies put forward for early privatisation, pre-selection vetting has ensured that managers and employees have an enthusiasm for privatisation. Although it has to be said that this often represents a limited understanding of the consequences of privatisation and the difficulties that they may face in the future, this positive display should not be underestimated. There is a striking realism among a growing section of the Romanian business community of the risks and benefits of privatisation and a willingness to face the challenges.

By initiating the top-down privatisation programme with a set of promising companies the Romanian government aims to set a tone for the whole programme. They are trying to balance economic realism with the wider political imperatives for reform. One prospect is that the lessons of the early privatisation programme will be translated into the policy of the State and Private Ownership Funds - focusing on the winners while retaining in the Funds the companies which need significant restructuring.

MANAGING THE PROGRAMME

While undoubtedly behind the rest of Eastern Europe in its programme, Romania is poised to exploit its advantages. Thus, it is intent on benefiting from the lessons others have learned, avoiding the pitfalls of other approaches to economic reform and selecting the methods which have performed well in the economic laboratory of Eastern Europe. Romania will also exploit the normally low level of debt in its state-owned companies which has resulted from the policies of the previous regime. While one consequence of this is significant investment requirements in many cases, the lack of a debt overhang may well attract foreign investors.

An interesting feature of the government's approach, being developed by the National Privatisation Agency, is to take action to ensure that companies are protected from some of the uncertainties of privatisation by prior discussion with both current suppliers and customers. Whether this approach can be sustained in the context of a full competition policy remains to be seen; it is, however, an important indicator of the attitude towards both privatisation and the foreign investor.

A further positive sign is the interest being shown by government in monitoring the future behaviour of state-owned companies. Failure to address this issue, often encountered in other countries in Eastern Europe, can jeopardise the success of privatised companies. In economies in transition, this incipient competition policy offers safeguards to both the foreign and domestic private investor that help reduce the risk to the investment decision.

As the privatisation programme unfolds in the next few months, much attention will be focused on Romania. Whether the programme can survive the ravages of political pressures remains to be seen. However, the evidence is that the Romanians are determined to catch up and to demonstrate to the international business community some of the key competitive advantages which the country possesses, including its size, population and level of education.

15

Property

Sinclair Roche & Temperley

Of major concern to many potential investors in Eastern Europe is the law relating to property ownership. Investors will wish to know whether they will be able to get 'good' title to property, whether they will be able to take effective security and whether there are likely to be adverse restitution claims following completion of any investment.

Unfortunately, although Romania has made rapid progress in establishing a legal framework for many aspects of investment, the situation as regards property law remains unclear and, from an investor's point of view, unsatisfactory.

The purpose of this chapter is to seek to clarify the current law to the extent that it may affect investment, and to highlight potential problem areas that an investor may encounter.

THE LAW RELATING TO AGRICULTURAL LAND

Prior to 1946 the ownership of agricultural land was principally by means of small landholdings, previously derived from large estates owned by a number of substantial landowners in Romania. After 1946 ownership of agricultural land was transferred to local co-operative holdings – a system of ownership which continued in Romania until the present day.

With February 1991 came the adoption of Law No 18 of 1991 – the Land Law. This Law marked a fundamental change in the ownership rights of individuals in respect of agricultural land and, in effect, returned the co-operative landholdings to the owners of the small holdings of 1946 in units of not more than 10 hectares per family (although such holdings may be increased by acquisition to 100 hectares per family).

However, the Law did not seek to implement a complete restitution process and did not recognise any claims in respect of land now controlled by state farms (which account for 50 per cent of agricultural land in Romania). The Law also prohibited any non-Romanian citizen or legal person, not resident in Romania, from acquiring an interest in agricultural land. If any such person should acquire an interest, it must be disposed of within one year of acquisition, failing which the interest will be transferred to the state.

Use of agricultural land

In addition to restrictions on rights of ownership, the Land Law also contains express provisions as to use of agricultural land.

Landowners are required to cultivate the land for agricultural purposes only and must take steps to protect the soil and avoid erosion. Failure to comply with these requirements may result in fines of between Lei 5000 and Lei 10,000 per hectare, annually.

As regards agricultural usage, Article 56 of the Law sets out specific requirements relating to agricultural use and allows change only in specific circumstances and only then with specific approval from the local agricultural control authority.

THE LAW RELATING TO NON-AGRICULTURAL LAND

As with agricultural land, the Romanian government has not recognised rights of restitution in respect of land previously confiscated by the state and, in consequence, claims of third parties against the state or existing 'owners' remain barred. However, the new Constitution does recognise rights of ownership in property.

Rights of private ownership

Private ownership rights are derived, initially, through the right to use property. Consequently, an individual, having a right to use the land on which his house is built, may demand the right to purchase that land from the state at a concessionary rate. Following completion of any such purchase, the individual owner is then free to transfer or sell that property to any other eligible owner – essentially, any party other than a foreign investor.

Effect of the Transformation Law

The Transformation Law transferred ownership of all assets of state enterprises to newly formed state-owned commercial companies formed under the Law.

Although Article 20 of the Transformation Law appeared clear in extending the rights of ownership to *all* assets, there was considerable confusion within Romania as to whether or not the ownership right extended to ownership of land. In consequence, the government issued a directive on 17 September 1991 (the 'Order Concerning Ownership Rights of Trade Companies Over Land') which amounted to an unequivocal statement to the following effect:

- The Transformation Law passed ownership of assets to the commercial companies incorporated under that Law.

- The ownership rights in respect of the assets referred to extended, without reservation, to rights of ownership in respect of land used by the commercial companies at the date of their incorporation – unless such land was specifically retained by the state.

- Commercial companies incorporated under the Transformation Law may use the assets vested in them in their absolute and unencumbered discretion.

In consequence of this directive, it is now clear that all state-owned commercial companies incorporated under the Transformation Law have vested in them full rights of ownership in respect of land and property used by such companies, unless such land and property has been specifically reserved by the state. Such companies may buy or sell land or create security interests over land, the proviso being that a foreign investor may not own land in Romania.

In practice, the government directive has done much to clarify the situation as regards land ownership by commercial companies in Romania. However, a fundamental weakness still remains in that there has been, to date, no effective system of registration of title and there are no certificates of title issued in respect of land.

In order to complete a sale of land it is essential to have a notarial instrument which will only be given once the notary is satisfied that the vendor has effective title to the land being sold. At present, it seems that one of the only effective ways of securing such confirmation in respect of a company set up under the

Transformation Law is for the relevant ministry controlling that company to confirm that, as at the date of the Transformation Law, the relevant company had a right of use in respect of the land being sold and that that right of use became an effective ownership right when the Transformation Law became effective. However, this method of deducing title is not guaranteed to be effective, and further government consideration to this aspect of the law is required as a matter of urgency.

RESTRICTIONS ON FOREIGN OWNERSHIP

As already stated, foreign investors are not allowed to own property under Romanian law. Where property rights in respect of agricultural land are inherited, Law No 18 requires that the interest be disposed of within one year of acquisition, failing which it should be transferred to the state.

However, while this prohibition of ownership would appear absolute, there is, in fact, no restriction on a foreign investor incorporating a wholly-owned Romanian subsidiary company which then acquires ownership rights in respect of Romanian property. By this means, an investor may effectively purchase both agricultural and non-agricultural land (although in the case of agricultural land the rights of ownership will be restricted to 100 hectares) and may also effectively take (and enforce) security from a Romanian party – security being created by instrument in writing in respect of a specified debt and over specified property.

In owning property through a Romanian company, the investor will also benefit from the terms of the Romanian Constitution which provides that the right of property is guaranteed and that expropriation may not be effected except in the event of public necessity (and then only upon payment of proper compensation).

POTENTIAL CHANGES

It is apparent that while Romania has made bold steps over the past two years to create a legal framework within which a free market economy may flourish, it has failed to develop essential property laws to match, for instance, the foreign investment and privatisation legislation.

At present, the uncertainty over registration of title and the ability to effectively complete a sale of land are unsatisfactory and, although a foreign investor can acquire land through the device of a Romanian company, it would be preferable from the point of view of promoting foreign investment if the government was to recognise the importance of ownership by a foreign investor and amend the legislation accordingly.

To date, the question of restitution has also been carefully avoided, possibly with elections later in 1992 being borne in mind. However, political considerations should not affect the fundamental requirement that a clear system of land ownership is essential for the stimulation of a free market economy and it is hoped that the Romanian government will soon take steps to put such measures in place.

16

The Fiscal Framework
Touche Ross

A crucial aim of the rapid and radical legal reforms undertaken since mid-1990 has been the transition of the Romanian tax system into one more suitable for a market economy. Tax policy was recognised at an early stage as a valuable tool, not only in raising state revenue but also in stimulating foreign and domestic investment.

Four important laws have already been passed as part of the reform programme:

1. A profits tax (corporate income tax) levied on all public and private enterprises was introduced on 1 January 1991 to replace the previous system whereby state enterprises made remittances from their profits to the state budget.
2. A salary tax was introduced on 1 January 1991 to replace the previous tax on the wage fund of state enterprises.
3. The turnover tax on the sale of goods was substantially revised on 1 November 1990.
4. The Foreign Investment Law, adopted in March 1991, contains generous tax incentives including profits tax holidays and import duty exemptions.

Further tax reforms envisaged include replacement of the present turnover tax by a value added tax based on the EC model, and the expansion of the present salary tax into a general personal income tax, both by 1993.

In this chapter, following a description of the tax incentives available to foreign investors, the principal taxes levied on business entities and individuals are explained. These are:

- profits tax on business enterprises;
- taxes on individuals; and
- turnover tax.

Some other relevant taxes including social insurance contributions and stamp duties are also discussed.

TAX INCENTIVES FOR FOREIGN INVESTMENT

The Foreign Investment Law (discussed in Chapter 7) contains quite generous tax concessions in respect of foreign investments, including branches of foreign companies as well as Romanian-incorporated trading companies with foreign participation.

Profits tax concessions

All foreign investments are granted a full profits tax holiday for periods varying between two and five years according to the sector of investment as follows:

- Profits from the industrial, agricultural and construction sectors are exempt for a period of five years from the beginning of productive operations.
- Profits from the exploration for and production of natural resources, and from communications and transportation, are exempt for a period of three years from the beginning of the respective operations.
- Profits from trade, tourism, banking and insurance, and other services are exempt for a period of two years from the beginning of the respective operations.

It is crucial to note that should a foreign investment go into voluntary liquidation within a period equal to twice the period for which it enjoyed a profits tax holiday, the foreign investor(s) will be liable to pay the tax in respect of all the profits derived throughout the life of the investment (including the tax holiday period). Such tax would be payable in priority to other payments from the liquidation or other rights of the foreign investor(s).

Similar, but in some cases less attractive, profits tax holidays are granted to wholly Romanian-owned enterprises under the Profits Tax Law.

Following the initial profits tax holiday period, further profits tax reductions may be obtained in certain circumstances. First, profits tax will be reduced by 50 per cent in respect of profits reinvested in Romanian enterprises set up with a view to expanding or improving productive technology or expanding activity to obtain additional profits, or in any investments aimed at securing the protection of the environment. Secondly, an annual 25 per cent reduction in profits tax is granted in respect of foreign investments if any one of the following conditions is fulfilled:

- At least 50 per cent of the necessary raw materials, energy and fuels are provided through importation.
- At least 50 per cent of the products and services are exported.
- More than 10 per cent of expenditure is disbursed on scientific research, the development of new technologies in Romania, or professional training.
- At least 50 per cent of the machinery and other equipment necessary for developing existing investments are obtained from domestic production.
- At least 50 new jobs are created by new investments or the expansion of existing production capacity.

Import duty concessions

An exemption from import duties is granted in respect of all imported machinery, equipment, installations, means of transportation and any other goods representing the participation of a foreign investor. All raw materials, supplies and components imported for the purposes of production during the first two years of the project will also be exempt from import duties.

Free ports have been established at Sulina, on the River Danube and Constanta Sud on the Black Sea. The laws governing these free ports are typical of similar laws regarding free trade zones in other countries – essentially storage, trans-shipment and manufacturing may take place in each free port, on application, without the payment of import duties.

Other concessions

The Foreign Investment Law envisages the possibility that the government may grant additional incentives for foreign investment in fields of special importance for the Romanian economy. UK businesses wishing to investigate the possibility of obtaining additional incentives for investment should approach the Romanian Development Agency in Bucharest.

PROFITS TAX

Profits tax is levied on business entities carrying out profit-making activities, including all forms of Romanian trading companies and foreign companies with branches in Romania, following an initial holiday period varying in length depending on the sector of activity and whether there is any foreign participation.

The Profits Tax Law differs somewhat from the corporate tax laws which apply in many Western countries. For example, income is recognised for the purposes of calculating taxable profits only when it is actually received by the company in cash, while deductible expenses may only be claimed once they are actually paid. This strict cash basis of tax accounting is clearly unsuitable where trade is conducted on credit terms, particularly under the monthly tax payment system (discussed below) which is based on the previous month's profit and loss result.

Determination of taxable profits

The profits tax liability of a company is computed on a self-assessing basis by the application of progressive tax rates to the company's taxable profits. The profits tax rates which are to apply from 1 January 1992 are summarised in Table 16.1.

Taxable profits are generally represented by the difference between the gross income collected in cash and the amount of deductible expenses actually paid during the relevant period. No definition is given in the Profits Tax Law as to what constitutes taxable income. However, those expenses which will be deductible

Table 16.1 *A summary of profit tax rates*

Band of annual profit (lei)	Rate of tax applicable to band	Cumulative tax (lei)
First 1,000,000	30%	300,000
Over 1,000,000	45%	–

in calculating taxable profits are specifically listed. They include the following:

1. Expenses relating to the activities carried on, or to the income collected, and that are acceptable costs according to the Law.
2. Taxes for the use of state land.
3. Expenses incurred for employees' professional and on-the-job training.
4. Expenses incurred on any of the following (if not already deductible as part of the enterprise's production or variable costs): costs of research and development projects falling within any high-priority programme of national interest; the establishment of development strategies; the improvement of product quality; and the development of new competitive products.
5. Commissions paid to enterprises with foreign trade activities.
6. Expenses of entertaining, advertising, and publicity within the limits set by the Ministry of Finance.
7. Child allowances paid by enterprises in cases where these sums are not otherwise reflected in costs.
8. Contributions to the company's reserve fund and other special funds that are legally required to be set up.
9. Unrelieved losses brought forward from previous years for up to two years.
10. Contributions and donations made for humanitarian purposes or to support social, cultural, scientific, or sporting activities, to the extent permitted by the annual budget law.
11. Duties incurred in respect of ownership of means of transport.
12. Other expenses as specified by the legal provisions currently in force.

Also deductible for profits tax purposes is the turnover tax actually paid by the company to the tax authorities.

Payment

The financial year for profits tax purposes is the calendar year. Profits tax must however be computed each month by applying the tax rates listed in Table 16.1 and the appropriate amount of tax must be paid over to the tax authorities by the 25th day of the following month. The tax payable in respect of each month is determined as the difference between the tax applicable to the estimated profit earnt since the commencement of the year to the end of the month in question and the tax already paid for the previous months of that year.

A final reconciliation of the financial year's actual taxable profits and the tax payable must be computed by 31 January of the following year, with an additional payment being made or a refund or credit given. Companies must also submit by 15 April in each year an income return for the previous year.

Dividends

Dividends must be paid out of post-tax profits. A withholding tax of 10 per cent is levied on dividends paid to non-residents under the Profits Tax Law. However, from 16 November 1991, a further withholding tax of 10 per cent has been introduced on all dividends paid to non-residents and Romanian residents, including individuals. Accordingly, it appears that dividends paid to non-residents are subject to a combined withholding tax of 20 per cent.

However, this may be overridden to some extent in the case of UK shareholders since the UK-Romania double tax treaty limits Romanian tax on dividends paid to UK residents as follows:

- 10 per cent of the gross amount in the case of a corporate shareholder controlling directly or indirectly at least 25 per cent of the voting power in the Romanian company;
- 15 per cent of the gross amount in all other cases (including dividends received by UK resident individuals).

It is important to note that the dividend withholding tax is levied independently of the various profits tax holidays granted in respect of foreign investments and, accordingly, foreign investors must bear the withholding tax even where the relevant dividend is paid during the initial tax holiday period.

It is currently unclear whether the 10 per cent withholding tax imposed under the Profits Tax Law also applies to the remittance of profits by a Romanian branch to its head office overseas. It does seem clear, however, that the further 10 per cent dividend withholding tax, introduced on 16 November 1991, does not apply to branches.

Taxation of UK resident of companies

A UK resident company should not be subject to profits tax merely because of the presence in Romania of a representative office which does not carry on any business but the activities of which are limited to, for example, the storage of goods for display, the purchase of goods, advertising, the collection and supply of information, or scientific research.

If, however, the UK company maintains a fixed place of business or branch in Romania through which it actively carries on business, any profits attributable to the branch will be subject to the Romanian tax regime.

TAXES ON INDIVIDUALS

There is currently no general personal income tax levied in Romania, although it is intended that such a tax will be introduced by 1993. In the meantime, the principal tax levied on Romanian individuals and foreign expatriates working in Romania is the salary tax.

Salary tax

Each month, salary tax must be deducted by employers from all salary or wage payments made to employees according to set progressive rates and must be remitted to the tax authorities, much in the same way as the PAYE scheme operates in the UK. Employees earning less than Lei2000 each month are exempt from this tax, while certain employees qualify for a 20 per cent reduction; for example, employees who are under 25 years of age or have one or more children.

Salary tax generally applies to any income in the form of salary or wages received in cash by an employee during the relevant month regardless of the period of employment to which the payment relates. Non-cash benefits such as the provision of accommodation or a motor vehicle appear to be excluded from the tax. Most payments made in connection with employment are considered to constitute salary, including bonuses, holiday pay and any payment for temporary disability or maternity. The earnings of certain employed professionals such as lawyers and doctors are also included.

Certain payments made to employees are exempt, including the payment of travel and necessary moving expenses, amounts received during any dismissal notice period, social security allowances, pensions, and meal allowances.

In the case of expatriates, salary tax will apply to all payments of salary or wages made by a Romanian employer in respect of activities carried out by the expatriate in Romania. If the expatriate is paid abroad under a non-Romanian contract of employment, salary tax will not apply. However, care should be taken if the non-Romanian employer attempts to on-charge such salary costs to a Romanian company since Romanian law in such cases requires a Romanian contract of employment to be executed with an accompanying salary tax liability.

The provisions of the UK-Romania double tax treaty (principally Articles 15 to 22) should be carefully considered in order to determine their possible impact in the case of a UK expatriate working in Romania. For example, a UK resident who is employed under a non-Romanian contract of employment but is paid in Romania would normally be subject to salary tax. However, so long as the expatriate is not present in Romania for a total period exceeding 183 days in the relevant year and provided his or her salary is not borne by a Romanian branch of the employer, salary tax would not apply to any salary received in Romania (Article 16(2)).

Dividends received by individuals

Finally, it should be noted that the 10 per cent dividend withholding tax introduced from 16 November 1991 applies also to dividends paid by Romanian companies to Romanian resident individuals. No further tax is levied in the hands of the recipient in such cases. Dividends paid to UK resident individuals after 16 November 1991 appear to be subject to withholding tax at 15 per cent (as discussed earlier).

TURNOVER TAX

The turnover tax on the sale of goods was significantly revised on 1 November 1990. The tax base was expanded and the tax is now levied on the sale of most goods produced within Romania, the import of goods, and the provision of services supplied within Romania. The sale of most primary raw materials (notable exceptions being oil and gas) are exempt. Exports and materials purchased to produce goods for export are also generally exempt (except, for example, where the material is of a type usually imported due to a shortage within Romania).

The turnover tax is responsible for raising over 40 per cent of total state revenues and is to be replaced by a value added tax system based on the EC model, probably in 1993. Turnover tax is levied at *ad valorem* rates (varying between 3 per cent and 15 per cent) and some exemptions are provided, apart from those mentioned above, in the agricultural, energy and defence sectors.

The turnover tax is no longer levied only on the final sale of goods to the consumer. However, the rates applying to intermediate sales and sales of capital goods are significantly lower than those applying to final sales of consumer goods.

Excise duties have recently been introduced on certain goods such as alcohol (30-60 per cent), tobacco and coffee (both 50 per cent). Goods subject to excise duty are not subject to turnover tax.

SOCIAL INSURANCE CONTRIBUTIONS

Employers (other than companies with foreign participation) must make social insurance contributions in respect of each employee at the rate of 22 per cent of the employee's gross (ie pre-salary tax) wages. In the case of companies with foreign participation, such contributions must be made in respect of its employees at the higher rate of 25 per cent. In all cases, each employee must contribute an amount equal to 3 per cent of their gross wages, this contribution being withheld at source by the employer together with the salary tax.

Unemployment fund contributions must also be paid in respect of all full-time employees. Again both employer and employee must contribute, at the rate of 4 per cent and 1 per cent respectively.

INTEREST AND ROYALTY WITHHOLDING TAXES

Romania imposes withholding tax on the payment of interest to non-residents at the rate of 15 per cent. The rate is reduced to 10 per cent under the UK-Romania double tax treaty where the interest is paid to a UK resident.

Copyright royalties paid to non-residents in respect of literary, artistic or scientific works (including cinema and television films and tapes for broadcast on radio) are subject to withholding tax at

25 per cent. All other royalties are subject to non-resident withholding tax at a rate of 20 per cent. These rates are reduced under the UK-Romania treaty to 10 per cent and 15 per cent respectively.

OTHER TAXES

Other taxes in Romania include stamp duty levied, for example, on certain licences, particular services, sales of motor vehicles, and inheritances of real estate. There are also municipal taxes, city land and building taxes and agricultural taxes. Land tax is levied according to the area of the land in question, while building tax is levied on the insurance value of the building.

17

Technology and Communications

Touche Ross and the Romanian Development Agency

The Romanian government, all political parties and other decision makers are fully aware of the crucial role that telecommunications play in today's international business world. This sector has therefore received special attention and is one of the most attractive for foreign investors – a number of which are already present in Romania (eg Siemens, Alcatel, Goldstar, Ericsson).

The medium-term objective is to achieve a European level of quality and structure of telecommunication services. The future prospects are good as Romania has obtained a loan of US$180 million from the European Bank for Reconstruction and Development to modernise its telecommunications. On the basis of a study made by the French company SOFRECOM, which has proposed a strategic approach for the development of telecommunications in Romania until 2005, the loan will be used for the modernisation of infrastructure and redesigning the network hierarchy.

Following this programme, by the end of 1993 eight main transit switchboard stations will be built (Bucharest, Timișoara, Craiova, Cluj-Napoca, Bacău, Brașov, Galați, Ploiești) and they will be interconnected by a fibre-optic based network. Work is under way to utilise the digital switchboard in Bucharest for international communications and to install two similar new stations in Cluj-Napoca and Galați.

OBJECTIVES FOR THE TELECOMMUNICATIONS SYSTEM

Government policy

Romanian government policy in the field of telecommunications is based on the following premises:

- Development of the telecommunications network is fundamental to the economy and its evolution over the coming years.
- Telecommunications investment is as important for industrial and economic development as are the more traditional forms of infrastructure investment such as railways, roads, water and electricity.
- Telecommunications represent a large and rapidly growing sector within the economy as a whole, giving rise to employment and the creation of wealth.

It is clearly understood that the need for information will spread across all sectors of the economy, not only within business but also in the private lives of Romanian citizens. This will cause far-reaching structural change in the way goods and services are produced and distributed, and is also expected to affect the administration and management of industry.

The Government has therefore decided to give a high priority to the telecommunications sector, and as a consequence intends to increase investment substantially in telecommunications capacity and equipment. The main targets for telecommunications development include:

- Achieving a direct exchange lines penetration of 30 per cent by the year 2000 (from the current level of just below 10 per cent). This increased level is regarded as the minimum necessary to support a market economy of the type Romania has in view for that time.
- Introducing digital technology as the basis for all new investment by the mid-1990s.
- Introducing a set of liberalisation initiatives for the telecommunications sector, with the aim of developing the sector in line with broader national goals for achieving a market economy.

The total investment required for achieving these targets is estimated at $11.5 billion.

Structural changes envisaged

To achieve the improvement of efficiency in the telecommunications sector, a number of reforms will be introduced:

1. separation of postal activities from telecommunications;
2. restructuring the telecommunications organisation into a commercial entity so that it can attract capital from the commercial markets, either in the form of loans or equity;
3. encouraging the entry of additional service operators, manufacturers, and network construction contractors;
4. allowing subscribers to provide capital investment for the network in their area;
5. separation of broadcast services and acceleration of the broader liberalisation measures.

Such measures aim to provide special status for certain types of networks in which participation of various operators will be permitted – ie mobile cellular radio, packet-switched teleconferencing and message handling systems.

Eventually, in line with evolving policy in the EC, all services other than basic telephone and telex will be open to free enterprise. Clarifying the role and degree of foreign ownership in this sector will become particularly important.

ORGANISATIONAL INFRASTRUCTURE

Prior to December 1989, the responsibility for telecommunications was highly centralised, and lay with the Ministry of Transportation and Telecommunications. This body conducted all telecommunications activities through the Directorate of Post and Telecommunications.

In January 1990, the government created a new Ministry of Post and Telecommunications, with the objective of establishing a coherent set of policies for the telecommunications sector. In June 1990, ministerial responsibility was again transferred, from the Ministry of Post and Telecommunications to a new Ministry of Communications.

In September 1990, following the general aim of the European Commission's Green Paper, telecommunications operations were removed from ministerial responsibility and vested in a newly created enterprise, ROM-POST-TEL (RPT). The Ministry of Communications is now responsible for strategic planning, human and financial resources, and overall government policy on telecommunications. At the same time, RPT has considerable autonomy regarding the purchase and supply of equipment, and full responsibility for operational matters.

ROM-POST-TEL

RPT, the national operating agency, is responsible for organising and operating postal and telecommunications services, and has technical control of radio frequencies and transmission systems for radio and TV broadcasting. In future it is intended that RPT will retain a monopoly only for the supply of basic telecommunications services such as telephone and telex.

Network construction

RPT is responsible only for maintenance of the network, while the construction activities are carried out by a separate company (Teleconstructia). This has demonstrated a peak construction capacity of 200,000 lines in its best year. The company engages in all internal and external construction activities, except for radio systems which are undertaken by a combination of RPT and an independent company specialising in the construction of towers and aerials.

Telecommunications manufacturing industry

The Romanian telecommunications manufacturing industry consists of several factories, the most important being Electromagnetica. Since 1975 Electromagnetica has been licensed by Bell Telephone Manufacturing (BTM, formerly owned by ITT, now Alcatel) to produce the Pentaconta crossbar exchanges which now constitute the main switching system in Romania. Production includes telephone sets and some transmission systems.

Analogue microwave and PCM carrier equipment is produced by ICRET, a small manufacturer under the control of the Ministry of Communications. A separate company is responsible for the production of cable.

Romanian industry is inadequate for meeting the future telecommunications needs of the country in terms of production capacity, manufacturing quality and design. For this reason, both the Ministry of Communications and RPT are interested in encouraging joint ventures to promote the supply of modern telecommunications equipment. In the past two years, several joint ventures with the object of producing digital switchboard equipment of small and medium capacity have been established (eg the Romanian producer Electromagnetica has established two such joint ventures with Seimens and Goldstar, and another Romanian producer, Datatim, is collaborating with Alcatel). To improve the infrastructure, organised tenders for buying telephone cables were set up and a Romanian–Italian joint venture with the object of installing cables will be established.

In radio communications, negotiations are currently taking place between COMSAT (USA) and the Regie Autonome for Radiocommunications to establish a joint venture for satellite communications.

TECHNICAL INFRASTRUCTURE

The existing telephone network

There are 2.34 million direct exchange lines (DELS) and 2.96 million telephone handsets in Romania; this corresponds to a density of 9.95 DELS and 12.85 telephones per 100 of population. Distribution of DELS is quite uneven: in Bucharest the density exceeds 25 DELS per 100 of population, while in the rural areas the density is only 2.7. The transmission network is almost completely analogue.

Romania has semi-automatic access to 109 countries for international traffic and a total capacity of 870 international circuits. Outgoing international traffic is switched semi-automatically through a manual switchboard in Bucharest, while all incoming traffic is routed automatically. A new digital international exchange (Siemens EWSD) with a capacity of 3000 lines was brought into service in 1990.

Romania has access to Intelsat satellites covering the Atlantic and Indian Ocean regions from two earth stations. Romania also became a member of Entelsat in May 1990.

The Romanian network requires a special kind of payphone for long-distance calls, and there are 6993 units for inter-urban calls and 22,310 units for local calls (of which 16,737 are located in urban areas).

Telex and data

The total capacity of telex and telegraph exchanges is 13,006 subscriber lines, of which 10,135 lines are employed by telex subscribers. All exchanges are automatic and the hierarchy exists on only two levels, national and international. The network provides full subscriber-dialed access to most countries in the world, with common exchanges handling telex and telegraph traffic.

Romania does not yet have any form of public switched data network, so customers must either use modems or develop their own facilities based on leased lines.

Leased lines

The public switched telephone network is complemented by a leased-line network which has a total length of 6,277,793 kilometres.

18

The Environment
Sinclair Roche & Temperley

In common with many of its Central and Eastern European neighbours, Romania's principal problem in connection with environmental control and regulation has not been a lack of legislation but rather a lack of enforcement and an apparent lack of a systematic environmental strategy within industry.

Legislation has been in place for some time regulating many aspects of the environment, including environmental protection (1973), fishing (1974), public health (1978) and use of pesticides (1982). At the time of writing, new environmental legislation is under consideration and, with a stated intention to seek associate status of the European Community as soon as possible, it appears that more urgent direction will be given to the government's environmental policy.

LEGISLATIVE FRAMEWORK

Although, for the past two decades, a legislative framework has existed for the regulation of the environment, it has only been since the Revolution of 1989 that the Romanian government has attempted to implement a full framework within which it is intended to control and regulate the environment and, in particular, environmental damage.

The adoption, early in 1990, of legislation regulating the environment within the Danube delta and other waterways was one of the initial steps directed at environmental regulation. A particular concern was the control of flooding and the protection of wildlife, while certain major construction works to link the Black Sea with the Rhine – Main – Danube Canal were being undertaken. The Land Law (Law No 18 of 1991) attempts to regulate, *inter alia*, the use of agricultural land and imposes duties on landowners to monitor and control soil erosion. Failure to comply with the new legal requirements carries financial penalties of between Lei5000 and Lei10,000 per hectare.

Law No 50 of August 1991 sets out a regulatory framework affecting construction of buildings and, in effect, imposes strict requirements for obtaining of planning permission in relation to any proposed building projects – all steps targeted at some form of environmental regulation. Similarly, the Foreign Investment Law of 1991 restricts the rights of foreign investors to invest in sectors of industry where such investment may adversely affect the environment and breach environmental regulations. To date, such regulations have not been clearly identified to potential investors and it may be that the adoption of the new Environmental Law later this year will more clearly define the regulations referred to.

The government's concern in connection with environmental matters is also highlighted by the fact that the Foreign Investment Law provides for a 50 per cent tax reduction on profits which are reinvested in investments 'aimed at securing the protection of the environment'. However, to date, there is no tax concession on initial investments that may benefit the environment.

REGULATORY CONTROL

As regards the implementation and enforcement of environmental legislation generally, the Ministry of the Environment was established in 1990, as was the Ministry of Public Works and Territories' Arrangements ('Territories' Arrangements' means, essentially, building control).

The principal function of the Environment Ministry is to co-ordinate environmental protection at national level. In co-ordinating such matters the Ministry is directed to undertake the following:

- to conduct studies and programmes for the assessment and creation of environmental protection;
- to create a new legal framework for the regulation of environmental concerns;

- to co-ordinate the redevelopment of environmentally damaged areas;
- to co-ordinate domestic environmental laws with internationally established standards; and
- to ensure compliance with environmental regulations by private persons, companies or governmental bodies.

Within the overall framework of the Ministry, separate departments have been established dealing, in particular, with waterways, forests, nuclear energy, the Danube delta and general environmental regulation.

Each individual department is charged with undertaking certain specific matters – for instance, the Environment Department (dealing with general environmental regulation) is required to ensure the co-ordination of the environmental legislative programme with international requirements and is required to monitor pollution emission in industry and manufacturing. Similarly, the Department for Nuclear Control is required to ensure nuclear security and protection against radiation, to monitor transportation of nuclear materials and radio active waste and, of importance from an investor's point of view, to grant authorisations for the conduct of business in the field of nuclear energy. It is also required to ensure compliance by established businesses with all relevant environmental legislation.

FUTURE LEGISLATION

Although these measures appear to create an established regulatory framework, the main concern from an international perspective has been that, to date, existing environmental legislation has not been fully enforced. In consequence, Romania is now seeking to adopt a new Environment Law having the following principal objectives:

- preventing, minimising and reducing environmental pollution;
- maintaining and improving environmental controls and ensuring compliance; and
- rebuilding and redeveloping areas damaged through environmental pollution.

As with previous legislation, the Ministry of the Environment continues to be the central body responsible for establishing rules and regulations for control of the environment and for ensuring compliance with such rules and regulations.

In draft form, the Law appears to require that companies should install and maintain equipment for the regulation of environmental emissions and imposes requirements to ensure that companies are themselves able to reduce environmental pollution. The draft also seeks to establish a more stringent authorisation procedure for businesses intending to establish in particular sectors of business and industry, where such establishment may have an adverse effect on the environment. For instance, authorisation will now become compulsory for any company undertaking any of the following businesses:

- construction and building development;
- undertaking natural resource mining, drilling or exploration;
- manufacturing or using any toxic or noxious substances or engaging in the transportation, importation and export of such substances;
- undertaking any business which may affect fishing, forestry or wildlife;
- undertaking any tourism activities within certain designated geographical areas; and
- undertaking any other activities which may adversely affect the environment.

Authorisation will be given by the Ministry only after it has undertaken certain technical and ecological studies in connection with the proposed business. Any authorisation will be valid for so long as may be stated in the authorisation itself (such period being dependent upon the type of business to be undertaken), provided that the circumstances in which the authorisation was granted remain unchanged. However, it should be noted that an authorisation will cease to be valid should the work for which the approval was given not be started within two years of the date of authorisation.

Particularly in respect of the manufacture and use of toxic and nuclear products, it is expressly forbidden to undertake such businesses without a prior authorisation and failure to obtain such authorisation may result in financial penalties being imposed.

GUIDANCE FOR INVESTORS

The environmental sector of industry represents a priority area for foreign investment in Romania (as illustrated by the preferential tax treatment given under the Foreign Investment Law for reinvestment of profits). Additionally, the government has indicated that the energy sector (with consequential environmental implications) is a stated priority area for development.

The new draft legislation appears to seek to create a more strict regulatory framework for investment, although until it is actually passed it is difficult to assess how effective the legislation will be in practice. With such a lack of enforcement to date, it is also unclear as to whether an investor may be made liable for environmental damage resulting from the actions of a previous owner or whether strict liability will be imposed.

It is hoped that, in due course, the government will clarify the basis on which liability will be imposed, and may even assume the liability for damage caused by businesses formerly under state control. However, in the meantime, investors should, in practice, seek to impose the most strict criteria possible in connection with any investment in order to reduce potential liabilities.

Most potential investors in industry are already fully aware of the merits of undertaking an environmental due-diligence investigation, whether entering into a joint venture arrangement, investment or acquisition. If potential environmental problems are discovered in the course of such a due-diligence assessment, it goes without saying that an investor may have to seek clarification of government policy at that time and may, indeed, have to reconsider the proposed investment.

19

The Labour Market
The Romanian Development Agency

Some 13 million Romanian citizens are of working age (defined as 16-59 years for men and 16-54 years for women). Of this total, 85 per cent, or 11.1 million persons, were economically active in 1990.

The level of employment is 87 per cent among men and 91 per cent among women, with the latter comprising 45 per cent of the work-force (and 41 per cent of paid employees). Women's share in the labour force is notably high; this reflects the former socialist ethic of non-discrimination, and also a policy of growth through the widest use of available resources.

Most workers are employed in the public sector (mainly in state enterprises). The share of this sector grew from 34 per cent of all those working in 1960 to 69 per cent in 1989. Agricultural co-operatives accounted for another 25 per cent of all employment while 6 per cent was in the private sector. The distribution of employed people by activity indicates that the industrial sector is the largest employer, accounting now for 38 per cent of all employment, followed by agriculture with 28 per cent. The low percentage of people employed in services – 33 per cent – is a specific inheritance of the former centrally planned economy.

Problems such as the lack of management skills are only likely to be remedied over time, probably with the assistance of foreign investment and training, while unemployment is likely to increase during a period of rationalisation and privatisation of Romanian industry.

EMPLOYMENT PRACTICES AND MOBILITY OF LABOUR

Labour markets, with employment levels and wages determined by supply and demand, have not existed in Romania. Instead, enterprises have been located near population centres and enterprise employment structures have been centrally determined by the specific technologies required to achieve output targets. Technological coefficients determined the number and skill-structure of employees, with each approved position having a rate of pay determined by reference to a central wage tariff. In practice, the coefficients used have resulted in substantial overmanning of enterprises.

So far, labour mobility has been extremely low in Romania: under the socialist system, virtually every worker was assured a job in the area he lived in and had little incentive to change jobs or move elsewhere. However, labour mobility has been hindered not only by job assurance, compressed wage scales, and benefits tied to the work-place, but also through active government policies to limit inter-regional migration. In 1976, a number of cities were declared closed to persons not already living within the city. Virtually all cities with populations in excess of 100,000 were 'closed' in this way. One of the first actions of the new government in January 1990 was to cancel this regulation.

Businesses have, until now, been reluctant to terminate contracts of employment for economic or profitability reasons. The institution of unemployment benefits, set up in February 1991, will soften the impact on the unemployed and facilitate redundancies.

Realising the need for regulation of the labour market and to assist the process of rationalisation of and investment in industry, the government introduced a basic legal framework covering matters such as employment contracts, trade unions and unemployment benefits.

THE LEGAL FRAMEWORK

An employer must comply with a number of employment-related laws covering employment standards, collective bargaining, human rights, health and safety, and workers' compensation. In addition, employers are required to contribute to a state-administered social security fund.

The new Romanian Constitution, passed on 21 November 1991, contained (in Article 38) the basic principles of employment:

1. every person has the right to employment in the business or sector of industry of his choice; and

2. all employees are entitled to certain minimum protection (for instance an eight-hour working day, health and safety at work, special working conditions for women and young people, a minimum wage, collective contracts guaranteed by law, statutory holidays, paid vacation, paid maternity leave and bonuses).

Generally, a working month is 170 hours, consisting of weekdays only. Employees are paid every two weeks, are entitled to additional pay for overtime and usually receive four weeks paid vacation per year.

Employers are required to take reasonable care for the safety of employees. In addition, employees themselves are expected to take reasonable health and safety precautions. Romanian law gives employees the right to refuse to perform work that would put them or others in danger. Employers may not discipline employees who properly refuse to work under dangerous conditions.

The right of employees to strike is also recognised (and regulated) by the Constitution. This represents a significant move away from the command-style regime with accompanying compulsory employment. The Constitution has also provided that no person may be employed if less than 15 years old.

Any foreign-owned company may employ Romanian citizens without authorisation. The Foreign Investment Law provides that no foreign citizen can be employed other than in a management or specially skilled role on the basis of a work permit issued by the Ministry of Labour and Social Protection.

The employment of foreign nationals working in Romania will be subject to the legislation of the foreign national and/or the investor unless the employee's contract of employment specifically states that Romanian labour law is to have effect. Employment of a Romanian work-force by a foreign investor will be subject to Romanian law although it should be noted that there are no legal restraints on an investor as regards the numbers of employees employed and/or retained by the investor or the business in which the investment is made.

Only persons having Romanian citizenship may hold public offices whether political, civil or military.

Contracts of employment

Contracts of employment can, according to Romanian law, be either collective or individual but, in any event, compulsorily contain certain specific terms imposed by law as embodied in the Constitution, the Civil Code and the Labour Code.

The following terms must be covered in both individual and collective contracts:

1. legal age;
2. minimum wage;
3. work conditions relating to holiday entitlement, bonuses, sickness benefits and special working conditions; and
4. scope of employment activity and required level of skill.

Any other conditions as agreed between the parties may be included in the contract. In all cases the contract of employment must be in writing.

Collective contracts of employment

In addition to covering the aspects referred to above, there are certain specific provisions relating to collective contracts of employment, which may be concluded either at national or local level.

In the event that a collective labour contract is negotiated with the work-force, it is compulsory for the contract to be entered into with all employees and not certain employees only.

The contract must be entered into for a specific period, which may not be less than one year, or for a specific project. At the expiration of the specified period the contract will be determined unless the parties agree to an extension.

The contract (which must be negotiated with the employer by an employees' delegation or trade union) must include provisions relating to protection of employment and strike procedures but will not be effective until registered at the Ministry of Labour and Social Protection. In no circumstances may the contract include provisions which are contrary to Romanian law, nor may it specify a wage which is less than the required minimum wage as set down by law.

There are no specified circumstances in which an employer must use a collective contract of employment, although it is common for such a contract to be used where the employer is a large private limited company or, more normally, an SA.

Individual contracts of employment

Normally used by a private limited company, an individual contract of employment cannot be used for the purposes of excluding the provisions of a collective contract of employment in the event that a collective contract exists for a particular company.

To date, it has been normal for individual labour contracts to be concluded for unlimited periods, although parties are at liberty to specify that the contract will be effective for whatever period they may agree in writing. With the changing requirements of employers in Romania and with the increasing level of foreign investment, it is likely that more and more contracts will be entered into for specific periods rather than on an unlimited basis.

The terms contained within an individual contract must satisfy the four general legal requirements mentioned earlier, and will usually include more detailed provisions as regards job specification than in a collective contract. The contract must be registered at the local Labour Ministry office and will not be effective until it is.

As regards termination of individual contracts, the contract will terminate at the expiry of the contract term or upon completion of the work for which it was entered into (if the contract is not unlimited). Alternatively, the dissolution or insolvency of the employer will also serve to terminate a contract. In the case of a contract for an unlimited term, it may be terminated by mutual agreement or by notice by either party.

Unless the contract states to the contrary, it may be terminated by an employee giving at least 15 days notice to an employer of his or her intention to terminate. However, an employer may only terminate an unlimited contract for one or more of the following reasons:

1. a reduction in the business activities of the employer or the insolvency of the employer (as evidenced in writing);

2. gross misconduct by the employee in the performance of his duties under the contract; or

3. incompetence of the employee in relation to the duties undertaken under the contract.

Termination by the employer will normally be by at least 15 days written notice sent to the local Labour Ministry office although, in the case of incompetence, termination may be immediate. The Labour Ministry office will then inform the employee of the termination of employment within five days of receipt of notice from the employer.

Where an employee receives maternity benefit from the state or sickness benefit for a child under three years, an employer may not terminate that employee's employment unless the employee's absence from work extends for a period of over one year.

Trade unions

Law No 54, passed in August 1991, seeks to set down guidelines for the establishment and regulation of trade unions. The Law recognises trade unions as legal persons, having the right to sue or be sued in their own name.

Trade unions may be established for the purposes of promoting and protecting professional, economic, social and cultural interests of the members of the union, subject to unions being independent of any state organisation or political party. All employees have the right to join a trade union or to organise themselves into such a union, subject to a union having a minimum of 15 members.

Employees of the Ministry of Defence, members of government and public officials may not join a trade union. Membership of a trade union by any other person is entirely discretionary and no employee may be forced to join a union against his or her wishes.

The Law recognises the rights of employees to be represented in labour disputes by a trade union but, in the case of employees of a company where there is no trade union, representation may be by representatives of the employees. The trade union will enter into conciliatory negotiations with the management of a company and, if no resolution is reached through negotiation (or if the management refuses to negotiate within 48 hours of receiving a demand), the trade union may effectively call strike action by the work-force. Strike action by the members of a trade union is entirely voluntary and employees are entitled to continue to work during the period of strike action.

A strike may not be declared for the purposes of achieving a political objective, for modifying collective labour contracts or for disputing any final arbitration decision as regards a labour dispute.

In the event that a labour dispute is not resolved within a period of 20 days of strike action being commenced, the dispute must be referred to the Ministry of Labour and Social Protection for arbitration.

Unemployment benefits and the social security system

Romania has established social insurance and assistance programmes which provide income support through unemployment benefits, pensions, and family allowances.

The rapid increase in the numbers of unemployed within Romania is of growing concern to the work-force and the state alike. It is estimated that the number of unemployed, which increased from 100,000 at the beginning of 1990 to 200,000 by April 1991, may have risen to 400,000 by the end of 1991. Accordingly, Law No 1 of 1991 seeks to address the problem of unemployment by providing for benefits to be payable to unemployed persons for a period of 180 days following termination of employment. Benefits are calculated by reference to the type of work previously undertaken, the length of time in employment, salary and the minimum national wage.

Unemployment benefits are paid by the Ministry of Labour and Social Protection and are funded by the following sources:

1. a contribution of 4 per cent of monthly salary of all companies, joint ventures, representative offices and other employers;

2. a contribution of 1 per cent of monthly salary payable by each employee; and

3. state contributions.

A certain proportion of the unemployment fund is also used for establishing unemployment offices to provide services for the unemployed and for retraining.

WAGES

In 1989, the average salary for public sector employees, who have traditionally constituted approximately 73 per cent of total employment, was Lei3063 per month. The highest average salaries in that sector were in the fields of public administration and construction (10 per cent higher than the overall average), while the lowest paid were in trade and municipal services (12–14 per cent below the sector average).

At present, the average gross industrial wage in Romania is Lei10,000 per month (approximately US$55), with the official gross minimum wage (which is indexed to inflation) being Lei8500 per month. However, it should be noted that foreign-owned companies generally pay significantly higher wages than those paid by local companies in order to attract the best workers. It should also be noted that, wage costs are being pushed upwards by the rate of inflation (319 per cent in October 1991 against September 1990) and by growing competition.

Although partially improved, salary legislation still provides for ceilings on wages, above which higher taxes are levied from companies.

Part III

The Options for British Business

Planning
Touche Ross

As the planning process moves forward, it will become apparent that the lack of hard data on many aspects of business and economic life makes it more difficult to find convincing evidence of how a venture is likely to perform. Past performance of state enterprises, for example, is often largely irrelevant. Likewise the breakneck speed in the transformation of the legal and economic situation can lead to even the most thorough plan needing to be updated on a more frequent basis than would be the case in the West.

Business life in Romania is full of rumours of all kinds which have implications for companies – political realignments, ministerial reshuffles, conspiracies and corruption of various kinds, new raw material supplies or shortages, new laws, decrees and so on. Much of these need to be taken with large amounts of salt but some provide early warning of important events. Having a feel for whether a particular rumour is meaningful is largely a question of experience and this is an argument in favour of building up a network of well-informed sources.

Whatever the peculiarities of doing business in Romania, planning for that business must be seen in the context of a company's overall planning process. Therefore the essential questions remain the same:

- What resources will we need to put in?
- What return can we expect?
- When can we expect to see the return?
- What risks are attached to the business?

- How would such a business fit in with our existing objectives and ambitions?

It is the answers to those questions that will highlight the differences between doing business in Eastern Europe and the West.

An LCCI document once neatly summarised this by advising that businessmen will need a considerable degree of long-term commitment to the Romanian market combined with an ability to identify Romanian requirements, which is by no means straight forward. In short, understanding and imaginative solutions are required.

THE MARKET

Taking a view

Romania, like other countries in the region, offers possibilities of both new markets and new production facilities for a variety of different kinds of companies. Since the Romanian economy will need to be comprehensively rebuilt over the next decade it is certain that a good number of fortunes will be made there in the next few years. However, this is unlikely to be the case for everyone. Some initially lucrative areas of business may already have disappeared through competition, others are not yet ready to produce real profits. In some cases, entry into Eastern European markets can be extremely risky, particularly for smaller firms which may become too exposed to projects that fail for no particular reason. Some experienced firms, notably in the commerce sector, have actually been forced to be very flexible in varying products, trading terms and prices as conditions have changed.

One result of the demise of the socialist system in Eastern Europe is that large differences between the countries have started to emerge. Each country will be attractive for a variety of reasons. Whether Romania is suitable for your venture will depend partly on the type of business being considered. Population, spending power, natural resources and the cost of labour will affect competitive advantage and determine whether Romania will be of interest.

Being so much larger than any other town in the country, as well as being the location of the national administration and the main international airport, Bucharest is usually the starting point for businessmen analysing their prospects in Romania. Yet other regions and towns may in fact prove of more enduring interest to British companies as they make contact with, for example, the clothes and shoe factories around Timișoara, the heavy engineering companies of Brașov and Craiova, the ports of Tulcea and Constanța or the paper and furniture enterprises near Brăila.

Romania, like the United Kingdom, was born from the union of a number of principalities and territories, each of which possesses distinctive features, political and industrial/commercial traditions, strengths and weaknesses. It may be the case that the smaller towns will be more responsive and flexible to investors' needs than Bucharest.

Market entry

The options available for starting business in Romania are hardly unique to the country, although many of the details may be.

Exporting to Romania

Exports to Romania have expanded a lot in the last two years. This expansion will probably continue, albeit at a slower pace, as industry is re-equipped and as companies, particularly the more affluent ones, look to upgrade their position. Exchange controls will mean that payment is likely to be a painful process for the Romanian client. Letters of credit are recommended, although not all Romanian customers will be able to take them.

Importing from Romania

The relatively large volume of exports to Western companies in the past means that there are quite a few enterprises used to exporting to international standards. Difficulties are more likely to revolve around getting payment to the supplier in a mutually acceptable way since most Romanian exporters do not like having to convert hard currency earnings at the National Bank and may look for other alternatives. Given the raw material shortages, timely delivery of goods may also prove problematic at times. The low labour costs, though, together with a British input of training and perhaps some materials, mean that it can prove very lucrative to import goods from Romania. Licensing and franchising can open up opportunities for local businessmen to capitalise on these advantages, but they are still largely unknown in Romania. Such methods will probably appear as the economy develops over the next five years, and will then prove useful in allowing ambitious Romanians to gain substantial turnover with an initially low capital and a solid international brand name.

Export distributorships

These have been relatively popular in Romania although initial success has been mixed as local staff do not always have the training necessary to perform as convincing sales people and to manage a new enterprise at the same time. As a way of getting round constraints in both production and marketing, importing components for assembly in Romania has been a traditional method for Romanian enterprise to export, with foreign technicians supervising the assembly of components/materials from abroad and with the production destined entirely for re-export to established markets.

Tenders

Given the great need for construction work on infrastructural projects, and given the increasing amounts of money coming into the country from international lending institutions like the World Bank, there have been a number of large contracts arranged by international tender. The procedures for these can seem mechanical and detached at times, and potential bidders should make sure that money for the projects genuinely exists before time and money are wasted in a wild goose chase. But the opportunities are real, particularly since competition is not yet intense.

Other possibilities

Beyond these arms-length type arrangements are ones involving a rather deeper involvement. By forming or buying a business entity under Romanian law, it becomes possible to own land (otherwise impossible for foreigners), to demonstrate to actual and potential partners a commitment to Romania and to hire staff to look after the interests of the venture full-time. This option does, however, expose the British side to legal and tax responsibilities which would otherwise be avoided.

One possibility which is only now starting to be available is to enter the market through the privatisation process. Every commercial company in Romania is to be sold off to the private sector over the next few years, and foreign involvement will form an important part of the process. Privatisation by trade sale to foreign companies or by sale to local purchasers with a foreign joint venture involvement are both possible options. Enterprises in heavy and light industry and in commercial and service sectors will be sold off from the middle of 1992 onwards.

DOING THE DEAL

Whatever the option chosen, particular care will need to be given to a number of issues in putting a deal together. Steps in the process will include:

- Valuations of businesses and assets. These will often be required in circumstances where historical information is unreliable and forecasts inadequate or non-existent. Valuation of intangible assets is a particularly thorny problem.

- Devising creative financial packages. To achieve the deal, it may be necessary to be creative in arriving at financial terms that are acceptable to both sides. Debt-equity swaps, local currency components and hedging instruments to deal with interest rate and/or exchange rate fluctuations might need to be considered.

- Negotiations with potential partners and/or sellers of assets or businesses. To be sure of protecting yourself and understanding precisely the nature of the commitments entered into, access to local language, legal, accounting and business advice will be essential. Issues which could arise include the nature and validity of contracts, previous owners' rights and hidden liabilities. It is advisable to move with some care and to ensure that a thorough due-diligence check is carried out.

- Completing transactions. Again expert advice and local assistance will be needed to ensure that contracts are water-tight and that commitments entered into are fully understood on both sides.

Timing

Given the present deep recession, the social and political unease, and the relatively undeveloped infrastructure for business, some people might wish to wait a few years before entering Romania. It should not be forgotten, however, that contacts and experience of local problems count for a lot in business in Romania. Many motivated, potential investors are already working out how to position themselves and identifying who they want to work with.

For as long as the perception of Romania abroad remains negative, assets within the country will be relatively cheap. Even a low level of contact with the market now may produce dividends when the larger opportunities begin to emerge. If a joint venture is contemplated it may take a couple of years before the Romanian side can be organised properly. The privatisation process will make available information on industry and enterprises that, for the present, is almost impossible for foreigners to access.

A key question concerns how long it will take to put a venture into operation in Romania; what return can be expected and over what period? In the early phase in most cases it is probably optimistic to envisage deals getting off the ground in less than six months to a year. Some larger projects which began to be negotiated in the middle or end of 1990 are still not finalised at the start of 1992. Having said that, there are also several examples of foreign firms being caught out trying to manage the explosive growth of their work in Romania. In consumer goods, for example, companies have often been surprised at the relatively high level of consumer demand for their goods, but at the same time are frustrated by the difficulties of establishing proper distribution channels.

GETTING STARTED

Making a decision about doing business in Romania is often more a question of getting a feel for the situation on the ground than of detailed desk research. A visit to Romania to have a look round at the conditions for doing business, at a potential partner's factory or shops and to talk to other people already doing business in the country is almost certainly a must. Thereafter, there are a number of ways of keeping in contact with the market without wasting time and money.

The first is to sit down for a couple of hours with a good lawyer or accountant to go through the basic ideas of a future deal to see whether there are any immediately obvious problems with the approach – for example, laws that might prove significant, or other issues that affect basic viability. A visit to the Romanian Development Agency would help in getting the English language texts of some of the more important laws.

Secondly, for market intelligence, it can be very cheap to hire a young English-speaking person to collect useful information from the press, the television or just rumours that are circulating. This can be added to a translation and interpretation role when appropriate, together with a lot of the basic legwork in finding the answers to some of the simpler business questions. Such a person can be found, perhaps on a part-time basis, at a low cost and is definitely recommended.

Thirdly, to keep down the biggest cost for visiting business people – hotels – it may be sensible to rent an apartment with a telephone, even if it will be used only a few days a month. In addition to the financial advantages, such a base also provides a venue for discussions and a place to store samples and documents.

These steps can minimise potential losses in the event that the deal does not work out, and enable opportunities to be seized as and when they appear.

Setting up an office

Finding decent space for a foreign company can be a frustrating business, with most properties on offer being relatively old, residential accommodation needing extensive renovation, refurbishing etc. Three main routes can be suggested:

1. Use some of the private property agents that have appeared and who generally deal with rented property. Their fees tend to be rather higher than the cost of personally going through newspaper advertisements, but at least the agents can usually speak English.

2. There is a government organisation with the primary purpose of helping the diplomatic community on property-related matters, but which also offers properties to anyone with hard currency. Again, they are not cheap.

3. One can try to get the word out through Romanian contracts that you are in the market for space and are prepared to pay commission for successful leads.

All three methods can be pursued at the same time, and this is probably the best approach.

As far as staff are concerned, there are a couple of points to be made. First, there are many expatriates who are genuinely happy in Romania, even though they may have been reluctant to go in the first place. Persuading staff to relocate is, therefore, perhaps the biggest obstacle. Most people who have spent time in the country seem happy to continue, given occasional breaks back to the West to stock up on the things that are still scarce in Romania. Finding local staff is often best carried out using contacts and offers of commission. The Embassy, Romanian organisations or other foreign workers in the country will almost certainly know of people as potential candidates. Alternatively, an advertisement can be placed in one of the higher circulation newspapers and response rates are usually high. Salaries should be paid either in dollars, or in a lei amount linked to a dollar original figure, as people try to protect themselves from inflation.

Expect to pay around $100 a month for a junior secretary, double that for a more senior personal assistant, treble that for a technical specialist and quadruple (or more) for a good management grade person. Competition between foreign firms is already creating a parallel labour market for people with foreign language skills, particularly English, so do not be surprised if these price levels move upwards more quickly than in the UK.

21

Marketing
Brittain Engineering Ltd

Romania, like most of its neighbours, has entered the post-communist era with only a vague idea of what exactly marketing is.

In the command economy, where all decisions on production and distribution were taken at the centre, with shortages of anything and everything the order of the day, the problem was not so much how to market one's products in the Western sense but how to convince the powers that be to include them in the next five-year plan.

Indeed, the whole idea of central planning was to eliminate 'wasteful' competition and most goods were produced in only a few factories, all grouped in the same 'Industrial central'. Standardisation was also used to produce identical goods, to specifications written years earlier, which largely explains the shoddiness of most products on the internal market and the lack of product innovation.

However, at the same time, Romania was a major exporter of quite a large range of products, including consumer goods, and although it was not possible to spend money on proper marketing abroad, a significant number of people have a reasonable understanding of modern marketing overseas. Also, some brand names have survived the years of command economy and newer ones have taken hold, suggesting both a strong tradition and a receptivity on the part of Romanians. Thus a grease gun is still a Tecalemit and brake pads are still brake Ferodo's, even though none of the originals have been sold into the country since the early-1940s. Similarly, one Xeroxes a document and builders request a Coles whenever they require a heavy mobile crane, pointing to some of the more successful exporters over the past 30 years.

Romania has a large pool of well educated people, most of whom understand at least one foreign language. Many speak English and some also French and Italian (to which Romanian is closely related), German and, in parts of the country, Hungarian. Even in the darkest days of Ceauşescu's dictatorship, Romanians kept abreast of what was going on in the outside world. The limitations are therefore likely to come much more from the lack of money than from a lack of awareness and consumer resistance to marketing and advertising.

After the 1989 Revolution, practitioners and academics joined together to create the Romanian Institute of Marketing, a professional body which attempts to set standards, lobby, run courses and organise exchanges with similar organisations abroad. At this stage, it is hard to judge just how successful the Institute is and how useful it will be in providing a pool of trained executives, but the very fact that they have made a start is commendable. It also proves that they are painfully aware of how much they have to catch up.

THE CONSUMER MARKET

Disposable income

The 1989 Revolution came at a time when there was a large liquidity overhang because of the lack of goods on the market. However, the influx of consumer goods and durables in 1990 and 1991 and accelerating inflation, have taken their toll and disposable income is reducing rapidly. Most income comes from wages and these now range between the equivalent of £50 and £150 per month per family. With inflation on the rampage (in the nine months to September 1991 price inflation reached 200 per cent while wages went up by 165 per cent) and unemployment on the increase, the immediate future is not particularly encouraging. However, it is only a matter of time before growth will resume again in the surviving industries, with services becoming more important than previously, and disposable income should start growing again from 1993 onwards.

Market research

Market research is in its infancy and at the time of writing there are no large market research organisations. Most Romanian producers place products on the market without any systematic market research and with no thought given to promotion, while shortages are such that unless the products are totally unacceptable (and this is sometimes the case), they are snapped up immediately.

As local producers increasingly feel the effects of competition from imported products, the demand for proper market research will increase and both local and foreign organisations will step in to fulfil this need.

Pricing

Inflation is on the increase, due both to the liberalisation of prices (only a few strategic commodities now have their prices controlled by the government) and the inefficiency of Romanian industry. Prices are still based on cost plus rather than what the market will bear and this has exacerbated inflation. However, there are already signs that some companies are feeling the backlash and, since December 1991, some prices (eg air fares) have been brought down. With the virtual devaluation of the leu in November 1991, imported goods are again relatively expensive, but if imports are further liberalised this too will put pressure on local producers to reduce costs, improve their design and, ultimately, reduce prices to consumers.

Distribution and retail

The system inherited from the command economy was highly centralised with both distribution and retail under the control of the Ministry for Internal Trade.

In the transition many producers have attempted to set up their own distribution and even retail networks but, often, this is almost as inefficient and wasteful as the system they are trying to replace. Retail and distribution are now being prepared for privatisation and no doubt the picture will change dramatically in the near future. Both will require extensive investment in transportation, warehousing and retail outlets.

Since 1990, a large number of private shops, roadside outlets and market stalls have sprung up and while their impact and total turnover cannot yet be assessed accurately, these too will grow in importance. Major foreign operators cannot be far behind.

INFRASTRUCTURE

Marketing and advertising agencies are very much at the artisan stage. The choice comprises Publicom, the publicity arm and exhibition organiser of the Romanian Chamber of Commerce, TIB the trade fair agency, agencies organised by local chambers of commerce, plus a multitude of private agencies that have sprung up, usually established by former (or existing) employees of the first three categories. The main problem is that none of the new organisations have a track record and practically all are small – just a few enthusiasts who do not have the financial muscle to hold out through lean periods. However, some good work has been done and no doubt if one looks carefully, one can find an agency to suit particular requirements.

THE MEDIA

Television

Most urban and many rural households now have television sets, although colour television represents only a fraction of the total. At the time of writing, television is practically under the control of the government and attempts to legislate for its independence and for an opening of the airwaves to private operators are under way. There are two channels on state television, both taking advertising, as well as a plethora of local stations and one private station (SOTI, which started broadcasting in December 1991), on the air for a few hours each day. A relatively large number of satellite dishes are being installed and most sets in border areas are tuned to neighbouring countries' frequencies.

Radio

Virtually all Romanians own or have access to a radio set and listen to broadcasts regularly. There are local radio stations (both state owned and, increasingly, private) throughout the country and all take advertising.

Press

The 1989 Revolution has unleashed a huge number of newspaper and magazine titles – at one stage over 1000. Romanians are avid readers of this output. The main titles with national circulation are *România Liberă*, *Adevărul*, *Tineretul Liber*, *Cotidianul* and *Azi*. All take advertisements.

ADVERTISING

Under the communist system, advertising was essentially another form of propaganda. Even today one sees advertisements on television for specialist products selling to a very narrow industrial market, which could not possibly benefit from exposure to the public at large. There is no guarantee that advertising expenditure will be accepted as a legitimate business cost so state-owned companies do it mainly for prestige reasons. There are very few professionals so most advertising is fairly amateur, except when foreign adverts are taken directly and translated into Romanian. No international agencies have yet set up in the country.

The main means of advertising (in order of importance) are: fairs/exhibitions, newspapers, television, radio, window displays, cinema, outdoor hoardings, public transport vehicles and (very limited) neon advertising.

MARKETING FOR THE EXPORTER

Marketing to industry and commerce

Doing business may prove difficult unless close contact is kept with potential customers, spread throughout Romania. With communications in a less than satisfactory condition and the sheer size of the country, reaching end-users is not exactly easy.

Assuming that preliminary market research indicates that there should be a market for one's product(s), the main problem is how to let the potential users and decision makers know of its existence and its main benefits. For a newcomer, the first step must be to join a trade mission organised by chambers of commerce (the London Chamber seems to be the most active in Romania), the CBI or trade associations. This will offer a chance to see the country, meet potential customers, agents and advertising agencies, and to seek advice from the older hands on the mission.

Contacts with relevant trade associations and universities in Romania, either directly or through their equivalents in the UK, can, in the longer run, produce quite spectacular results. These organise their own symposia and conferences and will be happy to let you present papers, organise mini-exhibitions, show films, etc, for nominal or relatively low charges.

There are two major trade fairs – TIBCO, for consumer goods (usually held in May) and TIB, the general trade fair (held in

October). In addition, Publicom, the exhibition and publicity arm of the Romanian Chamber of Commerce, organise specialised exhibitions, such as:

- Laborator (laboratory equipment, fine chemicals);
- Shop (consumer goods and durables);
- Autoservice (equipment and consumables for garages and service stations);
- Agra-vet (agricultural chemicals, veterinary drugs, agricultural machinery);
- Medicina (medical equipment, pharmaceuticals); and
- Informatica (computers, office machines, communications equipment and software).

Recently some smaller private companies have started organising specialised exhibitions and these may well be worth considering.

All regional chambers of commerce have more or less sophisticated exhibition facilities and publish newsletters, so contacts with them may prove a useful addition to monitoring the larger events in the capital.

Agencies and distribution networks

If the market is reasonably large, one may be well advised to look into agency/distributorship arrangements, either with a local company or a UK-based trading house with local connections. The British Overseas Trade Board has prepared a register of commercial houses trading with Central and Eastern Europe, available for £10.00.

If local representation is preferred, there are now plenty of private consultants, agencies and so forth registered in Romania.

Agencies and Distributorships

Sinclair Roche & Temperley

Frequently, potential foreign investors in a new market seek to 'test the water' through the creation of an agency or distribution arrangement rather than proceeding with a 'full-blown' investment by way of a joint venture or, possibly, the formation of a local subsidiary company. Normally, the risks involved in the agency or distribution arrangement will be expected to be significantly less than, say, the incorporation of a local company and, if unsuccessful, it is normally easier to terminate an agency or distribution arrangement than to go through the full process of winding up a local subsidiary company.

The purpose of this chapter is to consider agency and distribution arrangements as an alternative to the full process of incorporation and to provide a brief outline of the relevant Romanian legislation affecting such business structures.

AGENCY

The English concept of agency equates to the Romanian concept of mandate, regulated by the Civil Code. As the name suggests, the basic idea of mandate is that one party (the agent) should be authorised, by written mandate, to act on behalf of another party (the principal) in connection with the principal's business activities within a specified area.

The relationship between the principal and the agent is governed exclusively by the terms of the contract entered into between the parties themselves. As such, it is quite possible for the parties to agree terms to suit the particular circumstances of the individual parties. However, it is normal for a contract of mandate to be in respect of one of the two recognised forms of mandate:

- mandate with representation; or
- mandate without representation.

In the case of mandate with representation, the position is similar to the English concept of an agent acting for a disclosed principal. The agent is able legally to bind his principal who will be liable for the acts of his agent (subject to any limitation contained in the power of attorney appointing the agent). This limitation of liability is acceptable since the power of attorney appointing a representative will be registered with a notary in Romania and will, consequently, be a public document which may be inspected by interested third parties seeking to establish the extent of the mandate. Accordingly, if the agent exceeds his powers as granted by the power of attorney, the principal cannot be made liable for such over-reaching.

As regards mandate without representation, this concept is similar to an agent acting for an undisclosed principal. In such circumstances, the agent assumes unlimited liability as against a third party and, as long as the principal remains undisclosed, the principal will have no liability to such third party. Of course, the principal will remain liable to his agent under the terms of any contract appointing the agent to act.

REPRESENTATIVE OFFICES

In discussing the contractual arrangements between a principal and an agent, it is, perhaps, worth considering the steps by which a potential investor may set up a representative arrangement in Romania with a view to appointing a third party to act as agent.

Unlike the situation where a potential investor is seeking to establish a joint venture or subsidiary company in Romania, the establishment of a representative office or agency arrangement does not require approval of the Romanian Development Agency under the Foreign Investment Law. Instead, the foreign party must register the representation (whether by way of a representative office of the foreign party itself or by way of appointment of a local representative to act as agent for the foreign party) with the Ministry of Foreign Trade and Tourism.

Documents required for the establishment of a representative office are:

1. a copy of the memorandum and articles of association of the foreign party (or equivalent document);
2. a copy of the certificate of incorporation of the foreign party;
3. a notarised power of attorney in favour of the person who will act as a representative of the foreign party; and
4. a bank reference showing good standing of the foreign party.

Once approval is given by the Ministry, the representative arrangement may take effect.

As stated, the foreign principal will generally not be liable for actions of the representative where such actions exceed the term of the representative's authority under the power of attorney.

As regards taxation, transactions concluded through the representative office will be taxed on the value of profits deemed to accrue from the consideration payable in respect of such transactions. Where a representative office does not actually conclude transactions on behalf of the principal, tax will be payable on the number of employees employed by the representative office. Where no transactions are concluded through a representative office and where no employees are actually employed, tax may be payable on the basis that a representative office is deemed to employ at least one person.

DISTRIBUTORSHIP

There are no laws in Romania specifically regulating distribution arrangements.

Accordingly, as long as parties have the capacity to enter into a contract and as long as a contract is in writing and for consideration, parties are free to enter into such distribution arrangements. Thus, a foreign party seeking to establish a distribution network within Romania should consider the same points as should normally be considered when entering into a distribution arrangement in any territory within which the foreign party carries on business. After deciding whether there is, in fact, a market for the goods to be distributed, the foreign supplier may wish to bear in mind the following points:

- The territorial extent of the distribution arrangement. Is it to be an exclusive or non-exclusive arrangement and is it to be limited to a specific geographical area within Romania or Eastern Europe generally?
- Will there be minimum purchase and sale targets?
- What will the term of the contract be? Can the contract be terminated in the event of a failure to meet required targets?
- Governing law: although English Law may be stated to be the governing law of the contract (a point which is acceptable to the Romanian authorities) the supplier may wish to consider whether it would, in fact, be easier to enforce a Romanian Law contract within the specified territory.
- Payment terms: will payment be made within or outside Romania and who will be responsible for attending to exchange control requirements?

Additionally, the question of liability in respect of goods sold must be considered.

In the absence (at least initially) of a tested distribution network, a supplier may, in fact, feel that it is more appropriate to regulate the initial approach to a new market directly through its own representative network rather than through a newly established distribution arrangement.

23
Export and Import
Touche Ross and the Romanian Development Agency

BACKGROUND

Moving from the state monopoly on foreign trade to a market economy requires a new legislative framework and effective autonomy of economic agents.

The first steps to liberalise foreign trade started early in 1990 and legal provisions are now in force that entitle any private or state-owned company to engage in foreign trade. A new Company Law (issued in the spirit of the Commercial Code operating before the communist period) favours the establishment of new legal entities, most of which operate in foreign trade. At present, more than 15,000 economic agents are authorised to engage in foreign trade.

The small number of foreign trade enterprises have been replaced by a large diversity of private and state companies involving themselves in foreign trade, and internal convertibility has given a boost to Romanian exports. However, formalities are still extensive and payments are not always made on time. Even so, Romanian companies are willing to handle foreign trade transactions and are trying to comply with international standards.

Romania has created two free port zones; Sulina, on the Danube and Constanta Sud, on the Black Sea.

THE CHANGING ROLE OF FOREIGN TRADE ORGANISATIONS

Until 1990, only Foreign Trade Organisations (FTOs) were legally authorised to lead foreign trade transactions. Some advantages arose from this for Western companies, such as a single contact for specific operations, security of payments, and dealing with specialists. Since 1989, limitations on FTOs have been removed and they have diversified their businesses. On the other hand, some of their traditional suppliers have ceased dealing through them.

Only some of the economic agents authorised to engage in foreign trade are actually operating and most of these are joint ventures. There is a skill shortage and, under such circumstances, FTOs still play an important part in Romanian foreign trade. In 1991, only 16 per cent of Romanian exports were carried out by the private sector. In the long run, privatisation and growing competition will diminish the role of the FTOs, most of which will become private joint stock companies as they lose their monopoly and advantages.

It is important to note that some of the FTOs are still strong and reliable, while others have lost most of their specialised employees and contacts with domestic industry.

THE CUSTOMS TARIFFS

In 1990, Romania introduced a regime of customs tariff liberalisation, abolishing differentiations in the customs duties based on end use of the imported products and granting temporary reduction of duties on the import of goods in short supply on the domestic market.

From 1992, Romania's system of tariffs complies with the Harmonised System of Commodity Description and Coding of the Customs Co-operation Council in Brussels. This is a worldwide system of goods classification for duty and tariff purposes.

Romania is a GATT member and observes its tariff treatment rules. The customs tariff on imports is viewed as an important trade policy instrument during transition, especially as far as raw material prices are concerned.

The recently adopted customs tariff provides two categories of duty rates:

1. 'Duty rate': applies international standards with rates ranging from 3-60 per cent.

2. 'Duty rate applicable to 1992': applies substantially reduced duty rates; however, there may be exemptions for certain goods in short supply on the domestic market.

Most duty rates in the first category range from 10-25 per cent and are levied on raw materials and investment goods. Duty rates from 30-60 per cent are meant to protect some domestic industries (eg textiles, leather and furniture) and also to protect health (eg a 50 per cent duty applies to cigarettes). However, where Romania has entered into specific trade agreements, for example, with the EEC, customs duties apply according to their provisions – that is, some goods may be admitted at zero or reduced rates.

Some exemptions from customs duty are available – for example, equipment imported as a foreign investor's contribution to an investment, samples and advertising materials.

Goods can be temporarily imported (eg for trade exhibitions) if the importer guarantees to pay customs duty due should they not be re-exported.

Generally, customs clearance takes place at the border and is dealt with by the importer. Customs formalities are still time-consuming and border queues of trucks are commonplace.

THE IMPORT AND EXPORT REGIME

Imports

Most import restrictions were eliminated in 1991 under a new licensing regime. The issue of import licences by the Ministry of Trade and Tourism (MCT) is automatic and carried out only for statistical purposes. However, the MCT may establish temporary quotas or extra duties if there is a risk of a serious deficit on the balance of payments or if domestic industry is being injured by imports.

Import procedure is not particularly complicated and no special import document is required. The main difficulty concerns currency procurement as a result of foreign currency shortages. Sums larger than US$10,000 require approval from the National Bank. A priority system is operated and approval may take up to 30 days.

The Romanian government is willing to start negotiations with the US Co-ordination Committee on Multilateral Export Controls (COCOM) in order to facilitate its removal from the list of proscribed countries which normally require security export control. Such removal would result in a great benefit to the Romanian economy since high technology equipment could be imported without controls.

Exports

The export licensing regime has also been liberalised with export licences generally being eliminated as of 5 May 1992. Export licences may still be required in respect of trade with former socialist countries with which Romania has clearing agreements and in respect of exports to Romania's debtors.

Despite the general liberalisation, export quotas and other restrictions may apply in the case of shortages on the domestic market. At present, 36 products (all of which are subsidised) have been banned from export. Such products include raw materials for the energy industry, non-ferrous metals, cellulose, note books for school use, marble, leather, grain and basic food stuffs (including flour, sugar, oil, milk and butter).

Export quotas also now exist in respect of some wood products, medicines and livestock – such quotas being revised each quarter by the Ministry of Trade and Tourism in conjunction with the ministries concerned.

MCT is connected to the Geneva database and is able to check international market prices for both imports and exports.

Representation

Information on trading relationships can be obtained in the UK from the Romanian Embassy in London, and in Romania from the Department for Foreign Trade or the Romanian Development Agency. The main questions that UK firms should consider when trading with a new Romanian partner are delivery, timing and the quality of goods.

Even before 1989, major Western companies had established representative offices in Romania. The process was centrally controlled by MCT and a specialised agency. At present, representative offices are subject to the formal approval of MCT. UK companies can easily find an agent in Romania as English is widely spoken and good specialists are available.

Export promotion

As a result of the ending of the foreign trade monopoly, exports have fallen and imports have increased since 1989. Because exports are of crucial importance to Romania in the present economic situation, several export promotion measures have been adopted, either within the general reform programme or have been introduced specifically:

- internal convertibility at a new exchange rate representing a devaluation of the leu;
- exemption from turnover tax for raw materials and semi-processed products purchased by traders for export;
- a drawback regime for imported goods which are re-exported ie import duty can be reclaimed on re-export;
- the establishment of Eximbank to guarantee export credits and operate insurances and re-insurances;
- state subsidy of attendance at international fairs and exhibitions at national fairs.

24

Trade Finance
Commodities International

Before the 1989 Revolution, Romania was one of the few countries in the world which had a surplus balance of payments and reserve. That was soon exhausted. Under the National Salvation Front government: embargoes were placed on the export of foodstuffs and fertilisers; there was an influx of consumer goods in the first months of 1990; and the plummet in production made matters worse. The perception that the Romanian government was old wine in new bottles made aid, loans and credit difficult to come by. An already difficult situation was aggravated by the Gulf War; oil supplies were disrupted and the substantial amounts Iraq owes Romania are now in limbo.

FOREIGN EXCHANGE

The foreign exchange generated by exports, aid, loans and credits is insufficient to meet the needs created by the government's reform programme. In 1990, Romania had a total current account income of US$6824 million and expenditure of US$10,075 million, leaving a deficit of US$3251 million. The following year was no better and there are no immediate prospects of the balance of payments improving. The national debt is no bigger than it was only because of the lack of availability of more credits.

The EC, IMF, ECOFIN, World Bank, EIB and other multilateral agencies are providing finance selectively. The EC, for example, has approved ECU25 million for animal production and another ECU25 million for the health sector. The IMF has, *inter alia*, approved SDR (special drawing rights) 428 million to meet increased energy costs with a further SDR131 million if the country's balance of payments is adversely affected by increases in import prices of oil and gas. ECOFIN has pledged US$500 million plus, the EBRD has begun to look at the market, and the EIB is trying to identify projects for financing, especially in the oil sector.

In order to rationalise the allocation of foreign exchange available, Romania has already changed some of its banking policies. This has been conducted in a largely experimental way to date: as in the former USSR and Nigeria, dollar auctions are being used, although this cannot be a lasting solution.

Companies and banks are not allowed to hold foreign exchange accounts. This applies to foreign banks as well and could drive out those established in the market such as Manufacturers Hanover Trust and Société Générale. Some compromise is likely as these banks provide services that Romanian banks, even in their revised structure, cannot.

EXPORTING TO ROMANIA

Entering into a contract with most Romanian parties can be a tedious process. Even in cases where payment will be made by, say, the World Bank, the awarding of orders is more or less in Romanian hands. The usual horse trading takes place and, more often than not, the party with past Romanian connections gets the business, notwithstanding differences in prices and quality.

The margins of profit are high for any party that is finally able to get its goods into Romania. As a result there are more potential exporters to the market than foreign exchange available. This shortage of foreign exchange in the banks causes delays in the approval of letters of credit and transfers. In most cases a contract should not be considered operative until an acceptable letter of credit has actually been received. In other words, counter-commitments should be kept to a minimum. Confirmation should be arranged, as in most cases letters of credits will not be received confirmed by first class banks. Exporters need to shop around, especially looking to Swiss, Dutch and Belgian banks. It is clear that parties with past experience and connections are best able to organise this. Forfaiting is currently available for a maximum period of six months.

The successors to ECGD, NCM Credit Insurance Ltd, can only issue a policy cover for irrevocable letters of credit from Romania for about 2 per cent, subject to their usual terms and conditions. On the basis of such a cover, the incoming letter of credit could be discounted up to 180 days with certain banks.

Collection documents are subject to delays of approximately four months, that is the time taken between the moment the Romanian importer deposits the equivalent lei in the bank to the time of repatriation of foreign exchange. Although the collection experience of banks is generally good to fair, it is advisable that business is done on the basis of irrevocable letters of credit only.

It is often difficult to obtain finance even against letters of credit in the UK. For a budding exporter to Romania, European banks may be the best answer. It is useful to note that the Anglo-Romanian Bank (from its head office in the City of London) is very active in trying to promote trade with Romania. A rule of thumb followed by banks is that they look for companies with past trading experience. If you know the people concerned and if you know the hazards, banks will be more prepared to support you.

Countertrade used to be a big business because of Comecon links as well as special accounts with other countries. At the moment, it is not available.

It is too early to venture into leasing in Romania because of the inadequate legal frameworks. This could eventually become a major source of financing inputs for modernising outdated industries.

There is a trading business in Romania which is alive and kicking; oil production and refining. The surplus of refining capacity over production is being exploited by companies like Gotco, Marc Rich and Phibro, that are refining their crude and upgrading refineries as well. Romania is earning valuable foreign exchange in this way and the chances of being paid upfront are much better in the oil sector.

IMPORTING

Importing from Romania can be a frustrating business and can only be conducted successfully with the help of a specialist.

You may have booked some purchases at acceptable margins, but do not be deceived into considering that that is the end of the matter. As an example, you may have booked a small ship load of cement to be loaded at Constanța. Loading is fair to acceptable on the first day. On the second day, your ship is moved from its berth without any reason. To your utter frustration your competitor's ship is now being loaded with cement. Business can only be conducted successfully on the basis of well-made arrangements, right up to the stevedores' gangs.

The future of the Romanian economy is not so bleak. It used to be a rich country before totalitarianism and authoritarianism. After the political process has stabilised, it should not be very long before Romania is once again on the path to prosperity.

25

Licensing and Franchises
Sinclair Roche & Temperley

The transfer of technology, whether by way of licensing of intellectual property rights or know-how, is frequently regarded as one of the most important ways of stimulating economic growth and development in a newly emerging market. Subject to a local legal system being able to offer a licensor real protection, the transfer of technology allows an emerging market to have access to up-to-date technology for the purposes of creating a competitive manufacturing infrastructure. There may also be the additional attraction, from the licensor's point of view, that the licensee may be able to manufacture products at a cost which is significantly less than the cost of manufacture outside the territory of the emerging market (due, frequently, to lower labour costs, energy costs and raw material costs).

The purpose of this chapter is to examine the current legal framework for licensing of intellectual property rights and to consider certain fundamental questions which should be addressed by a potential foreign licensor entering into a licensing arrangement with a Romanian party. The chapter also briefly considers the legislative framework affecting franchises – another means by which a transfer of business know-how can be effected.

LICENSING

In the case of Romania, the concept of technology transfer is not a new one. The development of the RomBac 1-11 aircraft was the result of a licence granted by British Aerospace for the transfer of technology and know-how in the 1970s. In addition, with legislation affecting patents, trademarks and copyright having first been introduced in 1974, 1967 and 1956 respectively, Romania is not unused to the concept of intellectual property rights and their protection. However, early legislation regulated intellectual property within the framework of a communist society and it has only been with the adoption of a new Patents Act in October 1991 that the concept of protection of intellectual property rights, other than for the benefit of the state, has become real.

The new legislation recognises that the exclusive right to use an invention may be protected in Romania by a patent granted by the State Office for Inventions and Marks. Protection in respect of a new invention may be for a period of up to 20 years, depending upon the nature of the invention. Where the invention is to be used as an adjunct to an existing invention, the term is limited to the term of protection in respect of the invention which is improved (subject to a minimum period of protection of 10 years).

Most importantly, however, from a foreign licensor's point of view, the new Patents Act protects foreign parties, domiciled or with an international head office outside Romanian territory, through the application of the Conventions to which Romania is a party. The protection of a patent of a foreign party from a Convention country has priority from the date of the first deposit overseas if, within 12 months of the date of deposit, the inventor also applies for a patent of the same invention within Romania.

As regards licensing there are no restrictions on the rights of a potential licensor and a potential licensee in entering into a licensing arrangement in respect of intellectual property rights, save that the terms of the contract must not be such as to amount to an unfair practice under the terms of the Law on Unfair Practices. Accordingly, parties may impose such terms as they may agree in any contract relating to the licensing of intellectual property, although a potential licensor should consider, at least, the following points:

- restrictions on use of the property rights which are the subject of the licence;
- the term of the licence;
- the amount of any royalty payment to be made in consideration of the grant of the licence;
- whether or not the licensor will be obliged to update the licensed technology;

- who will be entitled to ownership rights in respect of developments and alterations made to the licensed property;
- confidentiality;
- whether or not the licence will be exclusive or non-exclusive;
- the geographical area in which the licence is to be effective; and
- whether or not the licensee will be entitled to grant any sub-licence in respect of the licensed property.

The licensor should also consider whether or not it will be able to enforce the terms of the licence created against both the licensee and any third party.

As regards the new Patents Act, potential licensors should also be aware that the new law allows any party to apply to the court for a compulsory licence to be granted in its favour in respect of a patent (if a patent has been obtained in Romania and if it has not been used adequately or at all either during the four years following registration of the patent application or during the three years following the grant of the patent – whichever period expires later). The owner must also have failed to give good reasons to justify the failure to so use the patent adequately and must have refused to transfer the patent. A compulsory licence granted in this manner will be non-exclusive and will be for such term as may be specified in it. The owner of the patent may, in turn, seek to have the compulsory licence withdrawn if a licensee fails to comply with the conditions for use as laid down in the licence itself.

FRANCHISES

In common with the position regarding distributorships, there are no specific laws in Romania regulating franchise arrangements.

A franchise arrangement may include elements of intellectual property licensing together with elements of agency and/or distributorship, while still remaining a unique form of establishing a business presence in a new territory.

The franchisor will attempt to find a potential party who, by means of the franchise, will be able to recreate a successful business concept in a new market, based on a tried and tested business concept as used previously by the franchisor. The franchisee will be obliged to commit its own funds to the development of the franchise operation but, in establishing a presence in a new market, the franchisor may still feel obliged to monitor closely the franchise arrangement as established by the franchisee.

Accordingly, the franchisor should consider the amount of control to be imposed over the franchisee, the extent to which the franchisee will be entitled to use the intellectual property rights of the franchisor, and a franchisor must, of course, consider many of the other commercial points which will also be relevant in establishing either an agency or distribution arrangement or, indeed, a licensing arrangement.

Forming a Company
Sinclair Roche & Temperley

In addition to conducting business through agency, distribution, licensing, franchising or representative arrangements, the Law Concerning Trading Companies recognises five basic legal entities by which businesses may establish a presence under Romanian law. The recognised legal 'corporate' forms are:

- a limited liability company;
- a joint stock company;
- a limited partnership;
- a general partnership; and
- a sleeping partnership.

In fact, the greatest amount of foreign investment (where conducted through a Romanian business enterprise) is conducted through the limited liability company. The supporting legal infrastructure for partnership has not been fully developed to date and the joint stock company equates more to a UK public company (with legislation being, consequentially, more demanding as regards such matters as share capital, control and appointment of auditors).

Accordingly, this chapter does not seek to address the method by which an investor may seek to establish a joint stock company or a partnership, but aims to provide a synopsis of the steps to be taken in incorporating a Romanian limited liability company.

INCORPORATION

The incorporation of a limited company by a foreign party is regulated principally by two statutes: the Commercial Private Companies Law (No 31 of 1990) and the Foreign Investment Law (No 35 of 1991).

Unless the intended activities of the company infringe environmental regulations, affect national security or harm public order (see Chapter 7) the company is free to invest in all sectors of business.

Constitution of the company

The rules and regulations regulating the constitution, capacity and business of the limited liability company are contained in the company's statutes of incorporation – a publicly registered document broadly similar to the memorandum and articles of association of a UK company.

Where it is intended that there will be two or more shareholders, it is also necessary to prepare a contract of incorporation containing details of any matters agreed between the parties to a joint venture or shareholders' agreement. Although the contract will also be a publicly registered document, the matters contained in it will be more of a personal nature (as between shareholders) than the statutes, which basically affect the company, its structure and its dealings with third parties. In both the statutes and the contract, it is essential to state the objects of the company, its capital (both authorised and issued) and the number of registered parts (shares) to be issued.

The address (registered office) of the company must be stated. It is, therefore, essential that any proposed investor must have investigated the availability of suitable premises before setting up the business. While it is not essential to have entered into a formal lease of the property (this is not likely to be possible until after incorporation), it is necessary to exhibit a letter of intent from a proposed lessor evidencing agreement with the proposed lessee.

Where part of the consideration for the issue of shares is constituted by non-cash contributions, the split between cash and other contributions must be specified in the contract and statutes.

Unusually (in comparison with the United Kingdom) it is also necessary to state the duration of the company's existence. This is necessary even if the investor intends that the company should continue to exist for an unlimited period. In such circumstances it is customary to indicate a specific period (say, 25 years) which may be extended by agreement of the members.

Certification of documents

Where it is intended that there will be one shareholder of the company, only the statutes must be certified. However, in the case of two or more shareholders, the contract of incorporation and any joint venture or shareholders' contract must also be certified.

Certification will normally be effected in Romania by a Romanian notary but may, in some circumstances, be effected by such person as may be authorised by a duly notarised and officially translated power of attorney.

The Romanian Development Agency

RDA investment approval is an essential element of a foreign investment. Chapter 7 deals in detail with the role of the RDA in the regulation foreign investment. However, by way of synopsis, the following documentation must be completed and/or exhibited:

- A printed form must be filled out detailing essential elements of the investment proposal - the amount of the proposed investment, the field of investment and the form of investment (in this case, incorporation of a limited liability company).

- Original confirmation from the investor's local Chamber of Commerce (or another competent office in the country where the investor has its principal place of business) of the investor's existence as a legal entity, its objects and share capital.

- Evidence of the investor's solvency provided by the bank where the investor has its principal account.

- A copy of the investor's balance sheet in respect of the immediately preceding financial year.

- The investor's memorandum and articles of association detailing the structure and activities of the investor (or a copy of the investor's partnership agreement, if appropriate).

- A certified power of attorney empowering a specifically named person to act on behalf of the investor and produce all the documents in its name.

Court procedure

Following registration of the investment proposal with the RDA it is necessary to obtain a Court decree prior to completing the incorporation process. The following documents are necessary:

- Certified copies of the draft statutes (and joint venture agreement/contract) of the company.
- Confirmation of RDA registration.
- Evidence of the intended address of the company (ie lease, contract or letter of intent concerning the property).
- Confirmation of payment of court dues.
- Evidence from the relevant Romanian bank at which the company will operate its account confirming that the minimum capital has been subscribed. The minimum capital required for a limited liability company is Lei100,000. This can be subscribed in cash or in kind (although contribution by way of assets must not exceed 60 per cent of the total value of the issued capital). Proof of valuation of assets contributed may be provided either by an expert's report or by submission of receipts proving the value of such assets. Cash may be subscribed in lei or in hard currency. If subscribed in hard currency, the contribution may be credited to a hard currency account which may be opened for the purposes of receiving share capital contributions only – no profits may be credited to the account. Where sums are paid to a hard currency share capital account, sums held to the credit of such account may be withdrawn by way of dividend, provided sufficient profits are available within the company.

Immediately following the grant of the Court decree, details of the application for incorporation must be published in the *Official Gazette* (*Monitorul Oficial*). Two copies of the decree must be filed and a publication fee of approximately Lei 3000 will be payable.

The Commercial Register

In addition to filing in the *Official Gazette*, the Court decree must be registered at the Commercial Registry in the district in which the company's head office is to be situated. Filing must be effected within 15 days of the date of grant. Additionally, the following documents must be filed:

- the statutes and contract of the company;
- documents of title or leases in respect of property from which it is intended that the company will carry on business;
- evidence from the company's bank that the minimum share capital has been subscribed and paid into the bank;
- proof of publication and payment of fees for the *Official Gazette*;
- RDA registration; and
- confirmation of payment of all dues at the Commercial Register.

It is only following registration at the Commercial Registry that the company will actually acquire legal status.

As regards Commercial Registry fees, it should be noted that US$500 (at the official rate of exchange) is charged in respect of any one business activity undertaken by a Romanian company. An additional US$100 is charged for any other activity adopted (subject to a maximum charge of US$900). The Romanian Registry recognises the following 5 business activities:

- production;
- internal commerce;
- import/export;
- services; and
- construction/buildings.

Within 15 days following completion of registration at the Commercial Registry, it will be necessary for the company's duly authorised representatives to deliver copies of their respective signatures to the Registry for the purposes of maintaining a record of authorised signatories on the company's file.

Tax registration and RDA certification

Simultaneously with the registration at the Commercial Register, a company must be registered at its relevant district taxation office, for the purpose of recording the company's existence and enabling the tax authorities to maintain tax files in respect of the company.

Finally, once the company is fully registered and established, the

Forming a Company 185

ROMANIAN DEVELOPMENT AGENCY (RDA)
Obtain 'Confirmation' for the investment registration with RDA

↓

NOTARY PUBLIC	→	Local Notary Public
Notarise the contract of association and the statutes.		

↓

BANK	→	Authorised Bank
Open a bank account in the name of the company and deposit its statutory capital.		

↓

COURT	→	Local Court
Register notarised documents and RDA's Confirmation. The appearance date established by the judge will be given within a week.		

↓

MONITORUL OFICIAL
Publish the contract of association and the statutes in the *Monitorul Oficial*

↓

COMMERCIAL REGISTER	→	Local Commercial Registry
Register the company. At this moment it becomes a legal entity.		

↓

TAXATION OFFICE	→	Local Taxation Office
Register your accounting books at the local Taxation Office.		

↓

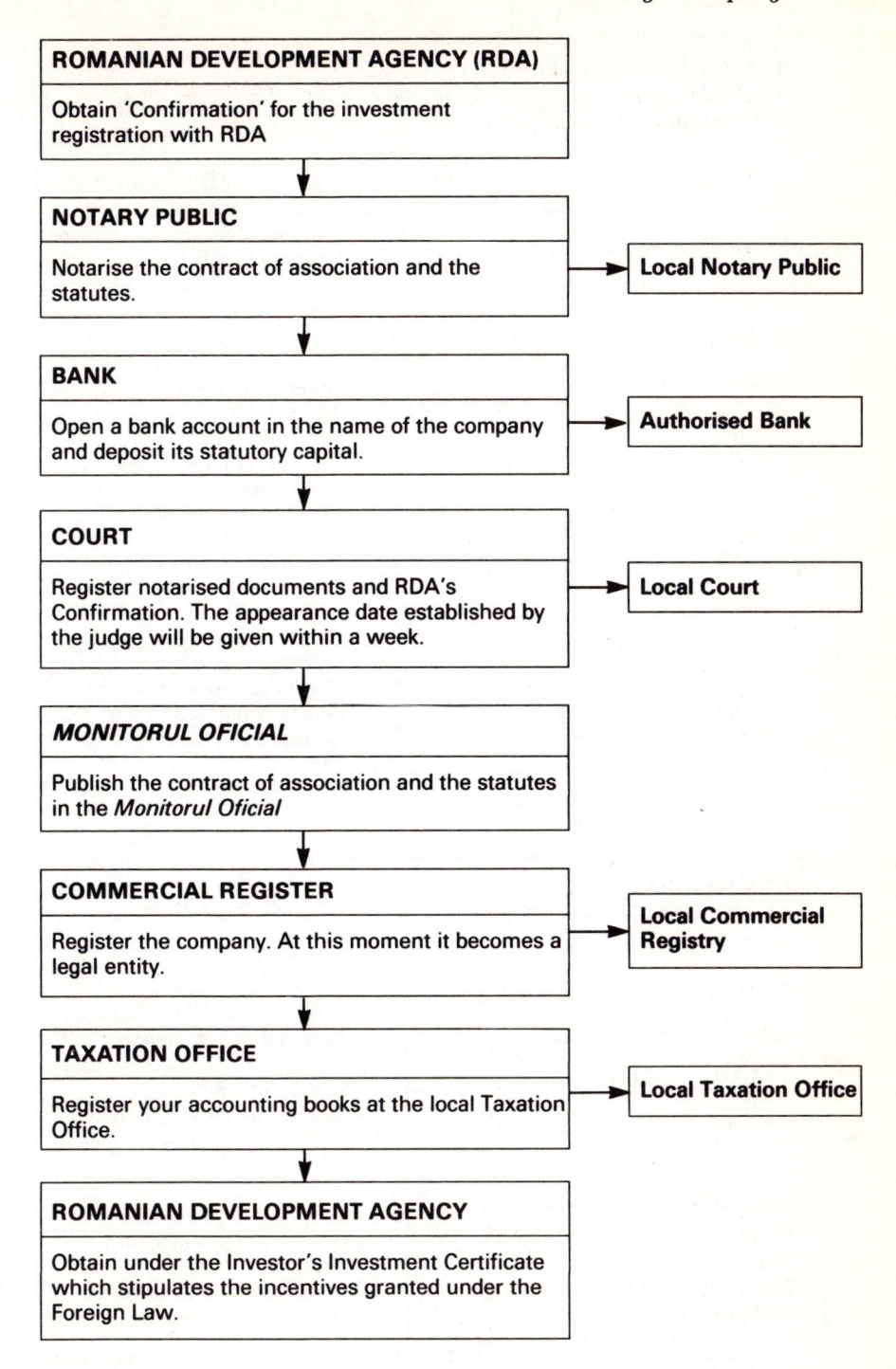

ROMANIAN DEVELOPMENT AGENCY
Obtain under the Investor's Investment Certificate which stipulates the incentives granted under the Foreign Law.

Figure 26.1 *The basic formalities of incorporating a company in Romania*

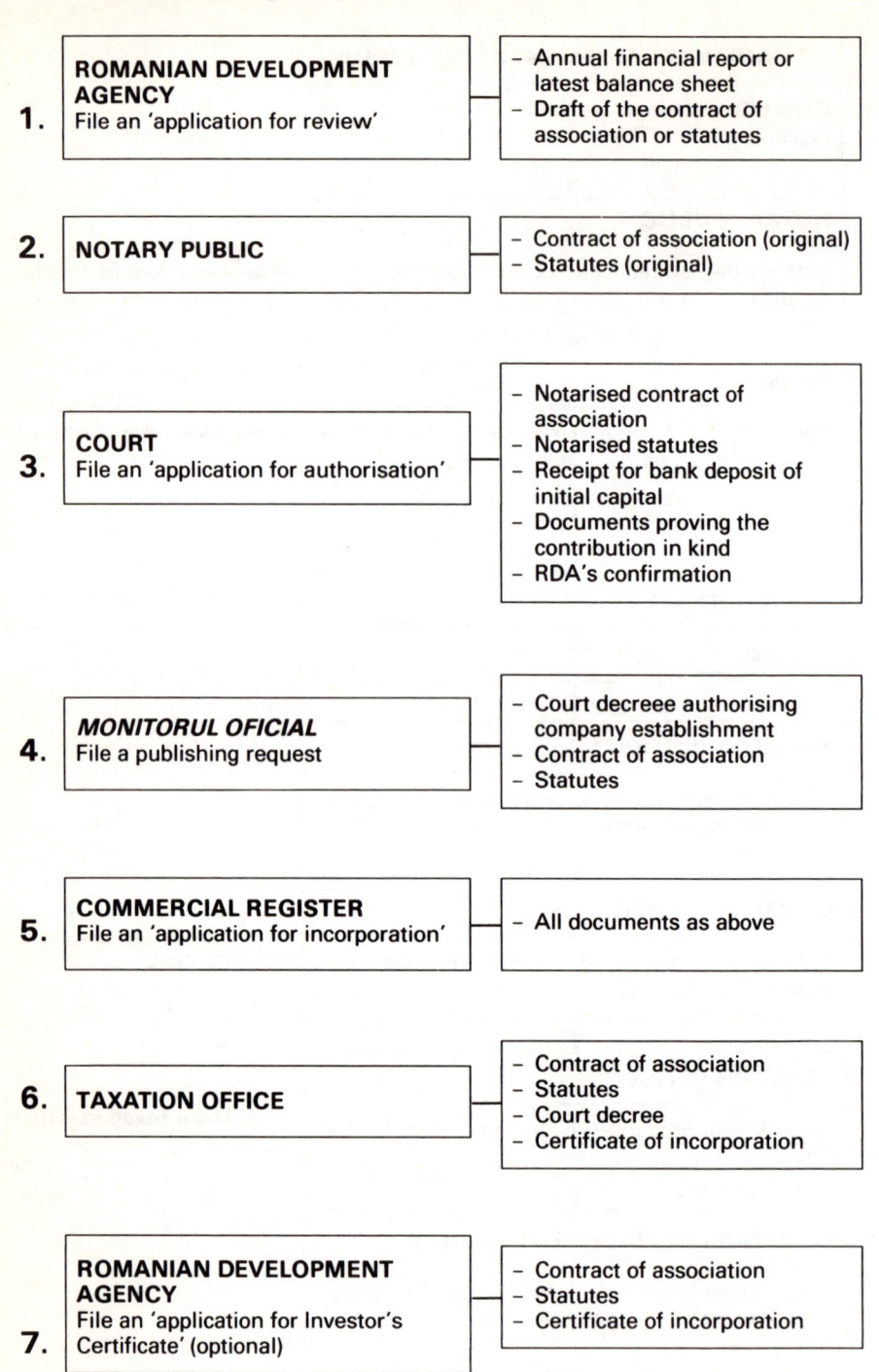

1.	**ROMANIAN DEVELOPMENT AGENCY** File an 'application for review'	– Annual financial report or latest balance sheet – Draft of the contract of association or statutes
2.	**NOTARY PUBLIC**	– Contract of association (original) – Statutes (original)
3.	**COURT** File an 'application for authorisation'	– Notarised contract of association – Notarised statutes – Receipt for bank deposit of initial capital – Documents proving the contribution in kind – RDA's confirmation
4.	***MONITORUL OFICIAL*** File a publishing request	– Court decreee authorising company establishment – Contract of association – Statutes
5.	**COMMERCIAL REGISTER** File an 'application for incorporation'	– All documents as above
6.	**TAXATION OFFICE**	– Contract of association – Statutes – Court decree – Certificate of incorporation
7.	**ROMANIAN DEVELOPMENT AGENCY** File an 'application for Investor's Certificate' (optional)	– Contract of association – Statutes – Certificate of incorporation

Figure 26.2 *Incorporation – the documents required*

RDA will issue the company with an Investor's Certificate, confirming the various tax and other incentives available to the business.

Timing

As regards timing for the incorporation of a limited liability company, the Foreign Investment Law and Companies Law each contain detailed provisions relating to time limits for lodging applications and obtaining certifications. However, the law does not set any time limit on the Court process and it is in this respect that most delay will be experienced by an investor, with periods of up two months not being uncommon for processing an application. This can make the overall time involved from first application to incorporation approximately three months.

In some circumstances it is possible to reduce the time taken for incorporation and, with more local professional practices being established, the incorporation process should be considerably reduced in future. In the interim, investors should consider the likely delay when preparing their business plans and, where a local presence is required urgently, an investor should consider an initial presence through the establishment of a representative office.

SUBSIDIARY COMPANIES

Where it is intended to establish a branch office or subsidiary outside the district where the company has established its head office, the directors of the company (the 'administrators') must notify the Commercial Registry within the district in which it is intended that the subsidiary or branch will operate and request that the branch or subsidiary be registered at that Registry.

Registration must be effected prior to the branch or subsidiary commencing trading operations and the representatives will be obliged to register their signatures in the same manner as for the parent company.

27

Financing a Company
Charterhouse

STRUCTURING A JOINT VENTURE

Foreign companies that wish to establish part of their operations in Romania may wish to enter some form of economic co-operation with an existing Romanian company, including a manufacturing agreement, a co-production arrangement, or a full-scale joint venture.

A joint venture is distinct from other forms of economic co-operation in that both the foreign and Romanian participants agree to become equity partners in a given company or project. However, because most existing Romanian enterprises lack the know-how to raise external finance and will generally limit their equity participation in the joint venture to a contribution in kind, the burden of raising external finance and of structuring the joint venture almost always falls on the Western partner.

The Western partner faces the difficult task of structuring the contractual arrangements of the joint venture and of 'selling it' to external sources of finance, whether commercial banks or potential equity co-investors. Generally, this is best done by the preparation of a comprehensive information memorandum which describes the planned operations of the joint venture, highlights its key strengths, and analyses potential risks and weaknesses, suggesting specific solutions. An information memorandum should point out the commercial rationale of a joint venture and highlight its strengths, such as:

- The Western partner's ability to participate in a Romanian enterprise's management and operations, perhaps improving its margins and profitability.

- The access given to the joint venture by the Western partner to new, possibly hard currency, markets with its products.

- The tax efficiency of the joint venture because of the tax holidays granted to joint ventures with foreign capital.

In addition, the information memorandum should address specific risk areas of the joint venture and identify solutions. The principal risks commercial bankers and external equity financiers will want to see addressed will include:

- Political risks: The Foreign Investment Law of March 1991 provides foreign investors in Romania with a specific expropriation guarantee, consisting of an undertaking from the government not to nationalise or expropriate investments other than in circumstances where it would be in the public interest, and even then only subject to payment of compensation equivalent to the value of the affected investment. However, foreign investors in Romania are acutely aware of sources of possible future political instability. The ECGD already provides cover against the risks of war, expropriation or changes in legislation on the repatriation of profits.

- Management risks: A risk faced by foreign investors in a joint venture is a break down in relations between the foreign and Romanian partners. A joint venture will be seen as a more viable proposition if the two or more parties involved know each other well and have worked together in the past in other forms of economic co-operations. The raising of external finance will also be facilitated if the foreign partner retains management control of the joint venture.

- Supply risks: Financiers and bankers may want to establish that the locally produced raw materials needed by the joint venture company in Romania will continue to be available.

- Devaluation risk: The Romanian currency reform of November 1991 has made transactions in foreign currencies within Romania illegal and all Romanian enterprises, including joint ventures, must now carry out all transactions in lei, greatly increasing a foreign investor's exposure to the risk of currency devaluation. Consequently, financial backers of a joint venture will want to know that the hard currency generated by the joint venture through exports will be sufficient to meet the company's hard currency obligations. Often, an offtake agreement or a letter of intent from a hard currency purchaser of the joint venture's products may also be required.

In addition, an information memorandum for bankers or other external financiers of a joint venture should provide investors with a cash flow forecast for the venture with a sensitivity analysis and a balance sheet to show the company's initial assets and liabilities.

SOURCES OF EQUITY

The primary source of finance for most joint ventures in Romania is the equity participation of the two or more parent companies. This is particularly true of joint ventures which aim to produce goods and services for the Romanian market. These joint ventures will be selling goods or services for non-convertible currency, at least in the short to medium term, and there will therefore be little scope for servicing any external financing in hard currency, whether in the form of interest payments or dividends to an equity co-investor. A corporation may have a strategic interest in such a joint venture to promote its products or brand name in Romania, but will find it difficult to raise external financing for the venture.

However, joint ventures with the backing of a strong Western corporate partner may be able to interest an investment fund as an equity co-investor. Although to date no investment funds have been established to invest solely in Romanian projects, a number of investment funds aim to make unlisted investments throughout Central and Eastern Europe. Some of these have been very active in Hungary, Poland and Czechoslovakia, and are now seeking investment opportunities in Romania or Bulgaria. Investment funds will generally seek to take a minority equity interest in a project, with a view to achieving a return on their investment through income or through a capital gain, by selling their investment at a profit when the venture is operational and the riskiest stage of the project has been overcome.

Fund managers realise that an investment in Romania will not necessarily generate hard currency immediately. They are prepared to take the long-term view – ie that the leu will eventually become convertible. Projects to produce goods for both Romanian and export markets are a good way of hedging against short and medium-term risks of devaluation, while waiting for opportunities in the future when Romania re-emerges as an important market.

In addition, investment funds will want to find a possible exit from their investment in a given time period before they will be tempted to invest in a project in Romania. Although the Romanian government has signalled its intention to develop a stock exchange within the next two years, this remains a remote prospect, in particular since at present Romania lacks the financial and institutional investor base for a stock exchange to operate in. In the absence of a functioning stock market, investment funds may wish to protect themselves from making a potentially illiquid investment in Romania by demanding a put option to sell their investment back to the corporate co-investor in the joint venture after the riskiest phase has been overcome. In other words, the project sponsor agrees to buy the investment fund's equity back after a certain period at a predetermined price. If funds are given an appropriate exit from an investment in a Romanian joint venture, they could be a valuable source of financing for a company that wishes to share with a third party the risks of the equity investment.

SOURCES OF DEBT

Although G24 countries had committed over US$2 billion to Romania in the form of commercial credits by November 1991, most bilateral credits have been used to finance the export of capital and consumer goods to Romania, and commercial credits to finance joint ventures remain difficult to obtain.

Commercial banks are generally still deterred from lending to Romanian projects on a medium to long-term basis. Consequently, possibilities for the project financing of joint ventures in Romania, without recourse to the balance sheet of the foreign company, remain limited. Generally, Western commercial banks will only lend to joint ventures in Romania if there is a guarantee from the Western parent of the joint venture or if the joint venture has secured an offtake agreement for its products. Consequently, exporters to Romania must seek to provide a 'financing package' which involves either a guarantee from a Western purchaser of goods from Romania, or a long-term commitment by a Western firm to buy the goods produced by the importers of equipment in Romania.

Multilateral agencies are an alternative source of financing for large, well-structured projects. Although to date most projects supported by multilateral agencies have been technical assistance projects, there are indications that this is now changing. Romanian projects are a priority for the recently established European Bank for Reconstruction and Development ('EBRD'). By the end of 1991, the EBRD had already approved two loans to Romania, amounting to approximately ECU150 million. Priority sectors until now have been infrastructure and telecommunications. In the future, the EBRD will support projects in a wider range of industrial sectors. The Bank has a London-based team which specialises in Romanian projects, and has recently set up a representative office in Bucharest, with the specific purpose of assessing the commercial and financial viability of projects in Romania. The EBRD aims to provide both debt and equity finance to projects in Romania, although its total participation cannot exceed 35 per cent of the project's value. It, therefore, aims to act as a financial catalyst, drawing other banks or equity partners into a given project.

Although Romanian joint ventures may now raise loans from either Romanian or foreign banks, there is little evidence suggesting that local loans have been taken up in the formation of joint ventures. Because the initial capital of the joint venture is generally used to purchase equipment in hard currency, local loans will probably be limited to financing its working capital requirements once a joint venture is already operational. Local banks may also, of course, be involved in the administration of a joint venture's current account transactions.

NEGOTIATING A JOINT VENTURE

Managers of Romanian state-owned enterprises should be encouraged to begin negotiations to form joint ventures with a foreign partner without obtaining the consent of the responsible ministry. The Transformation Law of 1990, which commercialised state-owned enterprises, kept the state as the owner of the enterprises' share capital, but established independent management structures. Consequently the ownership of the companies' assets is now unequivocally vested in the companies themselves.

In spite of this, there has been a general lack of understanding by the management of state companies, which has resulted in investment negotiations proceeding in the same way as before the

Transformation Law was passed, leading to considerable bureaucratic delay as managers waited for unnecessary approvals from ministries in respect of proposed joint venture agreements. Western businessmen negotiating with managers of Romanian state-owned enterprises should remember that in most cases, the only consent required for the formation of a joint venture is that of the management itself and the state's shareholder representative body.

It is often advisable for foreign businessmen to appoint a local adviser or consultancy firm to assist them in the negotiation process, in particular because an understanding of the local constraints and pressures in which Romanian businessmen operate can be of crucial importance in concluding a successful joint venture agreement and in understanding the Romanian partner's objectives in the negotiating process.

A problem which Western businessmen often face when negotiating a joint venture in Romania is that of valuing contributions in kind to the joint venture's share capital. Romanian managers tend to value assets at book value, irrespective of the assets' economic usefulness. Because book values in Romanian company accounts often overstate the real market value of a company's assets, this tends to be a common problem in negotiating joint venture agreements. This is not only because Romanian managers have been used to operating in a centrally planned economy, where productivity targets mattered more than profitability, but also because they may be sensitive to charges of selling assets 'on the cheap', a common accusation of the Romanian press and of Romanian politicians.

One solution to the problem of valuing contributions in kind to a joint venture may be to establish the joint venture as a new legal entity, with specific assets the economic value of which both parties can agree on, rather than to form a joint venture with an existing state enterprise.

Part IV
Case Studies

Case Study 1
Romanian Manufacturers SA

Report of an interview with Constantin Chesculescu, managing director, Romanian Manufacturers

Constantin Chesculescu is an *émigré* Romanian who is investing directly in the manufacture of leather goods in Romania. His joint venture, Romanian Manufacturers, is currently selling several million pounds worth of goods in the UK and is increasing sales in the rest of Western Europe. What has surprised him most since the Revolution is the buoyancy of consumer demand in Romania itself.

Constantin Chesculescu left Romania for the UK in 1974 at the age of 24, driven by two forces. He was fascinated by the idea of doing business across frontiers and he harboured the ambition of creating a business out of his university passion for leather jackets.

His first attempts to sell leather jackets were not successful. 'In Romania you were always suspicious of anything said outside the family. When I was getting negative replies from English buyers I invented motives for why they weren't buying the product. I wasted a bit of time with that attitude, until I found you could take people at their word. Once I realised that I started to make an impact.'

TRADING WITH ROMANIA

In 1978, having established himself as the sole UK distributor for the largest Brazilian producer of leather goods, Constantin Chesculescu returned to Romania for the first time. For the next 11 years he imported leather goods from Arpimex, the state trading organisation. 'I knew what was wanted for the British market. If I could provide samples, these were made up to specification and price. I was a bit restricted in the choice of materials because Romanians were only tanning pigskin, so I couldn't make a comprehensive range of leather jackets. The quality of workmanship was very good; Romanians have always had very good skills in clothing and textiles.'

'You could not deal with the factories direct, except to agree the technical specification: you could not sign a contract; you could not be invoiced; you could not even have a direct answer to a telex. Everything had to go through Bucharest. The first thing I did after the Revolution was to give each factory a fax machine.'

During the 1980s the world-wide manufacture of leather goods was becoming increasingly concentrated. The days of the simple trader were coming to an end, as large British buyers became more expert at importing direct. It was becoming necessary to be a primary producer in control of the manufacturing margin.

Leather clothing is still a labour intensive industry, as only cutting by hand ensures that flaws in a skin are detected. In the UK the unit cost of making a leather jacket is £15-£25. South Korea is well below that – it has cheap labour as well as a technological lead. Romanian costs are about half those in South Korea and are on a par with India and Pakistan. Romania is also much closer and, as a developing nation, allowed duty-free entry of leather garments to the EC. 'You were getting Indian costs in a European country' comments Constantin Chesculescu.

From 1985 he was operating on a CMT (cut, make and trim) contract, and by 1989 he was selling £3.4 million worth of goods. Cattle skins were being bought in Brazil, pigskins from Taiwan; goatskins from Pakistan, and lambskins from Italy and Spain.

DIRECT INVESTMENT

Although production was hardly disrupted by the Revolution, it had far reaching consequences for the way Constantin Chesculescu did business in Romania.

Decree Law No 96 of March 1990 made Foreign Trade Organisations 'the third man in a tango' by breaking their monopoly of trade and allowing Romanian companies to act on their own account.

To take full advantage of the new economic freedom, in August 1990 Constantin Chesculescu formed a joint venture, Romanian Manufacturers. His Romanian partners are: the manager of the factory he had worked with in Sebes-Alba, Sava Tipa (an old friend and the general manager of the newly formed company) and a lawyer friend, who is company secretary.

'An association with a state enterprise might have necessitated a drawn out, complicated setting up process with cumbersome decision-making procedures later on in the operation.' Constantin Chesculescu elected to invest in one of the factories he had previously worked with in Sebes-Alba. 'I deliberately chose a small, provincial town to avoid the problems of a big city and the wage drift you would get. In the provinces the family unit is stronger and people own their properties: they are very stable. In this part of Transylvania the business ethic is very good. They do a honest day's work for a honest day's pay.'

Constantin Chesculescu also opted for a smaller factory. He has enough work to keep 250 people busy without redundancies. 'I did not want to be in a position to say to a factory of 1200 "there's only work for half of you: who wants to go to the countryside?".' The factory was part of a larger combine that produced leather goods. Constantin Chesculescu's partners were adamant that they wanted to become an independent entity. 'There was nothing the large state enterprise could do; they just had to go along with the tide.'

Constantin Chescelscu is intending to get involved in the privatisation of the factory, although for the moment he has a letter of intent. The Privatisation Law allows employees first refusal on the capital of that company when it is sold. There has been no discussion as yet with the ministry and it is not clear how a market value is going to be established.

While the company is 100 per cent state owned at the moment, the target is that Constantin Chesculescu's British based company should own 40 per cent, a Spanish investor 40 per cent with 20 per cent held in Romania. He favours this structure for two reasons: he does not want a wholly owned subsidiary and the company should be run by Romanians on the spot, not from London. He also wants to concentrate on expanding his markets in Western Europe. 'On paper the legislation is superb and the advantages for a foreign investor are tremendous. It is turning that into reality which is the problem. For the present, investors have to find intermediate solutions. You can't at the moment go and buy a company outright. There aren't any up for sale.'

'The biggest risk involved is the political one. Will the country go back to a state monopoly? Will democracy succeed? It is a small risk. All the politicians agree on the need for a pluralist society, and they see that only a market economy and private enterprise produce the goods which everyone wants. There isn't really a way back. However, at the back of your mind is the possibility that the privatisation process could be discredited even before it has begun.'

RUNNING THE BUSINESS

Romanian Manufacturers was incorporated in August 1990 with capital of $600,000. To date, $450,000 has been invested largely in the form of Japanese sewing machines, cutting equipment, materials handling, vehicles and office equipment for production control and accounts.

At the end of 1991 the factory was selling 6000 leather jackets a month and making a profit for the year of Lei27 million. The target is to sell 8000 a month during 1992 generating an annual profit of Lei50 million. By 1993, Romanian Manufacturers are planning to sell 10,000 jackets each month.

The company is pressing ahead with plans to build a new factory and is currently looking at several sites. There are still problems with documents of title to the land and the factory may end up being built some five kilometers from the town on a farm now disused following the decollectivisation of agriculture. Constantin Chesculescu is anxious to make sure that the new factory is flexible enough to adapt to changes in Western demand by making other leather goods, such as bags, briefcases, shoes and gloves.

The priority for Romanian Manufacturers is to get productivity up. In 1990, 250 people were producing one jacket per day per man. Now it has improved to something like 1.5. The aim is to reach 4 within twelve months of the new factory becoming operational, achieved through effective use of time and the elimination of bottlenecks. The two main priorities for training are information technology and English. 'They must be able to speak the customer's language and work with computers.'

Romanians are 'a bit laid back' and did not understand the importance of responding to messages within 24-48 hours. Constantin Chesculescu has worked hard to impress on them that they are working for customers at all times and that managers need to know straight away if there is a problem. It has been like 'waging a battle', but he is getting results – and 'the fax is starting to talk back'.

Employees were used to taking orders from above and a survey of attitudes in the summer of 1991 brought about a tremendous change of mood. 'They were very flattered. It was the first time in their lives anyone had asked their opinion about anything.' Romanian Manufacturers wanted to find out:

- how many employees owned their own property;
- how they were getting to work;
- whether they would be prepared to work on Saturday mornings;
- how time was wasted in the factory; and
- what they thought of privatisation.

There was a nice suprise on the question of privatisation: only 7 per cent objected and the rest wanted it to happen quickly.

Before the Revolution workers were being paid Lei3000 a month; this had risen to Lei10-12,000 by March 1992. Romanian Manufacturers were paying Lei12-15,000, although with productivity increments. Cutters can earn as much as Lei28,000 a month. The general attitude is to pay a market rate, while providing excellent working conditions.

A critical factor for any newcomer to the market is to find 'a fixer' to get round the prevailing attitude of 'Oh no, it can't be done'. Finding a general manager is a formidable task. The previous system was geared to taking orders and not exercising any initiative. Sava Tipa previously ran the Youth Tourist Bureau and Constantin Chesculescu met him when he came to the UK to sign contracts in 1987. He is results-orientated and Constantin Chesculescu admits that he could not do better in Romania himself. At the moment Constantin Chesculescu is spending a week a month in Romania himself, although he and Sava Tipa will alternate in due course. 'You have to be realistic. You can't run a business from London. So we are acting as though they are running their own business. In the long term, there should be no need to keep going there so frequently. I will see the management reports once a month with a quarterly appraisal.'

For the moment the enterprise is relying on two credit lines with Midland and Banco do Brasil. In February 1992 Romanian Manufacturers applied for some currency by depositing a sum of lei worth about $200,000, which, in accordance with internal convertibility, came through two months later.

Logistics are relatively straightforward. Zips and trimmings are flown into the country once a week and skins are delivered by a Dutch carrier. There is no choice as yet of which airports and forwarding houses to use. There is also too much paperwork, 'which is really not necessary for something as common as shoes or clothing'. Once the operation is large enough, Romanian Manufacturers will use their own trucks to take out accessories and raw materials and to bring back finished goods.

CONSUMER MARKETS

Constantin Chesculescu's greatest surprise about the new Romania has been the strength of consumer demand. In the summer of 1991, faced with a flat market in the UK, surplus stocks of leather and sheepskin jackets were shipped back to Romania.

A small shop was set up in one of Bucharest's main arcades. It only has 700 square feet and is run by 5 staff. 'It sells enough merchandise in one month to pay the overheads of the factory in Sebes twice over!' The cost of running a shop in Bucharest is 2–3 per cent of turnover, so prices were virtually wholesale. In fact many wholesale customers have been buying hundreds of jackets through the shop. In addition, three truckloads of rabbit fur jackets, written off in the UK in the face of the green movement, were sold in two months.

For 1992 the Romanian sales budgets are twice as large as for the UK, in part because of the continuing recession here. Not all of Romanian Manufacturers' production could be sold in Romania, because of the need for the hard currency to buy skins. 'By now I could have five shops and double turnover overnight doing five times in Romania what I am doing in England. The lesson is that the recession in the UK is consumer induced, whereas the recession in Romania is caused by low production.'

THE FUTURE

Despite many uncertainties, Constantin Chesculescu is confident Romania will provide his company with 'a firm launching pad for growth in the rest of this decade'.

In business terms, he argues, Romania should be pictured as the future Taiwan of Europe, where you can get good industrial production for the types of product you no longer want to make in the UK because it is too labour intensive.

In the long term, Constantin Chesculescu would like to form a joint venture with a British tanner: there's no reason why skins being bought in the Far East should not come from Romania. He is also staying alert to any opportunities in property. There is no hotel in Sebes for instance. Property prices are going to increase by five to ten times in a few years time. It is an undeveloped property market; prices for office space are much the same everywhere. So there are great opportunities in getting prime positions for shops and offices now. This opens up the possibility of a joint venture with a hotel group.

Constantin Chesculscu's advice to Romanians thinking of emigrating is: 'You must be out of your mind! Everything is just opening up. Yes, you could make a living in the UK, but it is going to be slow. This is a structured society. It'll take you ten years to become somebody. In Romania, with an honest product and an honest price, you could make it in one to two years.'

Case Study 2
Shell Romania

Report of an interview with Egon Lust, area manager, Romania and Bulgaria, Shell International Petroleum Company Ltd.

Shell International Petroleum Company has taken the view that the prerequisites for a successful operation are being met in Romania. In early-1992, a 100 per cent owned local company was incorporated with a wide range of objectives to develop business.

This is not Shell's first involvement with the country. It first bought oil from Romania in 1903 and, by 1912, the country was the source of 17 per cent of all Shell oil production. This ended with World War II and Shell assets were nationalised by the communists. Relations resumed in 1969 in the form of an agency agreement for lubricants and, from 1971, there was a Shell expatriate representative in Bucharest.

Romania has significant oil deposits and has excess refining capacity, as well as potentially large consumer and industrial markets. Prior to the Revolution, Shell mainly traded bulk oil and chemical products. The company's objectives are now much more ambitious.

Shell has applied for one of the fifteen blocks offered for exploration and production in the Transylvanian basin. It is hopeful of agreeing the contract and starting exploration in the course of 1992. A fresh bidding round for blocks is under preparation and Shell is anticipating taking part.

Despite producing 7–8 million tonnes of crude oil a year, Romania imports 50 per cent of its energy needs – in large measure because of its extremely intensive use of energy. Romania needs almost three times more energy than OECD countries per unit of production. As Egon Lust comments: 'There is oil in the ground and with modern technology and know-how it should be possible to achieve a favourable energy balance.'

Romania has 35 million tonnes a year of refining capacity of which 50 per cent is not being used. Although it is an area Shell keeps under review, the company is concerned about environmental standards of plant and existing over capacity in Western Europe.

Automotive lubricants were launched in the first quarter of 1992. Shell is also actively marketing agrochemicals, petrochemicals, catalysts, additives and coal.

Real market prices are an essential condition to developing a network of petrol stations. When internal convertibility was established in November 1991, petrol subsidies were withdrawn and prices rose from Lei30 a litre to Lei130. The economics of retailing are still under review and Shell hopes to open its first station in one to two years.

Finding sites is not straightforward. In looking at existing stations there is the danger of environmental liability caused by oil that has soaked into the ground. The alternative of developing a new site is complicated by difficulties in establishing clear title to property. Furthermore, the organisation of reliable supply, storage and transport is hampered by the lack of a basic infrastructure for business in Romania.

SETTING UP A COMPANY

Timing market entry in Eastern Europe is all important according to Egon Lust. 'If you go in too soon, then there is some disruption or upheaval, you risk losing your investment. If you wait too long, then maybe your competitors have got in first and you are always trying to catch up.' Shell's objective now is to set up a business that will develop step-by-step with political and economic reform in Romania.

In line with this objective, initial share capital is on a scale of hundreds of thousands of dollars. Overall, fluctuations in the rate of exchange and the creditworthiness of the country are underlying concerns. 'We are an international business and that's our problem; if you can't convert lei into dollars, business stops and the whole thing falls apart.'

On the question of political risk, Egon Lust comments: 'After speaking to those in leading positions, I was very impressed by their clear perception and strong will. This has not diminished. On the contrary, the determination to go down the avenue of the market economy has gained even greater momentum. Most Romanians understand this, although I have to admit that it will take some time to persuade those working in the middle and lower bureaucracy to take decisions and accept the new direction.'

Setting up the company took about six months and was 'not straightforward', recalls Egon Lust. 'It is a country in transition. It's a learning curve for the authorities as well as you. Regulations do get adjusted, which makes things a little more complicated. You just need to persevere. Things are never as clear cut as you might initially think. Take it a step at a time.'

The application of Western standards is central to the development of the company. 'We could not have it said that we were exporting pollution. Similarly for health and safety, it would be inconceivable to get ourselves into a situation which suggested we valued a Romanian life less than one in the UK.'

ORGANISING THE BUSINESS

There is a shortage of reasonable office accommodation and Shell spent at least a year looking. Rentals are quickly adjusting to Western standards.

Telecommunications may appear bad, but at least they are not as bad as in some of the countries in the world with which Shell deals. Moreover, Egon Lust is confident that in five to six years Eastern Europe will have the same sort of standard as anywhere else on the continent.

Initially, Shell Romania took staff on from the representative office – including Guy Burrow, who ran the representative office and who is now the company's managing director. The company is now recruiting locals to bring staff up to about 20 by the end of the year. Ten of these will be sales representatives. Although Shell is bringing in resources from outside as required, the aim is to get locals running the business. Working for Shell is a radical change for Romanians. Before the state made decisions. Now it's up to them. The Shell philosophy is to decentralise responsibility and authority. That does mean giving recruits a thorough 'Shell grounding', with a special emphasis on the basics of a market economy – above all, financial management. In the medium term some will be given assignments abroad with a view to coming back eventually to work in the Romanian company.

The lack of hard currency does give Shell problems and the development of a reliable banking infrastructure is going to be very important. Knowing the way round the market has helped to overcome immediate financial problems. 'We sell in local currency and somehow manage the problem of converting it into hard currency enabling customers to buy again. It is one of the risk areas we have to take. You need hard currency for importing; for doing business in the country you work in lei.'

MARKETING

Prior to the Revolution there was little Shell activity on the ground. 'You just dealt with a few central authorities', comments Egon Lust.

Shell is effectively engaged in a start-up marketing operation in Romania. 'Now you are dealing with the customer, the people who use your products, so it's not just a question of supplying volume, you are marketing a product and service, the back-up and technical support, so you have to have people on the ground, whereas before it was just a question of signing things.'

In dealing with customers, there is a need to look into each individual case to try to find appropriate financing. In the absence of credit ratings for companies and even balance sheets, it is up to the people on the ground to make a judgement about customers. Shell's approach at present is to build relationships across as wide a spectrum as possible, explaining what Shell is and how it works. The company is taking care not to raise expectations, until it is confident of being able to deliver products.

Guy Burrow, the managing director in Bucharest, is concerned with introducing Shell to official bodies and the press. One of the benefits of this activity is that it goes some way to offsetting political risk by demonstrating that Shell is operating in the interests of the country as a whole. Exhibitions to specific customer groups are used. Last year there was a successful demonstration of laying a road in Bucharest with a bitumen/resin product, Shellgrip, followed by a seminar with the authorities and construction companies. The disparity between the pot-holed original and the end result made an impact, attracting wide press interest.

Opinion surveys show that the messages that Romanians respond particularly well to are internationalism, openness – 'the idea that you can talk to us' – and long termism.

No decision has been taken on TV advertising as yet but, as the retailing network develops, Egon Lust is sure it will come. 'The message of the campaign has to be appropriate to the country; it's not a question of taking the British one, translating it and putting it out in Romania. To start with Shell may well focus on particular cities through billboards and local radio.'

Case Study 3

The Wadkin Group

Report of an interview with Fabio Milone, export marketing executive, the Wadkin Group of companies.

The Wadkin Group, the UK's leading suppliers of wood processing machinery, decided to concentrate its efforts on Romania after conducting a review of East European markets in 1990.

In 1991, the first year of trading, Wadkin took orders for £3 million and Fabio Milone, the manager responsible, thinks that 'we could sign contracts in the next 18 months for £30–40 million if we had the ability to back it up with medium-term credit.'

WHY ROMANIA?

Wadkin decided to look at Eastern Europe because countries like Russia, Poland, Czechoslovakia and Romania are covered in forest and are all heavy users of the type of machinery Wadkin manufactures.

Eastern Europe was seen as a critical area globally; plant used is often 25–30 years old, so there is potential for a fast growth in demand for new equipment, although not necessarily for state-of-the-art technology.

About 30 per cent of Romania is covered in forest. In the late 1980s Romania was the fourth largest exporter of furniture in Europe and is still in the top ten in the world. 'All this with machinery 25 years old is quite an accomplishment.' Quality is variable. While some output is 'cheap and cheerful', Romanian sourced products are sold in up-market outlets on the British high street.

In 1989, 250 Romanian factories were exporting $400 million

worth of furniture, mainly to Germany, Italy and France. The minister for the wood industry told Fabio Milone that he is confident that output can be doubled. 'When we were in the factories we could see that orders from Germany were three times what they could physically produce', recalls Fabio Milone. 'The Romanians argue that if they take the machinery on, then the increase in output would more than pay for the investment.'

Wadkin also decided to concentrate on Romania because of 'a feeling that it was going to be the easiest to approach of the East European countries. They are still more centralised than elsewhere, which means that through knowing a few people, you can get more immediate results in terms of getting introductions and information.'

GETTING STARTED

The experience of Eastern Europe that Fabio Milone had built up with Ingersoll Rand and Fiat Earth Moving Equipment prior to 1989 was 'completely different, everything has now changed, you have to turn a new page completely.'

Milone went to the Embassy in London where someone is dedicated to following and promoting the Romanian wood industry. In October 1990 he went on a fact finding mission to the main trade fair and to contact the authorities. He met the minister of the wood industry, as well as people with the potential to become Wadkin agents. The one he selected is the former head of the state organisations for exporting furniture, so he knows all the factories and has all the right contacts.

It was decided that Wadkin should introduce its products to a large audience and, in December 1990, Fabio Milone gave a symposium to 100 factory managers at Braşov, where the university for wood technology is located. At the beginning of 1991 Wadkin started a regular series of sales missions. Save for one particularly large contract, orders have generally been for between £100,000 and £150,000. This is not for lack of demand, but because of difficulties in paying.

An agreement has been reached with a service company, so there is a local team of engineers familiar with Wadkin's machinery, which is invaluable for customers who can pay in lei. Three engineers were brought over to the UK to be given a week's training in each of Wadkin's three factories. When new Wadkin machinery is installed, a British engineer goes out to work with the local service company to pass on the know-how.

For the time being, Wadkin does not envisage making a direct investment in Romania, although it has identified one product for which there is a tremendous need and is considering finding a local manufacturer who could produce exclusively for the Romanian market.

Fabio Milone foresees problems buying companies in Romania, especially in one of the primary export sectors such as wood, where managers and employees have got the idea that they will become shareholders.

FINANCE

'We are very pleased that there is a great demand for our products in Romania, but our competitors have had one advantage over us: their governments support exports to Romania. As yet, Romania is not on ECGD cover, which means that it is harder work for the Romanians to buy our products since we cannot offer the same credit terms and we have to look for alternative forms of financing.'

Wadkin often found itself in a position where a Romanian factory is choosing between wood processing and panel processing plant. They often first buy the panel processing from a foreign competitor, which is on credit, in order to generate the revenue to buy Wadkin's products in cash. Nothing is shipped until Wadkin receives at least 90 per cent of the purchase price. Wadkin's agent has a recognised foreign currency account which is in credit; transfers to the UK from this account take 48 hours. If payment is routed through the recognised banking system, it takes about three weeks.

The introduction of internal convertibility caused initial confusion: 'Romanian companies, even the banks, did not have much idea of what it meant to start with, which put things back by two or three months.' Under internal convertibility, all hard currency receipts have to be surrendered. This has curtailed the practice of getting the Western customers of Romanian companies to pay Wadkin directly in hard currency.

Although companies can apply for their currency back, the project has to be justified, so the government can now isolate what is necessary and what is not. The problem for Wadkin is that Romania needs so much of everything that hard currency is likely to be used to finance bare necessities, as well as other industries less successful than furniture.

'A lot of our time is taken up with finding ways for customers to finance their orders, although some do just pay in cash. You just need to be flexible and inventive to get money.' Wadkin are hoping to set up a package of alternative finance from March 1992.

MARKETING

The best forms of promotion are showcases. 'We are exhibiting our machinery in the buyer's premises prior to going into production and the intention is to cover every area in the country where machines are sold. It enables Romanians to see their product being manufactured. Because of the centralised system, they are quite happy to invite companies that may not yet be, but are going to become their competitors. Managers have always been used to gathering together and being instructed in the latest techniques. We may as well grasp this opportunity while it is still available.' Wadkin undertakes the same exercise at trade fairs by tooling a company's products on the stand.

There is no technical press to advertise in at the moment, although there is considerable growth in the number of titles. It is difficult to know which one to use, as they do not have a target market as yet. Basically they are just trying to make money. The television advertising for machine tools by one of Wadkin's competitors does not appear to have had any great impact.

IMPRESSIONS

In a year's experience of doing business in the new Romania, Fabio Milone has formed a range of impressions of the ways things get done:

- In the industry Wadkin is serving, there is a great deal of professionalism and competence. Romanians are proud of what they are doing and know that they can do a lot better with Western technology.

- Culturally, the Romanians are second to none in Europe: they have a facility for languages and they are great extroverts. People are still relieved to be free, though there is a degree of frustration, as the removal of state supports exposes people to economic realities. Two years ago you got two small loaves for Lei1; now they cost Lei8 each.

- It is important to be humble and candid. Wadkins's approach has been to look at the problems they have, rather than to sell machines. As a result we are not only selling our own machines, but other people's as well.

- Wherever possible you should try to use Romanian skills. Despite the politics, most people are conversant with Western products and in some cases they know more then we do.

- Communications are terrible. Potential customers employing 5000–10,000 people may only have one telephone. It is better to telephone people at home in the evening.

- Don't think your trip ends in Bucharest, though be prepared for poor roads and for hotels below European standards. There are no problems in getting fed, as factories go out of their way to look after you.

- In Romania there is a bit of myth that they are preconditioned to buy German. Romanian officials are concerned that there should be an element of competition in the market-place, so that manufacturers do not end up depending on just German or Italian replacements and spare parts. The British do have a reputation for quality and fair dealing.

- Now is the time to invest for when, not if, the country will be standing on its own two feet. The danger is that the British will come to be seen as unfriendly because we are not assisting in the development of the country.

Case Study 4

Glaxo

Report of an interview with Rowland Hill, the Romanian country manager from 1986 to 1989, and with Steven Stead, Glaxo's current country manager.

Glaxo is the world's second largest pharmaceutical company with sales in 1991 amounting to £3.4 billion across the world. It is committed to expansion in Eastern Europe through setting up companies which are responsible for their own growth and organisation.

While recognising the obstacles to doing business in Romania, Glaxo does see it as a promising market in the long run by virtue of its size. There are some 45,000 doctors and Glaxo's objective is to build a field force of representatives who can contact those doctors who are likely to be in a position to use or prescribe Glaxo's products, either in the hospitals or the community polyclinics.

Romania's public health system faces terrible problems of shortages and inadequate facilities. The local pharmaceutical industry is also in poor condition. Raw material shortages and poor facilities result in a very limited range of generic and herbal remedies.

APPROACH TO THE MARKET

Glaxo is concentrating on promoting high quality, life-saving medicines, such as injectable antibiotics and asthma products, which can provide a real benefit to the Romanian people. Glaxo is also supplying less expensive products such as topical skin preparations which are of high quality and are needed in the local market.

The poor state of local facilities makes them unsuitable for the manufacture of Glaxo's products. The cost of building a new facility is, at present, unwarranted for a market that is in an early stage of development. Glaxo is intending to produce market specific, Romanian language packs in the near future.

Rowland Hill, then the area manager responsible for Romania, first visited Bucharest in the December of 1986. 'Glaxo may have been the UK's largest pharmaceutical company, but I met with a pretty indifferent reception in Bucharest. "Who are Glaxo?" they asked. We just kept going, until they got the message that we were committed.'

Having established a sales presence in Romania, Glaxo's next step was to set up a representative office in 1988. The only way to do this under the former regime was through Argus, then the official agency responsible for representing foreign companies. It took a year of frequent visits and interviews before a suitable local candidate was found. By November 1988 Glaxo had recruited a local woman manager with perfect skills. Her basic training was as a pharmacist with a subsequent PhD in pharmacology. She had also worked in West Germany for three years before acting as the representative for another western pharmaceutical company. She had been long enough in the business to know how it worked.

'Once she took over,' Rowland Hill recounts, 'she looked at the contacts I had made, some of which she saw as useful, others not. Local experience put us on the right track and provided a better focus to our activities. In our kind of business it was essential to have local staff in the market as early as possible.'

The Glaxo office was initially situated in the Argus building, because it was impossible to find accommodation elsewhere in Bucharest.

MARKETING

Before the 1989 revolution, all imported medicines were available only on prescription. They were exclusively purchased by Chimica, a foreign trade organisation which had a broad responsibility for buying and selling for the chemical and related industries.

'The problem of selling in Romania at the time,' according to Rowland Hill, 'was that there was a total decoupling of those who had the money and those who judged the quality. The tendency was to buy simply on price. With any luck patients get proper treatment third time round. Doctors and pharmacists in the hospitals who knew what was needed had limited input into the purchasing process.'

'In the 1980s, business partners such as Chimica, were obliged to operate under very severe financial constraints. As well as taking account of this, you had to appreciate their relative isolation from the rest of the world. These business conditions meant we had to work hard to meet their particular needs, as well as treating them with patience and understanding. When the first order came after two years, it was just for a few hundred pounds in value. We were elated all the same. It meant that we were starting to get positive results. Two years down the line politics might have freed up, but economic mechanisms are still weak, which still causes problems in winning business.'

'Glaxo's approach now is to concentrate on communicating the quality of Glaxo's products to users, such as hospitals, pharmacies and doctors, that now have a considerably greater say in the medical purchasing decision. This is now starting to yield results as the medical system becomes decentralised and the purchasing decisions move to users,' comments Steven Stead.

Glaxo plans to increase the number of representatives in territories outside Bucharest. The company also arranges regular symposia. Western experts always draw large audiences. Glaxo also regularly attends exhibitions. The Annual Medical Exhibition which attracted about 35 companies in the mid eighties has grown to 150. All the major European medical suppliers are now represented.

DEVELOPMENT OF OPERATIONS

The Argus office acted as 'a useful bridging operation'. Following legislative changes in 1990 Glaxo applied for local accreditation and terminated their arrangements with Argus.

Premises are a major problem in Bucharest with an almost complete lack of commercial property. In 1991 the company managed to secure office premises in the Hotel Bucharest. This started as one apartment but has since increased to accommodate the growth in activities and the numbers of staff. However, space continues to be a problem and Glaxo is constantly looking for better and more flexible accommodation.

Glaxo's business has now developed a healthy level of activity in Romania and the next step is to look at a greater involvement. Under the old regime joint ventures were the only way to establish an operation in the market. It is now possible to set up wholly owned subsidiaries and 'this is the long-term route to success'.

Decentralisation of healthcare and the ability to promote to a wider customer base means that Glaxo is in the process of developing towards a sophisticated company structure. 'The establishment of a local company is a major step and requires good knowledge of the local rules and regulations. Good financial and legal advice is critical in this difficult climate,' says Steven Stead.

For payment Glaxo has relied in the past on letters of credit, which never caused them problems. They never sold on open account.

Glaxo is presently developing a stock holding arrangement with a local partner which will allow sales to be made in lei. It will be the responsibility of the partner to change lei for hard currency, either through the banks or via countertrade type arrangements, which still remain important. The lack of money in the banks continues to be a major restraint on sales.

Intellectual property is an important consideration in a market such as Romania. There are no product patents and the adoption of European style legislation will represent a major improvement in the business climate.

Glaxo requires more high calibre employees. The recruitment of such people is difficult and in the early stages all employees were recruited through personal contacts. Glaxo prefers to conduct its own recruitment and training. At present Glaxo uses some external training for its new staff but hopes to introduce local training in the next twelve months.

Appendices

Appendix 1

Opportunities by Sector
Brittain Engineering Ltd

AGRICULTURE AND FOOD PROCESSING

The state farms have been converted into limited companies and there could well be scope for buying into some of the better ones and injecting expertise, supplying the food processing chains or creating one's own and supplying the home and export markets. In due course, Russia, Belarus and the Central Asian Republics of the former Soviet Union could become a major market, but just the home market and traditional Middle East outlets should be enough to provide an adequate return on investment. Furthermore, sooner or later some EC trade barriers to East European agriculture and food industry products will be lowered, if only because of the political pressures exercised by the three central countries – Hungary, Czechoslovakia and Poland – backed by sections of the press and the political establishment in Western Europe.

Both peasant farmers and state farms represent diverse sources of supply for independent food processors. Payment could be made in cash but also in fertilisers, animal feed, machinery and spares. Again, there is ample room for British interest as equipment suppliers, including in local manufacture of food processing equipment.

There is a tremendous shortage of adequate transport and storage facilities, including refrigerated facilities, and anything which will improve this will have a great future. This includes licensing or buying into some of the local manufacturers of refrigeration equipment, trailers and other equipment.

Romanian beer is now scarce and of poor quality, and there is a booming business in private firms' imports of canned lager from various sources including Turkey. While imports may be possible mainly for cheap brands and limited in volume for the time being because of the shortage of hard currency, buying existing breweries or setting up new ones with improved technology and strict quality controls may prove an excellent prospect. In the longer run, Bulgaria and the Ukraine should be the nearest export markets, but if, as expected, tourism takes off there may be more than enough customers without crossing any borders.

Food retailing is another area where the expertise and capital of our major players could pay dividends. While large out-of-town shopping centres are not a proposition because of lack of private transport, specialised outlets in towns, on main roads and tourist centres are likely to produce quick returns.

Romania has one of the best tractor industries in Eastern Europe, with traditional links with Fiat. They are busily designing equipment for the smaller farms of the future, but may find that improving current designs, for which they already have export markets and assembly lines abroad, are more lucrative. There should be room for a specialist producer of smaller units, which could in due course also export to Hungary, Bulgaria, Moldova and possibly further afield. There are at least two factories which could be considered for this purpose, but no doubt a proper investigation would reveal more. The same applies to other farm equipment.

Fertiliser and pesticide manufacture suffer from lack of raw materials and run-down facilities, but there are large units which could be made to work at full capacity. They do, however, produce mainly the basic chemicals, so specialised formulations in smaller packaging, more suitable for the peasant farmers, will either have to be imported or produced locally in converted or new units. There should be some opportunities there.

ENERGY

Romania shares with the other emerging democracies a shortage of energy, although its natural resources of oil and natural gas are greater than any of the other Central and East European Countries (excluding Russia). This is likely to be exacerbated in the future as deposits are further depleted, unless new ones are found and the technology updated.

Oil and gas

Offshore drilling could go some way towards solving the problem but there is a problem inherited from the post-war settlement. The Soviet Union annexed in 1945 a small island off the coast of Romania – the Snake Island – and this gives them continental shelf rights they would not otherwise enjoy. There was no treaty (except a protocol signed in 1947) on the subject. The legal position is therefore doubtful but, sooner or later, the issue will come up and complicate relations between the two countries. At some stage in the not too distant future, Romania and the successor to the USSR will have to settle the issue and there is no reason to believe that legality will not be restored.

Legislation on concessions for exploration and extraction of mineral resources is in place and bids for 15 concessions are currently being examined with contracts expected within the next few months and further auctions likely shortly thereafter.

Romania's refining capacity exceeds local oil extraction by some two to three times and ever since the accelerated debt repayment programme was implemented has suffered from a shortage of feedstock. The excess capacity did prove rather handy when capacities in the Gulf were put out of action, but longer-term arrangements will have to be arrived at. The facilities, built in the 1960s and 1970s were relatively modern at the time, but like all Romanian industry, have suffered from lack of maintenance and spares. Unlike exploration and extraction, refineries, restructured as limited companies, can be sold to bidders or joint ventures can be formed. So far, one deal, with Marc Rich & Co, is operational but further ventures cannot be far behind.

The distribution and retail networks, petrol stations included, are among the worst in Eastern Europe and, here again, only foreign involvement can put matters right. Another opportunity – both for the majors and for independent operators.

Power generation and energy efficiency

The new management of the electricity authority are looking into a retrofit programme but it is doubtful that they will, on their own, find the resources required. International aid will have a large role to play, in the form of both grants and loans, and this should open up tremendous opportunities.

Romania has quite an extensive industrial base to support the programme with two turbine manufacturers (one working to some

US-GE designs), two boiler manufacturers and a score of process plant manufacturers (heat exchangers, pipework, etc), all conversant with quality assurance systems to Western standards due to their involvement in the nuclear programme. Only Czechoslovakia, with Skoda and Sigma corporations, has an engineering base greatear than Romania's. ASEA-Brown Boveri has recently signed a joint venture agreement with five of the most important companies in the business and GEC-Alsthom another one, but there are still some extremely interesting companies waiting in the wings for similar ventures.

The energy efficiency of Romanian industry is generally extremely low and now that energy prices are on a par with those on the world market, there will be a greatly increased demand throughout industry for technologies and equipment that will reduce consumption to an acceptable level.

CHEMICAL AND PETROCHEMICAL INDUSTRIES

All the comments made in the 'Energy' section regarding the engineering base and availability of raw materials are applicable to the wider chemical industry.

A short visit to any petrochemical or chemical facility will underline the lack of maintenance and updating of plant. Unfortunately the dilemma faced by the government is that if it was to act solely on health and safety and environmental grounds, a large chunk of the industry would have to be closed down, but this would exacerbate an already precarious situation with hard currency earnings. If facilities can be kept open long enough and with some injection of capital and expertise, their hard currency earnings will enable them to embark on a programme of maintenance, repairs and upgrading.

At some stage in the traditional cycle, base chemicals will be in short supply and East European suppliers will become more important.

The pharmaceutical industry, like medicine generally, suffers from the additional problem of lack of funding for the health service. The internal market is therefore in a difficult position, which does not give cause for short-term optimism as regards exports to Romania or for investment in local facilities. This, however, cannot last for ever and the needs are so great that supplies from both abroad and from local producers are bound to grow. An improvement is likely to occur as soon as the assistance promised by aid agencies materialises.

ROAD, RAIL, AND WATER TRANSPORT

Romania has an extensive rail network, which carries a larger proportion of freight and passengers than is customary in the West. Extensive investment will be required to upgrade both the infrastructure and rolling stock. The mechanical and electrical engineering base to do it with is considerable.

The road system is possibly the worst in Central and Eastern Europe and recently the government approved a master plan for the building over 25 years of some 3000 kilometres (1800 miles) of motorways and 8000 kilometres (5000 miles) of roads. A start was made in June 1991 on the toll motorway from Bucharest leading, eventually, to Constanţa, built by a Romanian-Italian consortium, but this is a very small beginning and, in the not too distant future, bids will be invited for the major roads leading from the western and northern borders to Bucharest and beyond.

Bucharest-Otopeni and most regional airports are in need of modernisation and this should provide work for quite a few equipment suppliers, planning organisations and contractors.

The aircraft industry, with some foreign assistance, can supply short haul and commuter aircraft, while long haul aircraft are likely to be bought from the majors, with offset required for their own industry. A contract has been signed in 1990 with Airbus for three A310s but, undoubtedly, other aircraft will be required in due course.

The Danube, linked with the Rhine and the Black Sea, provide the main waterways to the West and the East. Some port facilities will need upgrading and overland access to the ports improved.

For all these projects, funding in the form of grants and loans from international organisations will be forthcoming in due course, so there are good reasons to believe that they will go ahead.

TELECOMMUNICATIONS AND ELECTRONICS

Like all countries in the region, Romania will have to invest heavily in telecommunications. Siemens, Alcatel and Goldstar already have joint ventures and are showing interest in deeper involvement, but there should be ample room for others in this and in the electronics industry generally. It is another area that will benefit increasingly from structural loans and grants.

The industrial base in telecommunication equipment and electronics generally has probably suffered most under the Ceauşescu regime, having been cut off from contacts with the outside world just when the technological revolution was taking place. There are, however, a large number of highly qualified people and skilled workers who could undoudtedly be put to better use than producing antiquated equipment no one wants. Worth mentioning is the joint venture with Control Data Corporation – Rom Control Data – manufacturing printers, which is one of the oldest joint ventures in Eastern Europe.

ENGINEERING

Although some branches of the engineering industry have already been touched upon, it is worth mentioning that other branches may also be worth looking into either as potential customers or as targets for investment in its various forms.

The aircraft industry

This has a long history of international co-operation – with Britain (BAe, Rolls Royce, Pilatus Britten-Norman), France (Aerospatiale, Snecma, Turbomeca, Messier-Hispano-Bugatti), and the USSR (Yakovlev, Mikoyan-Guryevich, etc). Although there are current difficulties, the skills acquired and some of the facilities available are well worth considering in future expansion plans.

The automotive industry

Romania is the only country in Eastern Europe where the French have had a big say in the car industry: Renault with the Piteşti Automobile Works and Peugeot-Citroën with the joint venture, Oltcit, in Craiova. Interest in renewal of links has been reported and apparently some talks are under way.

The truck industry, based mainly in Braşov manufactures trucks and diesel engines based on an old MAN licence. Both the engines and the trucks are sorely in need of updating.

The situation of indigenous automotive component manufacturers is slightly more complicated. Some were specifically set up for import substitution and will find it extremely difficult to hang on to the home market (British exporters, take note) never mind selling elsewhere, while others, with good management and flexible design teams, have already been searching with some success for foreign markets. Again, matters will become much clearer in the months to come, but it certainly is an area worth closer investigation. Overall, the automotive industry, after a promising start in the 1960s and early-1970s, has fallen further and further behind so some drastic action will be required.

Municipal Service Vehicles and Plant, including water and effluent treatment plant

It would not be surprising to see, at some time in the near future, some municipalities in the market for such items, despite financial problems. Again, opportunities will appear both for direct exports and local manufacture, and local companies could be considered for investment, possibly with chances of exports to some neighbouring countries.

Shipbuilding and ship repair

There are three major shipyards for sea-going vessels and several more on the Danube, and component suppliers throughout the country make virtually everything from engines to propellers, electronic equipment, navigation equipment, etc. All these are in relatively good shape and are well worth looking into. They have experience in working to the Lloyds Register of Shipping and are therefore conversant with international standards.

Other engineering branches such as tool-making, machine tools and many others should come under scrutiny and this will no doubt highlight other opportunities for exports, and local investment.

TEXTILES, CLOTHING AND FOOTWEAR

Romania has a long tradition in supplying both fabrics and clothing to the rest of the world. Its capacity to increase exports for hard currency is limited by the multi-fibre agreements and quota systems. The collapse of the Comecon market has brought in its wake some additional problems. Although the industry has seen a lot of investment in huge facilities, this all but ceased in the 1980s and some equipment is well past its prime.

Lately, former co-operatives and private entrepreneurs have

started producing on a smaller scale and these are likely to cater for the upper end of the market, rather than the mass market the large state-owned companies prefer to work for. Despite all the difficulties, the textile, garment and footwear industries are likely to attract a lot of interest when privatisation is finally under way and opportunities will appear both for equipment and accessory suppliers and for investors.

WOODWORKING, PAPER AND PULP

Woodworking has a long tradition in Romania and the industry has been developed considerably, both before and after the communist takeover. The facilities, like all Romanian industrial units, are desperately short of spares and new equipment and some may need to be closed down or replaced with smaller, more efficient units. This is an area where one expects local entrepreneurs to cash in on existing skills and move upmarket in small, flexible, units.

The paper and pulp industry will probably contract for lack of raw materials and energy, but a thorough examination of investment opportunities should be considered by the major players. Demand will grow and will have to be satisfied, either from local production or imports.

HOUSING AND BUILDING MATERIALS

Housing, as always, is in short supply and current public housing projects have all but ground to a halt. If market forces are allowed their play, more emphasis will be placed on smaller, individual housing. This will force the close down of some prefabricated concrete element factories and boost, for example, conventional brick, breeze-block, tile and joinery units.

Romania is a major exporter of cement but the low energy efficiency of factories built to the same designs as those in the 1950s and 1960s will certainly limit any expansion.

There will be opportunities to supply equipment for the smaller building materials factories and certainly for investment in local facilities, again with some exports possible to Eastern Germany and, mainly via German companies, to Russia, Belarus and Ukraine, where they have to build housing for the withdrawing Soviet Army and their dependants.

GLASS AND CERAMICS

Glass and ceramics factories are exporting quite a sizeable part of their production and are investing, whenever possible, in better equipment to replace the outdated facilities they have now. Contracts for equipment have already been placed by some of these companies and there are more in the pipeline for when they find the money. However, despite the fact that they are energy intensive, demand remains unsatisfied and an injection of capital, technology and marketing expertise could prove rewarding in the longer run.

DISTRIBUTION AND RETAIL OUTLETS

Existing organisations will soon be privatised and new, privately owned (by Romanians and some foreign investors) retail outlets come on the market every day. However, there is little experience and practically no facilities for modern, efficient, large-scale operations and the situation is such that it is impossible to solve the current problems by organic growth. Major companies would be well advised to examine the opportunities open to them. Growth in the economy should resume in the next two years and disposable income should increase enough to repay any investment decided upon now.

FINANCIAL AND ALLIED SERVICES

Romania's reform of the banking system opens the way for, on the one hand, training the staff from the National Bank down to the last teller in the old and newly established banks, and, at the other end of the spectrum, opening branches of UK banks and/or forming joint ventures with local partners.

There are, of course, a host of problems, not least the lack of indigenous capital and the precarious situation of an uncomfortably large number of potential customers. The Romanian government, however, is no doubt aware that none of the other reforms will succeed if the banking infrastructure is not developed rapidly and should therefore be more than willing to follow any advice on how to speed up the process and attract foreign bankers to the country.

Current plans call for the establishment of a Stock Market and Commodity Exchanges in Bucharest and major provincial centres and, here again, British expertise is second to none. One can envisage the day British stockbrokers will operate on the Bucharest floor and Romanian entities will again be quoted in London.

Attempts are being made to bring Romanian accounting standards into line with European practice and the major and possibly some of the lesser accounting firms in the UK will find that their services will be in greater and greater demand as time goes by. In the meanwhile there is much work to be done just in preparing for the day, training being just one of the facets of the task ahead.

The Romanian insurance industry, with a single monopoly supplier (now broken up), was rather basic and Romanians generally, either as individuals or corporate bodies were, to understate the case, under-insured. There is a large, almost virgin, territory waiting to be tapped.

The privatisation programme calls for the establishment of six ownership funds (one for state and five for private funds). An input to the management of these funds and finding imaginative ways of raising extra capital should be of interest to some institutions.

With the growth in the number of new private companies, some foreign owned, and of course the privatisation of existing ones, there will be a growing need for legal services.

Romanian lawyers will see the merit of joining forces with foreign counterparts, more versed in the workings of the market economy, and no doubt more British firms will be involved in joint practices before too long.

There are numerous sources of aid finance, such as the Know-how Fund, the PHARE Programme and others for consultancy, training and feasibility studies in all the above fields and these should be fully utilised to the benefit of both the Romanians and the British interested parties.

TOURISM

Tourism was, in the 1960s and 1970s, a major hard and soft currency earner and a large number of facilities were built in that period, particularly on the Black Sea coast. They are similar to facilities of the same vintage elsewhere (eg Bulgaria, Greece and Spain), catering for the package, low-budget, tourist.

The country is, however, ideal for year-round tourism, with major underdeveloped and underutilised attractions. Assuming that air, road and rail communications will eventually be sorted out (and this is a big assumption to make), there is a dire need for modern, decent accommodation and eating places on a huge scale, catering for group tourism and the independent traveller. Both the scale of investment required and the returns are too great to quantify here. There is, however, ample room both for small-scale, local and foreign investors and larger groups which can take advantage of their global marketing networks.

OTHER SERVICES

Services generally are likely to be the main source of job creation. Catering for the needs of the various branches of the services industry is going to be very big business. It is difficult to assess when exactly the boom will start, but start it certainly will, and the alert will reap rewards.

Appendix 2

Sources of Grants and Aid

To date, financial assistance from Western governments and international financial organisations has inevitably targeted those Central and Eastern European countries best able to demonstrate solid commitment to political and economic reform. The main criteria adopted have been the implementation of a democratic political system and the creation of a free market economy. Although Romania's own struggle to achieve these goals continues to gather momentum, internal political problems during the last two years have had repercussions on the implementation of foreign government and other aid and caused Romania to lag behind its neighbours in this respect. At the time of writing (March 1992) not all these problems have been resolved, although progress is being made.

This appendix discusses the main sources of financial assistance applicable to Romania, starting with international bodies and concluding with UK national sources.

EUROPEAN COMMUNITY FUNDS

PHARE

The PHARE secretariat has identified the following priority areas for Romania:

- agriculture and food supply (research, production technology, joint ventures);
- the environment;
- investment (transport, tourism, smaller enterprises);

- training (management, banking, tourism, communications, agri-foodstuffs industry); and
- improved access to markets.

Provisional sums have been set aside towards meeting these objectives as follows – ECU30 million for industrial privatisation and restructuring, ECU20 million for food aid, ECU20 million for small and medium-sized enterprises, ECU15 million for human resources.

In accessing the PHARE programme it is vital to remember that it is the recipient country, rather than the donor, which determines the need and priority of aid-assisted projects and programmes. One of the most effective ways of influencing the decision-making process on individual proposals is to liaise with the people on the spot. They are best placed to influence their national authorities about the priority of a particular project.

In Romania, despite the recent liberalisation, there can still be found a strong business ethos of 'wheeling and dealing' almost for its own sake, coupled, on occasions, with extreme secretiveness. This can create pitfalls for the inexperienced and it can often pay dividends to use the services of one of the British legal or financial companies who have set up representation in Romania or the new breed of general agent-cum-fixer who have begun to flourish in Romania. Several of these are British and the DTI Country Desk, British Embassy, CBI or London Chamber of Commerce and Industry can provide introductions on a 'without prejudice' basis.

In the context of PHARE, most of the consultancy work must go out to tender but the prospects of success for UK companies can be enhanced by suggesting initiatives, early input to project specifications and by good first-hand contacts, perhaps facilitated in Romania by the sort of expatriate agent mentioned above. Registration with the PHARE unit in Brussels is essential – the contact is:

Brigitte Despic
Directorate General for Development DG VIII
Rue de la Loi 200
B-1049 Brussels
Tel: 010 (322) 235 4926

In addition, there is a PHARE database of individuals with expertise relative to Central and Eastern Europe. To register you should outline your skills and experience in the region in no more than two to three pages and send it to Peter Kalbe, PHARE Information Unit at the above address - Tel: 010 (322) 235 0026. In Romania the contact point is:

M Virescu
Director External Relations
Romanian Development Agency
7 Boulevard Magheru
Bucharest Secteur 1
Romania
Tel: 010 (400) 15 93 67

Other EC Aid

In addition to PHARE assistance, Romania has received considerable amounts of *ad hoc* EC aid over the last 18 months on humanitarian grounds: eg ECU25 million for a reform programme to support the restructuring of the health system, pharmaceutical supplies, health care equipment etc; ECU25 million to assist with a reform programme in general privatisation, agriculture and tourism sectoral development; and ECU25 million for animal feed and agricultural assistance etc. EC assistance is being made available to help with the problems of the orphanages. Information on these initiatives should be sought from Brussels.

EUROPEAN BANK FOR RECONSTRUCTION AND DEVELOPMENT (EBRD)

EBRD has identified a long-term plan for its work in Romania which involves help for the National Privatisation Agency; bank restructuring including improvements in credit line operations involving small and medium-sized private sector borrowers; infrastructure improvements including Bucharest's Otopeni Airport, rail, roads and ports; marketing and distribution of agricultural products; and improvements in the telecommunications and energy sectors. As part of this long-term plan, EBRD is currently supporting two major projects: $133 million to First Telecom for the creation of a national digital telephone network and $39 million to GEC-Alsthom-IMGB to modernise Romanian technology for the production of steam turbines and energy generators. The bank is also negotiating possible loans with four or five other UK companies and their Romanian partners.

In reaching a decision whether to assist a project, EBRD takes into account the degree of commitment of the Western partner to the project, looking essentially for a 'joint venture' approach. The bank would also expect a reasonable level of gearing; good return on capital, with a sound cash flow; and the strong possibility of co-financing with other banks as joint preferred creditors. EBRD has a ceiling level of commitment of 35 per cent of a particular project and nominally a ECU5 million floor level of minimum project value. The bank tries to maintain a flexible approach, however, and is also willing to consider ways of helping finance the consultancy work required for feasibility studies, drawing up business plans and so on.

The initial contact at EBRD to discuss whether the bank can help you with a particular project in Romania or elsewhere in the region is:

Bogdan Baltazar
Senior Adviser
Merchant Banking
European Bank for Reconstruction & Development
122 Leadenhall Street
London EC3V 4EB
Tel: 071-338 6612

INTERNATIONAL FINANCE CORPORATION (IFC)

IFC is affiliated to the World Bank and is the world's largest source of direct project financing for private investment in developing countries. IFC typically invests in ventures costing at least $10 million but has funding available for smaller projects. It normally prefers to make both an equity investment and a loan but can, when appropriate, provide one or the other.

It normally only invests in a venture when appropriate arrangements exist for the repatriation of investment capital and related earnings. Since this is an area which can sometimes give rise to problems with Romania, informal discussion with IFC is recommended. Its Foreign Investment Advisory Service has studied and made recommendations on a number of issues affecting foreign investors in Poland, Hungary and Yugoslavia, so can be a valuable source of experience and expertise. The IFC representative in London is:

Christopher Bam
IFC
4 Millbank
London SW1
Tel: 071-930 8741
Fax: 071-976 8323

EUROPEAN INVESTMENT BANK (EIB)

EIB is an autonomous institution within the EC structure, established to finance capital projects that promote the balanced development of the Community; the member states all subscribe to its capital. Some ECU1 billion has been authorised for lending to capital investment projects in Poland and Hungary and EIB will also consider lending to Romania on identification of appropriate projects. Fuller details of EIB policies are available from the Bank itself:

> EIB
> 100 Boulevard Konrad Adenauer
> 62950 Luxembourg
> Tel: 010 (352) 4379

EIB regards itself as a complementary source of funds and aims to provide loans which will not exceed 50 per cent of the cost of a project. EIB has subscribed 3 per cent of EBRD's capital and has assisted in the latter's establishment.

INTERNATIONAL MONETARY FUND (IMF)

The IMF has taken a close and continuing interest in the economic development of Romania. The indicators of economic performance set by the IMF have been used not only by that body in deciding how much financial assistance to make available to Romania, but as a yardstick by other institutions too. The IMF has recently reported that, although Romania's initial obstacles to reform were worse than those faced by its neighbours, considerable progress has been made.

The IMF has committed some $800 million worth of credits, most of which has been disbursed, for economic stabilisation in Romanian. Part is being used to finance the purchase of strategic imports, including $130 million for oil and gas. Further IMF financial support is expected in the summer of 1992.

UK GOVERNMENT SCHEMES

The Know-How Fund (KHF)

The British government was first to introduce a structured system to give financial help to the economic reform process in Central and

Eastern Europe. Full details can be obtained from the scheme administrator:

> The Joint Assistance Unit
> Foreign & Commonwealth Office
> King Charles Street
> London SW1
> Tel: 071-270 3000

Romania became eligible for KHF assistance in May 1991. The JAU has access to a wide range of professional and expert advice which it uses to assess proposals submitted to it. Priorities in the region so far have been assistance to the financial services sector, advice on privatisation and the establishment of small businesses, management training and some assistance to the energy, industrial and environmental sectors.

The JAU is happy to provide guidance literature on the various schemes it administers, including the amount of financial assistance it can offer and the conditions imposed. For example, up to 50 per cent of the cost of a pre-investment feasibility study (PIFS) can be paid for from the KHF, similarly management training for key East European personnel who will run UK investment operations can be financed under the Training for Investment Personnel Scheme (TIPS). Both the PIFS and TIPS schemes, which are discretionary, are subject to a limit of £50,000 per approved application.

There has been a conscious effort on the part of the JAU to ensure that the conditions of their schemes are not onerous but obviously, in common with other bodies offering assistance to the region, the KHF will be looking for projects which are demand-led from the relevant country, meet the criteria of helping forward the economic reform process and appear financially viable. In normal circumstances the JAU is required to seek competitive tenders for a project from various sources of expertise in the UK.

Overseas Projects Fund (OPF)

This pre-dates the Know-How Fund and is available to assist UK companies with the cost of pursuing major projects (in excess of £50 million) anywhere overseas (except EC countries). It is therefore applicable to Central and Eastern Europe and can meet the costs of feasibility studies, consultancies and other pre-contractual activities. Where a contract is won with its help, OPF assistance is repayable together with a 15 per cent premium.

Officials of the DTI's Projects and Export Policy Division (PEP) are always ready to have preliminary discussions about the likely eligibility of projects under the OPF scheme. Contact:

> Department of Trade and Industry
> PEP Division
> Ashdown House
> 123 Victoria Street
> London SW1
> Tel: 071-215 5000

Hands on Training Scheme (HOTS)

PEP also administers this scheme which is basically designed to offer financial assistance in bringing key personnel from abroad (including Central and Eastern Europe) for in-house training in the UK. Contact PEP (HOTS section) at the above address for a brochure on the scheme.

World Aid Section (WAS)

WAS also comes within the responsibility of the PEP Division of the DTI. It provides a computerised source of up-to-date information on the availability of financial assistance for projects throughout the world. For descriptive literature or to visit the section by appointment, contact:

> Mike Marshall
> World Aid Section
> Ashdown House
> 123 Victoria Street
> London SW1
> Tel: 071-215 6520

The current WAS computer printout on Romania lists a dozen or so significant projects all or partly funded by overseas agencies, including the EC.

CONCLUSION

Although major strides have been taken in converting Romania to a market economy, it would be short-sighted to pretend that the road ahead will be easy either for the Romanians or their potential trade and investment partners. For example, British firms are currently waiting with keen interest the decision on whether ECGD will support medium and long-term credit cover for Romania.

As regards the agreed Western G24 $1 billion structural loan for Romania, the EC contribution of some ECU375 million is in the process of completion, but various non-EC G24 loans for the balance are still under negotiation. It cannot be over-emphasised therefore how important it is in dealing with Romania to seek specialist advice on the availability of financial assistance, whether it be grants, aid or credit lines.

Remember that Romania enjoys good cultural and political links with other Western countries in addition to the UK - eg France, Spain, Sweden, the USA and South Africa. These can sometimes provide alternative routes into the market. Spain, for example, recently had $1 million of credit available for agricultural investment in Romania and was quite prepared to allow utilisation of this by other Western nationals operating as traders of Spanish goods, sourcing sales through Spain.

Finally, it has to be recognised that Romania is, to all intents and purposes, a developing country, with the risks that implies, but one where the prospects for business success are correspondingly high. This success is only likely to go to those who can make the most flexible use of the not insignificant grants and other aid sources which are already available to assist investment.

Appendix 3

Bibliography and Sources of Further Information

BIBLIOGRAPHY

Books

The Romanians: A History, Vlad Georgescu, IB Tauris & Co, 1991.

Periodicals and Journals

Business Eastern Europe, weekly, Business International Ltd, London.
Central European Magazine, monthly, Euromoney Publications, London.
East European Investment Monthly, monthly, Dixon & Company, New York.
The Eastern European Newsletter, fortnightly, Eastern European Newsletter, London.
The Economist Intelligence Unit Reports, quarterly, The Economist Intelligence Unit, London.
Financial Times East European Business Law, monthly, Financial Times Business Information Ltd, London.
Financial Times Eastern European Markets, fortnightly, Financial Times Business Information Ltd, London.
Insight (Eastern European Business Report), monthly, Insight International Publishing, London.
'International markets' in *London Commerce*, London Chamber of Commerce and Industry, London.
Investing in Romania, Romanian Development Agency Report, Romanian Development Agency, Bucharest, March 1991.
Law Digest for Foreign Investors, Romanian Development Agency, Bucharest, June 1991.

Plan Econ, fortnightly, Plan Econ Europe Ltd, London.

The Parker School Bulletin on Soviet and Eastern European Law, monthly, Parker School, Columbia University, Transnational Juris Publications, US.

The Romanian Economic Digest, monthly, Center for Economic Information and Documentation, Bucharest.

Romania Economic Newsletter, quarterly, Cosmos Inc, US.

Romanian Insight, monthly, Romanian Chamber of Commerce and Industry, Bucharest.

Romania: Open for Business, DRT International in conjunction with the Romanian Development Agency, London, 1992, 2nd edition.

Romania Opens to Investors, Romanian Development Agency Report, Romanian Development Agency, Bucharest, March 1991.

Romanian News (English Language Supplement) weekly, Collets, Wellingborough.

Technical Assistance/Critical Imports Loan, World Bank Appraisal Report, London, June 1991.

The White Book of Romanian Reform, The Council for Reform, Public Relations and Information, Bucharest, May 1991.

SOURCES OF FURTHER INFORMATION

DRT International

Archibald Campbell
DTT Eastern Europe Liaison
Touche Ross & Co
Hill House
1 Little New Street
London EC4A 3TR
Tel: 071-936 3000
Fax: 071-583 8517

Rick Olcott Deloitte & Touche
Bulevardul Unirii Nr 10
Bloc 7B, Sc 2, Etaj 2, Ap 29
74128 Bucuresti
Romania
Tel/Fax: 40 (0) 12 40 40

Audit and Accounting Services:
Nigel Johnson
Touche Ross & Co
Hill House
1 Little New Street
London EC4A 3TR
Tel: 071-936 3000
Fax: 071-583 8517

Corporate Finance Services:
Martin Clarke/David Douglas
Touche Ross & Co
Friary Court
65 Crutched Friars
London EC3N 2NP
Tel: 071-936 3000
Fax: 071-480 6958

Environmental Audit Services:
Ken Beecham
Touche Ross & Co
Peterborough Court
133 Fleet Street
London EC4R 2TR
Tel: 071-936 3000
Fax: 071-583 1198

Management Consultancy Services:
Brian Pomeroy/Stuart Mungall
Touche Ross & Co
Peterborough Court
133 Fleet Street
London EC4R 2TR
Tel: 071-936 3000
Fax: 071-583 1198

Taxation Services:
Peter Parsons/Paul Glover
Touche Ross & Co
Hill House
1 Little New Street
London EC4R 3TR
Tel: 071-936 3000
Fax: 071-583 8517

Tourism and Hotels Services:
Graham Wason
Touche Ross & Co
Peterborough Court
133 Fleet Street
London EC4R 2TR
Tel: 071-936 3000
Fax: 071-583 1198

Sinclair Roche & Temperley

Legal Services:
Ian Gaunt/Richard Thomas/
    Campbell Steedman
Sinclair Roche & Temperley
Broadwalk House
5 Appold Street
London EC2A 2NN
Tel: 071-638 9044
Fax: 071-638 0350/1/4

Sinclair Roche & Temperley
    (Romania) Limited
Representative Office
Radu Cristian Str Nr1
Bucuresti 2
Romania
Tel: 40 (0) 120411; 135554
Fax: 40 (0) 120412

Corporate Finance Services:
Richard Thomas/Campbell
    Steedman
Sinclair Roche & Temperley
Broadwalk House
5 Appold Street
London EC2A 2NN
Tel: 071-638 9044
Fax: 071-638 0350/1/4

Environmental Audit Services:
Richard Buxton/Gerard Hopkins
Sinclair Roche & Temperley
Broadwalk House
5 Appold Street
London EC2A 2NN
Tel: 071-638 9044
Fax: 071-638 0350/1/4

Taxation Services:
David Relf
Sinclair Roche & Temperley
Broadwalk House
5 Appold Street
London EC2A 2NN
Tel: 071-638 9044
Fax: 071-638 0350/1/4

Other Advisers

Corporate Finance Services:
David Nussbaum/Ion Florescu
Charterhouse Bank Ltd
1 Paternoster Row
St Paul's
London EC4M 7DH
Tel: 071-248 4000
Fax: 071-248 1998

Environmental Audit Services:
Carlo Motara
Basinvest SpA
Via Cerva 28
20122 Milan
Tel: 39 (2) 76 0091 41
Fax: 39 (2) 76 0090 51

Gaëton de Boysson/Annik Bolard
Financière Saint Dominique
48 bis, rue Fabert
75007 Paris
Tel: 33 (1) 49 55 70 53
Fax: 33 (1) 45 55 62 41

Other areas

Management Consultancy Services:
Cess Jon de Bruis/Ion Florescu
IFRC
Veerkade 7
PO Box 23341
3001 KH Rotterdam
The Netherlands
Tel: 31 (10) 414 4544
Fax: 31 (10) 433 2879

Razvan Magureanu/Vasile Hreamata
CoDIF
Radu Cristian Str Nr1
Bucharest 2
Romania
Tel: 40 (0) 120411; 135554
Fax: 40 (0) 120412

Paul Beza
Brittain Engineering Ltd
PO Box 367
509 Footscray Road
London SE9 3UJ
Tel: 081-302 0310
Fax: 081-309 1321
Telex: 898300

Hari Mohan Saraff
President
Commodities International Limited
Mabledon
London Road
Tunbridge Wells
Kent TN4 0UH
Tel: 0732 368888
Fax: 0732 367890

Mr Niculae Tinca
Impexrom Enterprise for Foreign Trade
(Commodities International Limited)
Bvd N Balcescu Nr 16
Bucharest
Romania
Tel: 40 (0) 146855
Fax: 40 (0) 121450

Ion Nestor
Associated Business Consultants SRL
44 Transilvaniei Str
Et3, Ap12
70778 Bucuresti
Romania

Department of Trade and Industry
Overseas Trade Division 3/5B
Kingsgate House
66–74 Victoria Street
London SW1E 6SW
Tel: 071-215 5000
Fax: 071-222 2531
Telex: 8813148

East European Trade Council
Suite 10
Westminster Palace Gdns
Artillery Row
London SW1P 1RL
Tel: 071-222 7622
Fax: 071-222 5359
Telex: 291018

Confederation of British Industry
Initiative Eastern Europe
Centre Point
103 New Oxford Street
London WC1A 1DU
Tel: 071-379 7400
Fax: 071-240 1578
Telex: 21332

London Chamber of Commerce and Industry
69 Cannon Street
London EC4N 5AB
Tel: 071-248 4444
Fax: 071-489 0391
Telex: 888941

Romanian Embassy
4 Palace Green
London W8 4QD
Tel: 071-937 9666

European Commission (London Office)
8 Storeys Gate
London SW1P 3AT
Tel: 071-973 1992

European Bank for Reconstruction and Development
122 Leadenhall Street
London EC3V 4EB
Tel: 071-338 6282
Fax: 071-338 6105/6115

European Investment Bank
100 Boulevard Konrad Adenauer
62950 Luxembourg
Tel: 010 (352) 4379

PHARE
World Aid Section
DTI
Room 402
1 Victoria Street
London SW1H 0ET
Tel: 071-215 4255/5369

The Know-How Fund
The Joint Assistance Unit
Foreign and Commonwealth Office
King Charles Street
London SW1A 2AH
Tel: 071-270 3000

International Finance Corporation
4 Millbank
London SW1
Tel: 071-930 8741
Fax: 071-976 8323

Anglo-Romanian Bank Ltd
42 Moorgate
London EC2R 6EL
Tel: 071-588 4150
Fax: 071-628 1274
Telex: 886700

Romanian Development Agency
B-dul Magheru 7
Bucharest
Tel: 40 (0) 151686
Fax: 40 (0) 132415
Telex: 11027

National Agency for Privatisation
Str Ministerului 2-4
Bucharest
Tel: 40 (0) 136136

General Direction of Customs
Str N Iorga 19
Bucharest
Tel: 40 (0) 592080

National Commission for Statistics
Str Stavropoleos 6
Bucharest
Tel: 40 (0) 134253

State Office for Inventions and
    Marks
Str Ioan Ghica 5
Bucharest
Tel: 40 (0) 159066

National Commission for
    Standards, Metrology and
    Quality
Bd Nicolae Bălcescu 21
79019 Bucharest
Tel: 40 (0) 153265

Institute for World Economy
B-dul Carol I Nr 12
Bucharest
Tel: 40 (0) 142005

Romanian Bank for Foreign Trade
Calea Victoriei 22-24
Bucharest
Tel: 40 (0) 149190
Telex: 11235

Bank for Agriculture
Str Smirdan 3
Bucharest
Tel: 40 (0) 144260

Commercial Bank
Bd Carol I Nr 14
Bucharest
Tel: 40 (0) 156675

Romanian Bank for Development
Str Doamei 4
Bucharest
Tel: 40 (0) 158750

Bankcoop
Str Ion Ghica 13
Bucharest
Tel: 40 (0) 597640

Mindbank
Calea Plevnei 46-48
Bucharest
Tel: 40 (0) 130788

Ion Tiriac Bank
Str Doamnei 12
Bucharest
Tel: 40 (0) 142833

Eximbank
Str Lipscani 23
Bucharest
Tel: 40 (0) 154767

Romanian-American Bank
Str Doamnei 9
Bucharest
Tel: 40 (0) 139204

National Bank of Romania
Str Lipscani 23
Bucharest
Tel: 40 (0) 130410

British Embassy
Str Jules Michelet 24
Bucharest
Tel: 90-120304

American Embassy
Str Tudor Arghezi 7-9
Bucharest
Tel: 90-104040

Ministry of Economy and Finance
Piata Victoriei Nr 1
Bucharest

Ministry of Industry
Calea Victoriei Nr 152
Bucharest
Tel: 90 505020
Fax: 90 503029
Telex: 11109

Ministry of Trade and Tourism
Str Apollodor Nr 17
Bucharest

Ministry of Agriculture and Food
B-dul Republicii Nr 24
Bucharest

Ministry of Education and Science
Str General Berthelot Nr 30
Bucharest

Ministry of Public Works and Land Improvement
Str Apollodor Nr 17
Bucharest

Ministry of Environment
B-dul Libertății Nr 12
Bucharest

Ministry of Culture
Piata Presei Libere Nr 1
Bucharest

Ministry of Labour and Social Protection
Str Onesti Nr 2
Bucharest

Ministry of Youth and Sports
Str Vasile Conta Nr 16
Bucharest

Ministry of Health
Str Ministerului Nr 1-3
Bucharest
Tel: 90 141526
Fax: 90 156192

Department of Foreign Trade
Str Apollodor Nr 17
Bucharest

Department of Domestic Trade and Tourism
Str Apollodor Nr 17
Bucharest

Department of Food Industry
Str Walter Maracineanu Nr 37
Bucharest

Department of Building Materials
Str Radu Calomfirescu Nr 9
Bucharest

Department of Machine Building Industry, Electronics and Electrotechnics
Calea Victoriei Nr 152
Bucharest

Department of Geology and Recycling of Materials
Calea Victoriei Nr 152
Bucharest

Department of Metallurgical
  Industry
Str Mendeleev Nr 21-25
Bucharest

Department of Chemical and
  Petro-Chemical Industry
Splaiul Independentei Nr 202A
Bucharest

S.N.C.F.R. (Romanian Railways)
Bd Dinicu Golescu 38
Bucharest

Regia Autonomă de Electricitate
  (Electricity Board)
Bd Magheru 33
Bucharest

*Chambers of Commerce and
  Industry in Romania:*
Romanian Chamber of Commerce
  and Industry
B-dul Nicolae Balcescu 22
79502 Bucharest
Tel: 40 (0) 154707
Telex: 11374

Alba County
Str IC Brătianu 1
2500 Alba Iulia
Jud Alba
Tel: 968-11772
Telex: 36220
Contacts: Mr Ilarie Oargă,
  President

Arad County
Town Hall
Bd Revoluției 75
Room No 90
Arad
Jud Arad

Argeș County
Piața Vasile Mile 1
0300 Pitești
Jud Argeș
Tel: 976-2400

Bacău County
Str Libertății 1
5500 Bacău
Jud Bacău
Tel: 931-46262
Telex: 21239

Bihor County
Str General Magheru 7
3700 Oradea
Jud Bihor
Tel: 991-17381
Telex: 34227

Bistrița-Năsăud County
Hotel Bistrița
Str 1 Decembrie 2
4400 Bistrița
Tel: 990-17640

Botoșani County
Prefectura
Piața Revoluției 3
6800 Botoșani
Jud Botoșani
Tel: 985-13630
Telex: 24211
Contacts: Mr Dan Andrașcu,
  President and Mr Doru Floareș,
  Exhibitions Department

Brașov County
Bd Eroilor 5
2200 Brașov
Jud Brașov
Tel: 921-17046
Fax: 921-13416
Telex: 61220
Contacts: Mr Mircea Florescu,
  President

Brăila County
Piața Independenței 1
6100 Brăila
Jud Brăila
Tel: 9465-35900

Buzău County
Bd Nicolae Bălcescu 48
Entrance C
Room 18
5100 Buzău
Jud Buzău
Tel: 974-15229

Caraș-Severin County
Centrul Doman 2
1700 Reșita
Jud Caraș-Severin
Tel: 964-13776
Telex: 74227

Călărași County
Str Sloboziei 9-11
8500 Călărași
Jud Călărași
Tel: 911-11301
Fax: 911-14533
Telex: 86208

Cluj County
Bd Eroilor 2
3400 Cluj-Napoca
Tel: 951-11472
Fax: 951-12214
Telex: 31456
Contacts: Mr Ioan Muntean,
    President and Mr Gheorghe
    Mureșanu, Foreign Relations
    Dept

Constanța County
Str Ștefan cel Mare 36-40
8701 Constanța
Tel: 916-16018
Telex: 14215
Contacts: Mr Cornel Florea,
    President and Mr Cezar
    Catargiu, Secretary General

Covasna County
Piața Libertății 4
PO Box 70
4000 Sfântu Gheorghe
Jud Covasna
Tel: 923-15670
Telex: 68299

Dâmbovița County
Bd Castanilor 5
0200 Tăgoviște
Jud Dâmbovița
Tel: 926-68644
Telex: 17266

Dolj County
Str Ialomicioarei 6
1100 Craiova
Tel: 941-34386
Telex: 41210

Galați County
Str 23 August 26
6200 Galați
Jud Galați
Tel: 934-13904
Telex: 51230

Giurgiu County
Str Parculi 1
8375 Giurgiu
Jud Giurgiu
Tel: 912-13094
Telex: 15739

Bibliography and Sources of Further Information

Gorj County
Str Eroilor 36
1400 Târgu Jiu
Jud Gorj
Tel: 929-12017

Harghita County
Str Timișoarei 15
4100 Miercurea Ciuc
Jud Harghita
Tel: 958-15092
Telex: 67282

Hunedoara County
Str 1 Decembrie 35
2700 Deva
Jud Hunedoara
Tel: 956-14865
Telex: 72278

Ialomița County
Str Matei Basarab 29
8400 Slobozia
Jud Ialomița
Tel: 910-12170
Telex: 13218

Iași County
Str Cuza Vodă 10
6600 Iași
Tel: 981-12170
Telex: 22212

Maramureș County
Str Gheorghe Șincai 37
4800 Baia Mare
Jud Maramureș
Tel: 994-12557
Telex: 33258

Mehedinți County
Str Cantemir 8
1500 Drobeta-Turnu Severin
Jud Mehedinți
Tel: 978-14100

Mureș County
Piața Victoriei 1
4300 Târgu Mureș
Jud Mureș
Tel: 954-265016

Neamț County
Str Alexandru cel Bun
5800 Piatra Neamț
Jud Neamț
Tel: 936-16663
Telex: 25227

Olt County
Str Nicolae Titulescu 45
0500 Slatina
Jud Olt
Tel: 944-11001
Telex: 47227

Prahova County
Str Republicii 2
Room 424
20000 Ploiești
Jud Prahova
Tel: 971-26331

Satu Mare County
Piața 25 Octombrie 1
3900 Satu Mare
Jud Satu Mare
Tel: 997-14036
Telex: 38219

Sălaj County
Piața 1 Decembrie 1918 No 7
4700 Zalău
Jud Sălaj
Tel: 996-14612
Telex: 39227

Sibiu County
Str Telefoanelor 1
CP 164
2400 Sibiu
Jud Sibiu
Tel: 924-16447
Telex: 69255
Contacts: Mr Ghoerghe Ionaș,
    President

Suceava County
Str Ștefan cel Mare 36
5800 Suceava
Jud Suceava
Tel: 987-10148
Telex: 23230

Teleorman County
Str Dunării 178
0700 Alexandria
Jud Teleorman
Tel: 913-11862
Telex: 16166

Timiș County
Piața Victoriei 3
1900 Timișoara
Jud Timiș
Tel: 961-11413
Telex: 71385
Contacts: Emil Mateescu,
    President; Sergiv Palcău, Vice-
    President

Tulcea County
Str Păcii 20
8800 Tulcea
Jud Tulcea
Tel: 915-11960
Telex: 53254

Vâlcea County
Str Tudor Vladimirescu 72
1000 Râmnicu Vâlcea
Jud Vâlcea
Tel: 9947-12901

Vaslui County
Str Ștefan cel Mare 79
6500 Vaslui
Jud Vaslui
Tel: 983-11442
Telex: 26223

Vrancea County
Str Dimitrie Cantemir 1B
5300 Focșani
Jud Vrancea
Tel: 939-13210

Index

accounting standards, legislation 99-102
  accounting requirements 101
  background 99
  general provisions 100
  penalties for non-compliance 102
  valuation methods 101-2
advertising 161
agencies and distributorships 152, 159, 162, 163-6
  agency 163-4
  distributorship 165-6
  representative offices 164-5
agrarian reform *see* agriculture
agriculture 11, 13, 27, 30-1, 221-2
  the Bank for Agriculture and Food Industries 95, 96
  and food processing 221-2
  and property law 113-14
  use of agricultural land 114
aid 17, 35
  foreign assistance and investment 40-1
  sources of 232-9
    EC funds 232-4
    European Investment Bank (EIB) 172, 236
    International Finance Corporation (IFC) 235
    International Monetary Fund (IMF) 24, 40, 63, 172, 236
    UK government schemes 105, 230, 236-8
aircraft industry 17, 226
Anglo-Romanian Bank Ltd 97, 174
Anti-Trust law 12
Apsa SA 110
Argus 215
automotive industry 226-7

Banca Italo-Romena 97
Bank for Agriculture and Food Industries 95, 96
Bank for Small Industry and Private Enterprise *see* Mindbank SA
Bankcoop SA 96

banking and financial services 40, 48, 93-8, 229-30
  foreign banks 96-7
  interest rates 97-8
  local banks 94-6
  new banking structure 93-4
bankruptcy 12
Banque Franco-Romaine SA 97
bottom-up privatisation 109
British business, the options for 147-93
  agencies and distributorships 152, 159, 162, 163-6
  export and import 151-2, 167-71, 173-5
  financing a company 188-93
  forming a company 180-7
  licensing and franchises 176-9
  marketing 157-62, 207-8, 212, 215-16
  planning 149-56
  trade finance 172-5
Brittain Engineering Ltd
  marketing 157-62
  opportunities by sector 221-31
  Romania and its potential 17-35
building materials 228
business culture 50-6
  communications 55-6
  mentalities 53-5
    prices and values 54-5
  structures 51-3
    co-operatives 52
    joint ventures 53
    private companies 52-3
    state enterprises 51-2
business infrastructure 75-146, 159-60
  accounting standards 99-102
  banking and financial services 40, 48, 93-8, 229-30
  commercial law 43-4, 77-81
  convertibility of the leu 11, 39, 71-2, 82-7
  the environment 134-8
  the fiscal framework 118-27
  the labour market 139-46
  marketing and advertising 159-60
  prices, rents and wages 88-92
  the privatisation process 103-7

property 113-17
technology and communications 128-33

case studies 195-217
  Glaxo 214-17
  Romanian Manufacturers SA 197-203
  Shell Romania 204-8
  the Wadkin Group 209-13
Ceauşescu, economy under 36-8
Centracoop 96
Central Economic Union of Trade Co-
    operatives 96
ceramics 229
certification of documents 182
chambers of commerce 58, 59, 150, 160, 161
Charterhouse
  banking and financial services 93-8
  convertibility of the leu 82-7
  financing a company 188-93
  prices, rents and wages 88-92
chemical and petrochemical industries
    214-17, 224-5
Civic Alliance 28
civil code 43
clothing and footwear 110, 227-8
  Romanian Manufacturers SA 197-203
co-operatives 52, 96
Co-ordination Committee on Multilateral
    Export Controls (COCOM) 169
Comecon see Council for Mutual Economic
    Assistance
commerce, marketing to 161-2
commercial law 43-4, 77-81
  competition 80-1
  contract 77-9
  security 79-80
commercial register, the 183-4
Commodities International
  trade finance 172-5
communications 55-6
communications see telecommunications
companies 27, 45, 45-6, 167
  financing 188-93
    negotiating a joint venture 192-3
    sources of debts 13, 35, 191-2
    sources of equity 190-1
    structuring a joint venture 188-90
  formation 180-7
    incorporation 181-7
    Shell Romania 205-6
    subsidiary companies 187
    Wadkin Group 210-11
competition law 49, 80-1
Confederation of British Industries (CBI)
  Initiative Eastern Europe 12, 13-14
Constitution 11
  the new Romanian 27, 43, 140-1
  and the role of the NPA 106-7
constitution, company 181-2
construction industry 137, 228
consumer market 158-9, 202
  disposable income 158
  distribution and retail 159

market research 158-9
  pricing 159
contract law 77-9
  creation of a contract 78
  liability and damages 78-9
contracts of employment 141-4
  collective 142
  individual 142-4
convertibility of the leu 11, 39, 71-2, 82-7
  lack of hard currency 82-3
  moves towards 83-6
  repatriation of profits 87
  retention of profits 86
copyright see intellectual property
Council for Mutual Economic Assistance
    (Comecon) 23
  and the West, Romania's trade with 62-3
Council for National Union 25
court procedure, company formation 183
customs tariffs 168-9

debt, sources of 13, 35, 191-2
Democratic Agrarians 27
Democratic Convention 28-9
Democratic Union of Hungarians in
    Romania 28
demography 20-1
direct investment 198-200
disposable income 158
distribution and retail system 159, 229
distributorships 152, 162, 163-6
  agency 163-4
  representative offices 164-5
dividends 123
  taxation on individuals 125
Dossier d'Information on Romania 59
double taxation treaty 123, 125

Eastern European Trade Council 58
economy 29-41
  agriculture 30-1
  foreign trade 34-5
  forestry 31
  industry 33-4
  mining 31-3
  natural resources 29-30
  power 33
  transformation of 36-41
    economic performance 40-1
    foreign assistance and investment 40-1
    pillars of reform 38-40
    under Ceauşescu 36-8
Electromagnetica 131
Electromontaj 110
electronics 225-6
employment practices and regulations 47-8,
    139-40
energy 222-4
  oil and gas 30, 125, 174, 223
  power generation and energy efficiency
    110, 223-4
engineering 18, 226-7
  aircraft industry 226

Index

automotive industry 226-7
   municipal service vehicles and plant 227
   shipbuilding and repair 227
environment, the 134-8
   future legislation 136-8
   guidance for investors 138
   legislation 48-9, 134-5
   regulatory control 135-6
equity, sources of 190-1
European Bank for Reconstruction and Development (EBRD) 128, 192
European Community (EC)
   funds 172, 232-4
      other EC aid 234
      PHARE 59, 105, 230, 232-4
   Romania's trade with 63, 65-6
European Investment Bank (EIB) 172, 236
export and import 151-2, 167-71, 173-5
   background 167
   changing role of FTOs 167-8
   customs tariffs 168-9
   import duty concession 120
   the regime 167-71
      exports 170-1
      imports 169-70
   trade finance 173-5
Export-Import Bank of Japan 40

financial and allied services *see* banking and financial services
financing a company 188-93
   see also trade finance
fiscal framework 118-27
   interest and royalty withholding taxes 126-7
   other taxes 127
   profits tax 121-4
   social security insurance contributions 126
   tax incentives 119-21
      import duty concession 120
      other concessions 120-1
      profits tax concessions 119-20
   tax registration and RDA certification 184-7
   taxes on individuals 124-5
   turnover tax 125-6
food processing 221-2
footwear 110, 227-8
foreign banks 96-7
foreign exchange 172-3
foreign investment 13, 45, 66, 68-73
   environmental guidance for 138
   historical perspective 68-9
   legislation 11, 45, 47, 69-73, 138, 164, 189
      areas of participation 69
      incentives 70-1
      registration and the RDA 72-3
      restrictions on 70
      rights of investors 71-2
   tax incentives 119-21
foreign ownership of non-agricultural land 116

foreign trade 11, 34-5
   in the 1990s 63-5
   and investment (1850-1947) 61-2
   patterns of UK/Romanian trade 35
   see also trade finance
Foreign Trade Organisations (FTOs) 39, 51, 83, 167-8
forestry 31
forfaiting 173
franchises and licensing 176-9
Frankfurt-Bucharest Bank 97
free trade zones 120, 167
furniture making 209-13

gas 30, 125, 223
geography 18-20
glass and ceramics 229
Glaxo 214-17
   approach to the market 214-15
   development of operations 216-17
   marketing 215-16
grants and aid, sources of 17, 35, 232-9
   EC funds 172, 232-4
      PHARE 59, 105, 230, 232-4
      European Investment Bank (EIB) 172, 236
      International Finance Corporation (IFC) 235
      International Monetary Fund (IMF) 24, 40, 63, 172-3, 236
   UK government schemes 105, 230, 236-8

Hands on Training Scheme (HOTS) 238
health-care 89-90
history, a brief 21-9
   after the revolution 25-9
   before the revolution 21-5
housing and building materials 137, 228

incorporation, company 181-7
   certification of documents 182
   the commercial register 183-4
   constitution 181-2
   court procedure 183
   and RDA rules 182
   tax registration and RDA certification 184-7
   timing 187
individual taxation 124-5
Industrial Finance Reconstruction Corporation (IFRC) 9
industry 33-4
   marketing to 161-2
inflation 41
infrastructure, business *see* business infrastructure
insurance 173-4, 230
   social security system 126, 144-5
intellectual property 46-7, 176-7, 210-11
interest
   rates 97-8
   and royalty withholding taxes 126

Index

International Finance Corporation (IFC) 235
International Monetary Fund (IMF) 24, 40, 63, 172-3, 236
investment *see* foreign investment
Investment Bank, the 95, 96

Joint Assistance Unit (JAU) 237
joint ventures 24, 53, 97, 226
   negotiating 192-3
   structuring 188-90

know-how 46-7, 176-7, 210-11
Know-How Fund (KHF) 105, 230, 236-7

labour market 139-46
   employment practices and mobility of labour 139-40
   legislation 140-5
      contracts of employment 141-4
      trade unions 144
      unemployment benefit and social security system 144-5
   wages 145-6
land law 39, 113-17, 135
leased telephone lines 133
legislation
   accounting standards 99-102
   banking 48
   the civil code 43
   commercial law 43-4, 77-81
   competition 49, 80-1
   the Constitution 11, 27, 43, 106-7, 140-1
   employment regulation 47-8
   environmental 48-9, 134-8
   foreign investment 12, 45, 47, 69-73, 138, 164, 189
   intellectual property 46-7, 176-7
   labour market 140-5
   a new legal framework 42-9
   other legislation and outlook 49
   privatisation 12, 46, 103-6
   property law and land ownership 48, 113-17, 135
   trading companies 27, 45-6
   transformation law 44-5, 80
liability and damages 78-9
licensing and franchises 176-9
living standards 37-8, 88-90
local banks 94-6

Manufacturers Hanover Trust 96, 97, 173
market intelligence 57-60
   market research 158-9
   obtaining information 57-8
   sources 58-60
      external 58-9
      internal 59-60
marketing 207-8, 212, 215-16
   for the exporter 161-2
   the media 160
   options for British business 157-62
      advertising 161

      consumer market 158-9
      infrastructure 159-60
   see also planning
maternity benefit 143-4
media 160
Mindbank SA 96
mining 30, 31-3
Ministry of Trade and Tourism (MCT) 169, 170
Misr Romanian Bank SAE 97
mobility of labour 139-40
Monitorul Oficial (*Official Gazette*) 183, 184
municipal service vehicles and plant 227

National Bank of Romania 40, 48, 71-2, 84-5, 86, 93-4, 97, 169
National Commission for Statistics 59-60
National Liberal Party (PNL) 23, 27
National Peasant Party (PNT) 23, 26, 28
National Privatisation Agency (NPA) 8, 40, 105, 109
   the role of 46, 106-7
National Salvation Front (FNS) 25, 26, 28-9, 82-3, 172
natural resources 29-30
NCM Credit Insurance Ltd 173-4
New Economic and Financial Mechanism (NEFM) 37
newsletters 59-60
non-agricultural land, property law and 114-16
   effect of Transformation Law 115-16
   rights of private ownership 114-15

Official Gazette 183, 184
oil and gas 30, 125, 174, 223
   Shell Romania 204-8
opportunities by sector *see* sectoral opportunites
Overseas Projects Fund (OPF) 237-8

paper and pulp 228
patents *see* intellectual property
petrochemical industries 18, 61, 224-5
PHARE programme 59, 105, 230, 232-4
pharmaceutical industry 214-17, 224-5
'Plan Comptable Générale' 100, 101
planning 149-56
   doing the deal 153-4
   getting started 154-6
      setting up an office 155-6
   the market 150-2
      market entry 151-2
      taking a view 150-1
political parties, Romanian 21-9
power generation and energy efficiency 33, 223-4
press, the 160
prices, rents and wages 88-92
   price controls 13
   prices and values 54-5
   recent evolution of 90-2

regional differences 92
  standards of living 88-90
pricing 159
Private Ownership Funds 104, 106, 109
privatisation process 8, 11, 39-40, 46, 103-12
  constitution and the role of the NPA 106-7
  foreign opportunities 106
  legislation 12, 103-6
    employee participation 105-6
    implementaion of the privatisation programme 105
    private ownership funds 104
    state ownership fund 104
  in practice 108-12
    bottom-up privatisation 109
    managing the programme 111-12
    top-down privatisation 109-11
  private companies 52-3
profits 86-7, 121-4
  repatriation of 87
  retention of 86
  tax 72, 118, 121-4
    concessions 119-20
    determination of taxable profits 121-2
    dividends 123
    payment 122-3
    taxation of UK resident companies 124
property 48, 113-17
  agricultural land 39, 113-14, 135
  non-agricultural land 114-16, 202-3, 217
  potential changes in law 116-17
  restrictions on foreign ownership 116
  and security 79-80
public utilities 110
Publicom 159-60, 162

radio 160
regia autonoma see state enterprises
representative offices 164
restitution *see* land law
retail outlets 229
road, rail, and water transport 225
Rom Control Data 226
Rom Telecom 55
ROM-POST-TEL (RPT) 131
Romania 15-73
  business culture 50-6
  the country and its potential 17-35
  economic transformation 36-41
  and foreign investment 68-73
  and its trading partners 61-7
  and market intelligence 57-60
  a new legal framework 42-9
Romanian Bank for Foreign Trade (RBFT) 83, 93, 95, 97
Romanian Commercial Bank 93, 95-6
Romanian Development Agency (RDA) 59, 154
  company formation rules 182
  labour market 139-46
  and registration 72-3
  tax registration and RDA certification 184-7
  and Touche Ross
    export and import 167-71
    technology and communications 128-33
Romanian Economic Newsletter 59
Romanian Institute of Marketing 158
Romanian Manufacturers SA 197-203
  consumer markets 202
  direct investment 198-200
  the future 202-3
  running the business 200-2
  trading with Romania 197-8
Romanian National Agency for Privatisation *see* National Privatisation Agency (NPA)
Romanian National Unity Party 28
'Royal Dictatorship' 22
royalties and withholding taxes 126

salary tax 118, 124-5
satellite communications 132
  television 160
Savings and Loans Bank 94, 95, 97
sectoral opportunities 221-31
  agriculture and food processing 221-2
  chemical and petrochemical industries 224-5
  distribution and retail outlets 229
  energy 222-4
  engineering 226-7
  financial and allied services 229-30
  glass and ceramics 229
  housing and building materials 228
  other services 231
  road, rail, and water transport 225
  telecommunications and electronics 225-6
  textiles, clothing and footwear 227-8
  tourism 230-1
  woodworking, paper and pulp 228
Securitate 215
security
  over immovable property 79
  over movable property 80
  in respect of debts due 80
  retention of title 79-80
Shell Romania 204-8
  marketing 207-8
  organising the business 206-7
  setting up a company 205-6
shipbuilding and repair 18, 227
Sinclair Roche & Temperley
  agencies and distributorships 163-6
  commercial law 77-81
  the environment 134-8
  foreign investment 68-73
  forming a company 180-7
  licensing and franchises 176-9
  a new legal framework 42-9
  privatisation process 103-7
  property 113-17

Index

Romania and its trading partners 61-7
Social Democrat Parties 28
social security system 126, 144-5
   contributions 126
Socialist Labour Party 28
societate comerciale see state enterprises
Société Générale bank 96, 173
SOFRECOM report 128
State Committee for Standards and Quality 18
state enterprises 11, 51-2
   see also Transformation Law
state ownership fund 104
State Planning Committee (SPC) 37
subsidiary companies 187

taxation *see* fiscal framework
technology and communications *see* telecommunications
telecommunications 55-6, 90, 225-6
   objectives for 129-30
     government policy 129-30
     structural changes envisaged 130
   organisational infrastructure 130-2
     manufacturing industry 131-2
     network construction 131
     RPT 131
   technical infrastructure 132-3
     the existing telephone network 132-3
     leased lines 133
     telex and data 133
Teleconstructia 131
television 160
telex and data 133
tenders, infrastructural project 152
termination of employment 143
textiles, clothing and footwear 110, 227-8
TIB and TIBCO trade fairs 60, 160, 161-2
Tiriac Bank SA 96
Touche Ross
   accounting standards 99-102
   business culture 50-6
   fiscal framework 118-27
   market intelligence 57-60
   planning 149-56
   and the RDA
     export and import 167-71
     technology and communications 128-33

Romanian economic transformation 36-41
tourism 110, 137, 169, 230-1
toxic or noxious substances legislation 137-8
trade associations 161
trade fairs 60, 160, 161-2
trade finance 172-5
   exporting to Romania 173-4
   foreign exchange 172-3
   importing 174-5
trade unions 144
trading companies 45-6
trading partners, Romania and its 61-7
   foreign investment (1990s) 66
   foreign trade (1990s) 63-5
   foreign trade and investment (1850-1947) 61-2
   Romania, Comecon and the West 62-3
   Romania's trade with the EC 65-6
Transformation Law 44, 80, 115-16
turnover tax 118, 125-6

UK government aid schemes 236-8
   Hands on Training Scheme (HOTS) 238
   Know-How Fund (KHF) 105, 230, 236-7
   Overseas Projects Fund (OPF) 237-8
   World Aid Section (WAS) 238
UK resident companies, taxation of 124
unemployment benefit 144-5

valuation methods, accounting 101-2

Wadkin Group 209-13
   finance 211-12
   getting started 210-11
   impressions 212-13
   marketing 212
   why Romania? 209-10
wages 145-6
water and effluent treatment plant 227
water transport 225
withholding taxes 126
woodworking, paper and pulp 170, 209-13, 228
World Aid Section (WAS) 238
World Bank 24, 63, 172